Battlefield Events

Battlefield Events: landscape, commemoration and heritage is an investigative and analytical study into the way in which significant landscapes of war have been constructed and imagined through events over time to articulate specific narratives and denote consequence and identity. The book charts the ways in which a number of landscapes of war have been created and managed from an events perspective, and how the processes of remembering (along with silencing and forgetting) at these places have influenced the management of these warscapes in the present day. With chapters from authors based in seven different countries on three continents as well as comparative case studies, this book has a truly international perspective.

This timely longitudinal analysis of war commemoration events, the associated landscapes, the travel to these destinations and their management strategies will be valuable reading for all those interested in war landscapes and events.

Keir Reeves holds a chair in Australian History at Federation University Australia, where he is the director for the Collaborative Research Centre in Australian History (CRCAH). Prior to this he was the director of the Australian and International Tourism Research Unit at Monash University, Melbourne, Australia and held teaching and research positions at the University of Melbourne, Australia.

Geoffrey R. Bird is Associate Professor at the School of Tourism and Hospitality Management at Royal Roads University in Victoria, BC, Canada.

Laura James works as a researcher in the National Centre for Australian Studies at Monash University, Melbourne, Australia.

Birger Stichelbaut is a post-doctoral researcher at the Centre for Historical and Archaeological Aerial Photography – a collaborative initiative between Ghent University, the In Flanders Fields Museum and the Province of West-Flanders – and is engaged with aerial photography, archaeology and the conflict landscape of World War I.

Jean Bourgeois is Professor at Ghent University in Belgium and Head of the Department of Archaeology.

Routledge advances in event research series
Edited by Warwick Frost and Jennifer Laing
Department of Management and Marketing
La Trobe University, Australia

Events, Society and Sustainability
Edited by Tomas Pernecky and Michael Lück

Exploring the Social Impacts of Events
Edited by Greg Richards, Maria deBrito and Linda Wilks

Commemorative Events
Warwick Frost and Jennifer Laing

Power, Politics and International Events
Edited by Udo Merkel

Event Audiences and Expectations
Jo Mackellar

Event Portfolio Planning and Management
A holistic approach
Vassilios Ziakas

Conferences and Conventions
A research perspective
Judith Mair

Fashion, Design and Events
Edited by Kim M. Williams, Jennifer Laing and Warwick Frost

Food and Wine Events in Europe
Edited by Alessio Cavicchi and Cristina Santini

Event Volunteering
*Edited by Karen Smith, Leonie Lockstone-Binney, Kirsten Holmes
and Tom Baum*

Battlefield Events

Landscape, commemoration and heritage

Edited by Keir Reeves, Geoffrey R. Bird, Laura James, Birger Stichelbaut and Jean Bourgeois

LONDON AND NEW YORK

First published 2016
by Routledge

2 Park Square, Milton Park, Abingdon, Oxfordshire OX14 4RN
711 Third Avenue, New York, NY 10017

*Routledge is an imprint of the Taylor & Francis Group,
an informa business*

First issued in paperback 2018

British Library Cataloguing in Publication Data
A catalogue record for this book is available from the British Library

Library of Congress Cataloging in Publication Data
A catalog record for this book has been requested

ISBN: 978-1-138-90059-2 (hbk)
ISBN: 978-1-138-59223-0 (pbk)

Typeset in Times New Roman
by Fish Books Ltd., Enfield, Middlesex.

Contents

Figures

Contributors

Julien Barbara is a Senior Policy Fellow in the State, Society and Governance in Melanesia Program based at the Coral Bell School of Asia Pacific Affairs – College of Asia and the Pacific at the Australian National University in Canberra. Prior to joining ANU Julien had a career as a diplomat for the Australian Department of Foreign Affairs and Trade (DFAT) and an aid official with the Australian Agency for International Development (AusAID), which included a posting with the Regional Assistance Mission to Solomon Islands.

Geoffrey R. Bird is Associate Professor and Head of the School of Tourism and Hospitality Management at Royal Roads University in Victoria, BC, Canada. Geoff completed a PhD in anthropology in 2011 at the University of Brighton, UK where he studied the relationship between tourism, remembrance and landscapes of war. In addition to teaching for the past 13 years, included in his work history was a period serving in the Canadian military and as a heritage interpreter at the Canadian War Memorial at Vimy Ridge, France. Geoffrey's research interests include heritage tourism experiences, the politics of remembrance and meaning associated with landscapes of war.

Kevin Blackburn is an Associate Professor in History at the National Institute of Education, Nanyang Technological University, Singapore. In 2012 he authored *The Sportsmen of Changi* (UNSW Press) and co-authored, with Karl Hack, *War Memory and the Making of Modern Malaysia and Singapore* (NUS Press).

Jean Bourgeois is a professor at Ghent University and Head of the Department of Archaeology. He is Francqui research professor for 2010–13. He is a member of the Royal Flemish Academy of Belgium for Science and the Arts, a corresponding member of the German Archaeological Institute and president of the International Union of Prehistoric and Protohistoric Sciences (2011–17). His research concentrates on the Bronze Age and the Iron Age in Western Europe as well as in the Altay Mountains. He is also active in aerial photography in Flanders (archaeological aerial photography as well as World War I aerial photography).

Lloyd Carpenter is a New Zealand-based researcher at Lincoln University, Te Whare Wānanga o Aoraki, Canterbury, New Zealand in the Department of Tourism, Sport and Society, Faculty of Environment, Society and Design where he is a lecturer in Māori Studies. His work includes trans-Tasman nineteenth-century mining history – an aspect of his PhD dissertation undertaken at the University of Canterbury – as well as Māori and colonial history. His Iwi is *Ngati Toarangatira*.

Joseph Cheer is a lecturer and director of AITRU at Monash University, Melbourne, Australia. His current research interests are sociocultural anthropology, cultural geography and development studies. His research examines the tradition–modernity binary and the implications for present-day livelihoods. His forthcoming book is on cultural tourism and sustainable livelihoods in the Pacific Islands and it draws on his PhD that used an ethnographic approach to sustainable livelihoods and cultural tourism in Vanuatu.

David Cragg is Assistant Secretary of the Victorian Trades Hall Council. He has been involved in planning for commemorations of the Centenary of the 1916 and 1917 Referenda on Conscription in Australia.

Hannelore Decoodt is a Belgian heritage researcher at the Flanders Heritage Agency. Since 2002, her main focus has been the inventorying and protection of World War I heritage in Flanders, such as military cemeteries, memorials, bunkers and other remaining war infrastructure.

Marc Dewilde is a Belgian heritage researcher at the Flanders Heritage Agency. Archaeology is his specialism. Since 2002 the archaeology of the 'Great' war became an important part of his research.

Warwick Frost is an Associate Professor in the Department of Management and Marketing at La Trobe University, Melbourne, Australia. His research interests include heritage, events, nature-based attractions and the interaction between media, popular culture and tourism. He has co-written four books and co-edited two others with Jennifer Laing, and is a foundation co-editor of the Routledge Advances in Events Research Series. Their latest book is *Imagining the American West through Film and Tourism* (Routledge, 2015). Warwick is a member of the editorial board of *Journal of Heritage Tourism* and a co-convenor of the International Tourism and Media (ITAM) Conference.

Piet Geleyns was trained as engineer-architect and master in conservation of historic towns and buildings. He has been working as a policy officer at the Flanders Heritage Agency since 2004. His main field of expertise is UNESCO's World Heritage Convention.

Koen Himpe is a landscape-architect (1989, PHITS Anderlecht), and has worked at the Flemish Heritage Agency as a researcher on inventorying and protection of landscape heritage (cultural landscapes, gardens, parks, trees and war cemeteries) since 2004. Previously he was retained as a landscape expert by Vlaamse Landmaatschappij and as a landscape consultant by Belconsulting-Antea-group.

Toyah Horman currently works as a research assistant in the areas of Cultural Heritage and Cultural Diplomacy at the Cultural Heritage Centre for Asia and the Pacific, Deakin University, Melbourne. She participated as a mentor in the Kelabit Highlands Museum Project and has since co-written various articles on the outcomes of the project, as well as featured in the student made documentary, 'A World Within No More'.

Laura James is a PhD researcher in the National Centre for Australian Studies at Monash University, Melbourne, Australia. Currently involved in the 'Anzac Remembered' Australian Research Council-funded project led by Professor Bruce Scates that includes Rae Frances and Keir Reeves, Laura's research is focused on regional remembrance of Anzac Day within Australia, looking at how remembrance of the day has changed and developed over time. Her research interests include the relationship between war heritage and tourism, and the development of war commemorative practices in Australia.

Jennifer Laing is a Senior Lecturer in the Department of Management and Marketing at La Trobe University, Melbourne, Australia. Her research interests include travel narratives, the role of events in society, health and wellness tourism and rural and regional development through tourism, events, heritage and wine. Together with Dr Warwick Frost, Jennifer is a foundation co-editor of the Routledge Advances in Events Research series and they have co-written four books and co-edited two others. Jennifer is a member of the editorial boards of *Journal of Travel Research*, *Tourism Analysis* and *Tourism Review International* and a co-convenor of the International Tourism and Media (ITAM) Conference.

William (Bill) Logan, FASSA, is Professor Emeritus and UNESCO Chair in Heritage and Urbanism at Deakin University, Melbourne, Australia. He is a fellow of the Academy of Social Sciences in Australia and formerly member of the Heritage Council of Victoria and president of Australia ICOMOS. He is co-editor of the Routledge Key Issues in Cultural Heritage series and the *Blackwell Companion to Heritage Studies*. His research interests include World Heritage, heritage and human rights, the heritage of war, and Asian heritage, especially the urban heritage of Vietnam and the management of intangible cultural heritage in Southeast Asia's borderlands with China.

Rowena MacDonald has worked in the Australian museum sector for more than 20 years. With qualifications in history and museum studies, she specialises in exhibition development, and has worked as both a curator and an exhibition project manager at the National Museum of Australia, Museum Victoria and the National Archives of Australia. In 2012 she completed an assignment as an Australian Volunteer for International Development, working with the staff of the Solomon Islands National Museum in Honiara to develop a new permanent exhibition about the history and culture of the Solomon Islands, and a display about the Solomon Scouts and Coastwatchers in World War II.

Samuel Merrill is an interdisciplinary researcher working on the cultural memories, heritages and geographies of a widely conceived underground. He currently holds a post-doctoral position in the Department of Sociology at Umeå University, Sweden. He has an undergraduate degree in Ancient History and Archaeology from the University of Birmingham, a graduate degree in World Heritage Studies from the Brandenburg Technical University and a doctorate in Cultural Geography from University College London. He was awarded first prize in the 2014 Peter Lang Young Scholars in Memory Studies Competition and his first book is on the 'buried memories' of the railways beneath London and Berlin.

Marnix Pieters is a soil scientist and archaeologist. At present he is a senior advisor in maritime heritage at Flanders Heritage Agency and as such involved in the French-Belgian project team that strives to get a selection of World War I sites along the Western Front inscribed on the World Heritage list of UNESCO.

Keir Reeves holds a chair in Australian History and is the Foundation Director of the Collaborative Research Centre in Australian History (CRCAH) at Federation University Australia, Ballarat. His undergraduate training was at Monash University where he took a double degree in arts and economics. He also has a MA and a PhD from the University of Melbourne. He has held academic roles at Monash University as a senior research fellow and prior to that at the University of Melbourne in the former Department of History. He is also interested in thematic history, heritage in Asia and the Pacific. In 2013 he was a Visiting Fellow at Clare Hall, Cambridge and a Visiting Researcher at the McDonald Institute for Archaeological Research, University of Cambridge, where he worked with the Cambridge Heritage Research Group in the Department of Archaeology and Anthropology.

Jennifer Rowe is currently undertaking a PhD in Anthropology with the School of Social Science, University of Queensland. She participated in the Kelabit Highlands Community Museum Development Project field school as a Masters student at Deakin University, co-curated the project's student photographic exhibition '"World Within" No More', and was the 2012 recipient of the Roslyn Lawry award for excellence in the Cultural Heritage and Museum Studies program at Deakin University.

Bruce Scates, FASSA, holds the Chair of History and Australian Studies at Monash University, Melbourne, Australia and is the Director of the National Centre for Australian Studies. He is the author/co-author of several studies of war and memory and is the lead chief investigator on an Australian Research Council project charting the history of Anzac Day in Australia and Aotearoa/New Zealand. He also served as the Chair of the Military and Cultural History panel advising the Anzac Centenary Board and leads the 100 Stories project at Monash University.

Birger Stichelbaut was a research assistant at the Research Foundation Flanders and obtained his PhD 'World War One Aerial Photography: an Archaeological Perspective' in 2009. His general research interest are archaeological prospection, aerial photography for archaeology and conflict archaeology. He currently works as a post-doctoral researcher at the department carrying out a large-scale landscape analysis of World War I sites in West Flanders using historical aerial photographs (1915–18). This project is a collaboration between the In Flanders Fields Museum, the Province of West Flanders and the UGent Department of Archaeology.

Jonathan Sweet is a Senior Lecturer at Deakin University, Australia. His work in recent years has focused on heritage and development issues in Southeast Asia. He has published in the journal *South East Asia Research* and contributed case study chapters to the *Handbook of Research on Religion and Development* (Edward Elgar 2013) and the forthcoming *Oxford Public History Handbook* (Oxford University Press). He is currently completing a book on the subject of museum development and cultural representation for Ashgate Publishing UK.

Yannick Van Hollebeeke is a research assistant in the Archaeology Department of Ghent University, where he is working on historical aerial-photographic coverage of the Région Nord-Pas de Calais (France). His main interest is in the archaeology of modern conflict with a focus on heritage perception and management. He has carried out several projects in Antwerp and Comines-Warneton (Belgium) inventorying and studying the preserved World War I heritage.

Luc Vandael studied architecture and urbanism. After working as an independent consultant at various design companies in Belgium and abroad he joined the Flanders Heritage Agency in 2010. As a policy officer he focuses mainly on World War I heritage.

Hilde Verboven is a researcher at the Flemish Heritage Agency. In 2009 she started a project exploring the relation between (heritage) landscapes and World War I in Flanders. In the meantime she has published several articles on this topic.

Damien Williams is an historian and lecturer in the National Centre for Australian Studies at Monash University, Melbourne, Australia. In 2012 he travelled to London to research the dedication of the RAF Bomber Command memorial in Green Park, London, funded by an Australian Research Council Grant exploring pilgrimages to the memory sites of World War II. He has a PhD in history from the University of Melbourne.

Caroline Winter is a senior lecturer in tourism studies in the Business School at Federation University Australia, Ballarat. She is interested in identifying the ways in which visitors commemorate those who have fought in war – particularly World War I of 1914–18, and has conducted studies in Melbourne, France and Belgium. Caroline has previously taught at universities in New South Wales and Queensland in the areas of tourism, leisure and health, sociology and research methods. Prior to joining Federation University Australia she taught at La Trobe University in Melbourne.

Acknowledgements

This book has been supported by a number of individuals and organisations. The editors thank the Academia Belgica and then Director Professor Walter Geers for hosting a successful event in September 2012 in Rome. Special thanks to Antoinette Dillon for her research assistance on this book.

We also wish to thank Frederik Vervaet, Ann Dillon, Denise Logan, Jolanta Nowak, Colin Long, Geoff Sparkes, Meriam and Tanna Evergreen, the Australian Research Council, the Monash Fellowship Scheme, National Centre for Australian Studies Monash University and the School of Tourism and Hospitality Management, Royal Roads University.

The project 'Great War Heritage Research in Comines-Warneton' was conducted by Ghent University Department of Archaeology for the city of Comines-Warneton. It was funded by the Département du Patrimoine, Direction de l'Archéologie, Service Public de Wallonie (subvention N° 11/49996). The support of the Société d'Histoire de Comines-Warneton et de la région, of the inhabitants of Comines-Warneton and especially of Jean-Claude Coussee, forester of Bois du Gheer, was much appreciated during the research and fieldwork in the region.

Lloyd Carpenter acknowledges the staff of the Tauranga Public Library, New Zealand, who provided invaluable help in this project. The research completed by Debbie McCauley for the 'Tauranga Kete' blog pointed him in the right direction for several aspects of this study. Lee Switzer and Debbie McCauley were also very generous in making photographs of the commemorations available for use in his chapter.

Warwick Frost, Jennifer Laing and David Cragg would like to thank the Victorian Trades Hall for their assistance and Julie Kimber of Swinburne University, Melbourne, Australia for sharing her experiences with them.

Damien Williams thanks Edgar Pickles, John Arnold, Brian and Mary Troath, the RAF 550th Squadron, Godfrey Woods, Penny Claire and Councillor Alistair Moss from the Westminster City Council.

Bruce Scates' chapter is an outcome of the National Centre for Australia Studies, Monash University–led project titled 'Anzac Day at Home and Abroad: A Centenary History of Australia's National Day'. The chapters by Damien Williams and Keir Reeves and Joseph Cheer draw on research undertaken as part of the Australian Research Council Discovery Project 2010–13. Keir Reeves is a chief investigator on a project titled 'Revisiting Australia's war: international perspectives on heritage, memory and ANZAC pilgrimages to the cemeteries, sites and battlefields of World War II (WW2)'.

William Logan's chapter is in part an outcome of an Australia Research Council-funded project entitled 'Australian Heritage Abroad: Managing Australia's Extraterritorial War Heritage' conducted by the author in collaboration with Professor Andrea Witcomb and Dr Bart Ziino, both of Deakin University, Geelong, Australia, and Professor Joan Beaumont of the Australian National University, Canberra, Australia. Logan is indebted to Dr Nguyen Thanh Binh for enabling access to Vietnamese views of death, grieving, remembrance and memorialisation in the published Vietnamese-language literature, internet discussions and interviews, some of which can be found in their earlier joint paper on Dien Bien Phu (Logan and Nguyen 2012).

1   Introduction

Landscape, commemoration and heritage

Keir Reeves, Geoffrey R. Bird
and Birger Stichelbaut

The origins of this book began at a 2012 conference held at the Academica Belgica in Rome titled 'Landscapes of War'. The conference was successful in exposing the range of issues in our understanding of commemoration, remembrance as sites of remembrance. In the years that followed, editors found themselves thinking about acts of remembrance (see Winter 2006), and the landscape of war as a site of commemoration. Three years later, we arrive at this book, with many of the authors involved in those initial discussions in Rome, well into the World War I centenary and the upcoming seventy-fifth anniversaries related to World War II.

Battlefield Events: Landscape, Commemoration and Heritage focuses on war heritage events, commemoration, landscapes of war and the way they are experienced in the present day through tourism and travel. The book is an investigative and analytical study into the way in which significant landscapes of war have been constructed and imagined through events over time to articulate specific narratives and denote consequence and identity (see also Anico and Peralta 2009). This book charts the ways in which a number of landscapes of war have been memorialised and managed from an events perspective, and how the processes of remembering (along with those of silencing and forgetting) at these places have influenced the management of these warscapes in the present day.

Through a survey of the existing literature this chapter sets out the issues and key themes of this book: battlefield events, commemoration, landscapes of war and heritage and explaining the motivations for visiting these battlefields at commemorative events in the present day. In doing so we provide a critical summation of literature to date and how this book advances the knowledge in the area of commemorative battlefield events. It will also set up a framework that argues the best way to understand the interplay between the key themes of this book is through interdisciplinary approaches. This combines heritage, history, landscape, travel and tourism, commemoration and events.

Throughout the world World War I centenary commemoration strategies can be seen through the lens of public memory. However, in areas such as Flanders there are also political and tourism development agendas behind commemorative battlefield events. For example, the Fromelles commemoration is international in reach and involves major transnational strategies of commemoration. Planning and organizing for key events have been under way for several years and predictably involve tourism to key events on an unprecedented scale. Elsewhere commemoration strategies that evaluate workers' service in World War I, such as the Victorian Trades Hall in Melbourne, Australia, are best understood as evolving, longitudinal, intangible heritage practices as much as they are commemorative events.

In this introductory chapter the editors will to provide a set of reference sources and ideas including intergenerational, post-memory motivations for visiting battlefield events as well as the need of many travellers to attend these events *in situ* in the respective warscapes. We use Marian Hirsch's idea that 'post-memory' is a form of retrospective remembrance, those family stories that have come to assume a life of their own. This involves historians employing non-conventional techniques to capture the complexities of what Jay Winter has called 'collective remembrance'.

An obvious example is the mass visiting of the Gallipoli Peninsula in Turkey for the centenary of the Anzac landing. We will also introduce and contextualize other battlefield commemorative events from the New Zealand Wars, World War II, the American-Vietnamese War and the more recent Solomon Islands conflict in the Pacific.

By way of a transnational comparative approach, the authors of this book consider how a number of groups and individuals have drawn meaning from different locales and destinations in their understandings of war and conflict. These comparative case studies will intersect with theoretical discussions on several themes, including remembrance, cultural memory and war-related travel to commemorative events. They also provide new insight into the methods and practices of managing and orchestrating commemorative events. In a sense this book sits as a companion piece to another book in this series *Commemorative Events: Memory, Identities, Conflict* (Frost and Laing 2013) and is informed by research into heritage and war explored by Ziino and Gegner in *Heritage and War* (Gegner and Ziino 2013). Where the book you are holding contributes is in examining the complex relationships that surround the management and meaning of war landscapes and events in the twenty-first century.

However, in the era of the centenary of the World War I, issues relating to the increasing trend of battlefield tourism will also be addressed and examined. This will be done through an examination of the mechanisms that help to create and support heritage tourism, such as key commemorative events. This investigation involves discussion of not only the World War I battlefields of Europe, but twentieth-century landscapes of war worldwide. This book will demonstrate the difficulties of reconstructing the past, and the issues surrounding the protection, commemoration and interpretation of the battlefield landscapes into the future.

This book is quite deliberately aimed at both general and academic audiences. Because of its wide scope thematically, detailing a number of case studies on the commemoration of war and management of warscapes internationally, this book will appeal to those in Europe, North America, South East Asia and Australia equally. With the centenary of the outbreak of World War I, the need for a book of this nature is essential as it provides a longitudinal analysis of the war commemoration events, the associated landscapes, travel to these destinations and discussions of management strategy. It should be noted that increasingly the media frames understandings of commemorative war events and this phenomenon in turn has amplified the profile of events commemorating the centenary of World War I (for a contextual discussion see Andrew Hoskins' 'Ghost in the machine: television and war memory' Hoskins 2007).

Literature review

During the past decade a plethora of literature on war and commemoration has been written. Understandably, this in large part has been driven by the centenary of World War I (itself a veritable commemorative industry in certain parts of the world). The level of public awareness overshadowed governmental and academic scholarly responses to the commemoration of World War I. Literally millions of visitors are travelling to the former Western Front as part of the one-hundredth anniversary celebrations; in April 2015 tens of thousands of Australians and New Zealanders (along with others from Allied countries) travelled to Gallipoli in Turkey to mark the ill-fated landings there. However, another force at work is the inevitable synthesizing of theories, concepts and ideas from the various disciplines and fields of study that have each explored these issues but, in a relatively 'siloed' fashion. Our literature review is to present some of the watershed concepts and insights over the years that allow us to advance our understanding of war remembrance, events and sites of memory.

First, we need to start with what is seemingly an odd term: 'battlefield event'. In the context of heritage and remembrance, a battlefield event is quite simply a formally orchestrated activity on a former battlefield. Such activities are often based on tradition, set into the commemorative calendar and following well-known rituals of music, liturgy, symbols, messages and a collective and known performance of remembering. In this context, commemorative events are a motivation to visit as well as a time to participate in the ritual acts of remembrance.

A battlefield event is typically a commemoration, as most of the chapters in the book examine. However, future areas of research could look at the world of re-enactment, as both an experientially participatory, and a controversial form of remembrance. Typically, unless dealing with a battle such as Waterloo, the American Civil War, or earlier battles, twentieth-century battlefields are not enlisted as a site for re-enactment. Sites such as Pearl Harbor, or the beaches and towns of Normandy, are not yet over the trauma sufficiently to even consider that type of event. As well, there is significant law enforcement relating to what uniforms visitors strolling the streets of the Normandy region are allowed to wear: for example, German uniforms are not allowed to be worn unless permission is granted, and then only in certain 'closed' events.

But commemorative events are certainly a central, ritual aspect of remembrance. Annual commemorations attract significant numbers of international visitors who participate for a variety of reasons: as a marker of the anniversary of the battle, as ritual and as part of the tourist performance. The practice of commemoration is different from other markers such as memorials, cemeteries and museums, in that it is situated in a place at a specific time.

For Connerton (1989: 53), the symbolism and meaning of commemorative practices is where 'myth and ritual diverge', and the voices of the state and religion, veterans and the community at large come together and formally remember. However, for Winter and Sivan (1999) commemoration, as a form of collective remembrance, may involve gathering as a group on a particular day, but what is remembered varies from individual to individual. There can be dissonance in the meaning of commemoration, as Frost *et al.* (2009) note, based on various stakeholders participating in the memory work. Their research, involving a case study of commemorations related to Anzac Day, acknowledges growing criticism of what is viewed as inappropriate behaviour at commemorative events, coupled with conflicting ideas of what is being commemorated. This infers that a certain degree of 'solemnity and moral worthiness' (Frost *et al.* 2008: 170) is expected at such events, leading to gatekeeping with regard to who should be allowed to participate and how.

Whereas tradition largely shapes the form that commemoration takes, what is remembered is defined by who is involved in organizing, as well as those participating in, the memory work (Winter and Sivan 1999). In explaining these points, two perspectives are offered below: the multi-vocal character of commemorations; and sustaining fictive kinship in war memory.

A characteristic of commemorations is their employment as a political instrument. In this context, Hobsbawm and Ranger (1983) point to the invention of various ceremonial traditions as a way of legitimizing the state. Examples of these are the two-minute silence and the wearing of poppies (see Cannadine 1981; Iles 2008). Alternatively, public commemorations may involve various political interests, an example being November 11th Remembrance Day, a Commonwealth holiday, that may evoke the heroic memory of individuals fighting for the nation juxtaposed against the pacifists' call 'never again' (Winter and Sivan 1999). Related to this is the appropriation of sites of memory for new causes, reflecting the multi-vocal character and evolution of memorialized sites (Koshar 2000). Ultimately, Winter (2009: 64) argues that commemorations dealing with war remembrance represent 'a chorus of voices... some louder than others, but they never sound alone'. Thus, there are top-down and bottom-up elements to commemoration, with regional and local twists to the commemorative discourse – what Sturken (1997) might refer to as representing the dynamic, contested element of cultural memories of war that plays out in the ritual of commemoration.

Lemelin's discussion of dissonant heritage (Lemelin *et al.* 2013) is 'to examine the omission of Indigenous narratives in battlefields and sites of conflicts while also highlighting how certain battlefields and sites of conflicts have attempted to address dissonant heritage by diversifying interpretation strategies and implementing elements of collaborative management approaches, thereby addressing Indigenous erasure'. Writing from a Canadian perspective, yet with a global resonance, the authors explore how indigenous people greatly helped British and Canadian militia and other fighters in battlefields and sites of conflict. However, owing to diversifying interpretation of touristic strategies and management, indigenous narratives in battlefields are ignored. Winter (2000) offers the concept of the commemorative process, the means by which ritual becomes established, as central to sustaining the war memory over time.

These acts point to the role of the state in mediating major commemorations. However, there are many towns with their own war memorials and commemorations. Winter (2006) argues that it is often a local *collective* of individuals who have come together to memorialize and commemorate. This *fictive kinship* is formed because they share a common experience, either as next of kin or as veteran comrades of those who were killed. The challenge to sustaining remembrance is whether the commemorative ritual is adopted by the next generation.

In his study of the Verdun battlefield as a site of memory, Prost (1998) provides a different perspective on the evolution of the commemorative process. He recognizes that there is an evolving process of remembering that involves a range of communities and forms of commemoration. For example, ceremonies at Verdun offer 'three distinct and complementary memories of the battle: the official, patriotic narrative; the veterans' meditative, memorial memory; and the historical memory that is imparted to tourists' (Prost 1998: 394). The distinction between official and veterans' memory is discussed by Pickering (1997) who notes how the veterans' narrative can stand in contrast to the official narrative, stripped of hyperbole, and presenting events in more personal terms (ibid. 205). Thus, over time, the official narrative gains hegemony with the passing of the wartime living memory, as the community involved in memory work evolves and responsibility for the memory is committed to the care of the state. Farmer (1999) illustrates this when she describes the involvement of the state in establishing as a national memorial the martyred village of Oradour-sur-Glane, where the townspeople were massacred and the village destroyed by the Nazis in June 1944.

Seaton (2009a: 96) argues that what distinguishes thanatourism from other forms of tourism is the 'auratic quality' of the site, what can be defined as a socially constructed meaning attributed to the site by its association with death. This Otherness of Death, 'the most powerful of all Others' owing to 'the universality of death' (ibid. 83) is 'the defining feature of thanatourism and... evoking and conserving its auratic impacts are the central tasks of management' (ibid. 75). Auratic quality can involve four attributes. First, it exists in people's imagination, and is collectively shared by a community (see Anderson 1983). Second, the meaning of the space is socially constructed through the influence of individuals, groups and cultures. Third, the meaning of the space is temporal, changing over time. Finally, the significance of the site is subjectively attributed by the individual in the manner he or she chooses, 'often without much reflection' (Seaton 2009a: 96). Seaton is concerned with how tourism manages this aura, which involves addressing issues of commodification as well as the politics associated with remembrance (2009a: 75; 2009b).

Caroline Winter, a contributor to this book, is another who has written about travel to World War I commemorative events. Her work engages with dark tourism as a developing field of theory and research, dealing with the relationships between tourism and death. Between 2014 and 2018 commemorations of the various centenaries of World War I will be held and millions of visitors will travel to participate in these commemorations. In the past, people did not consider some battlefield visitations as being for leisure because many people grieved at graves and war memorials and prayed for those killed. However, not all people will join in commemorations as a form of pilgrimage because some tourists seem to be attracted by entertainment and interest rather than by seeking graves when they visit battlefields. For some a personal connection between visitors and the conflict is important and could mean a shift from pilgrimage to tourism. Not many people have had a personal connection with a person who actually witnessed a war because that generation has now passed away. Pilgrims and tourists are conceptually different in their behaviour. The practice of pilgrimage can be conceived as an effect of social conditions and generational need. While pilgrims focus on spirituality, tourists focus on education and understanding, so pilgrims and tourists can both have their own forms of remembrance (Winter 2011 – for a more general discussion of remembrance see Marshall's (2004) 'Making sense of remembrance').

A key purpose of Winter's article is 'to measure some of the motivations and characteristics of a sample of battlefield visitors' (Winter 2011). As tourists tend to be interested in entertainment rather than graves when they visit battlefields, it is important to adequately identify the motivations for their visit. The theory of dark tourism provides 'a framework through which the motivations and experiences of battlefield tourists for remembrance and education as well as leisure can be better understood' (Winter 2011). Likewise dark tourism is one explanation for the enduring fascination with war heritage and attendance at commemorative war events.

Walton's recent work on Polish war memory describes war memorials in Poland and analyzes Polish historical memory (Walton 2013). In Poland, there are some battlefields, but unfortunately as tourist destinations they are neither organized nor well-known. For Walton the idea of battlefields and their associated commemorative events has a broader significance that recognizes that 'an understanding of the role of memory and commemoration is fundamental for all of modern European history' (Walton 2013). Throughout most countries in Europe are a high level of public commemoration and interpretation of history and battles, all of which in some respect promotes dark tourism. For example, in France and England there are monuments or memorial statues to war dead in every major town or village. In addition, the towns and cities where most of the deaths occurred in World War I have lists of the dead prominently carved in stone.

Holyfield and Beacham 'examine the commemoration of the American Civil War through symbolic structure of "fragmented" and "multi-vocal" commemorative sites' (Holyfield and Beacham 2011). American Civil War memorials are remembrance of the most difficult past faced in American history because American-African people were included in the war and slavery existed. Therefore, people are now struggling over how people remember the Civil War, its causes and results. The African American Civil War Memorial and Museum exists as a multi-vocal site because, in that museum, there are many kinds of historical material such as housing artefacts, documents, and displays of heroism and sacrifice that are relevant to all Americans. Visiting museums or battlefields encourages people to understand what happened in the past, catch ancestors' appeals and feelings and obtain correct knowledge and precise details.

Hau's work investigates relationships between nationalism and war commemoration in Latin America (Hau 2013). In Europe, war commemoration is quite important for tourists or pilgrims, and there are a lot of statues, monuments, street names on roads, in cities, etc. but in Latin America war commemoration has not been important to the memory work in the region. Accordingly, battle scenes and the names of military heroes are rarely found on streets, in cities or village names, so war commemoration in Latin America does not play the major role in local nationalism that it does in Western culture. Instead, Latin America focuses on textbooks to get knowledge about war commemoration, so almost all students learn the history of the country's wars, national heroes, battlefields, war commemorations and so on from textbooks. Yet for many, visiting a museum or a battlefield commemorative event is their primary and often most enduring experience of war and the primary way of understanding past conflicts.

Morgan and Dunkley (2011) explore the motivations and experiences of tourists who visit battlefields and conflicts. As mentioned above, there are two types of tourists, pilgrims and personal tourists. Pilgrimage has spiritual characteristics and prayers for the war dead figure deeply in pilgrims' individual experiences. On the other hand, personal and collective remembrance is represented not from feelings but from moral obligation to the dead. Determining specific motivations is difficult because it depends on highly personal experiences that are rooted in individual perceptions. Dark tourism has a wide intellectual currency but the term includes negative connotations. At the same time, more memorial museums have opened all over the world to show historical materials originating from battlefields. Therefore tourists can get a chance to see historical materials and experience the past. This paper demonstrates 'how battlefield tours offer opportunities for pilgrimage, collective and personal remembrance and event validation' (Morgan and Dunkley 2011). Morgan and Dunkley also observe that pilgrimage is a task to be done annually. It is not leisure, enjoyment or satisfaction. The pilgrimage is something sacred and ceremonial and is embedded within a process of commemoration. Having a special or historical interest in the conflict or battlefield sites was a motive for participants in this study. The special interest was rooted in the individual's socialization or current lifestyle. Others such as Winter have suggested that the use of the term 'pilgrim' to denote a battlefield tourist is erroneous and, by extension, to attend a war commemorative event is not a pilgrimage but instead a personal visitor experience.

For Murakami the types of purpose for which tourists visit battlefields include pilgrimage, sociality and materiality of commemoration and personal and perspective commemoration (Murakami 2014; see also Bird 2011). Pilgrimage is a social practice of commemoration where the dichotomy between the sacred and the profane, good and evil, blurs. The pilgrims can provide a place and time to pray for veterans, for the war dead, or for family, as well as memorial services. The most significant role of pilgrimage is related to religion.

Battlefield pilgrimages are a personal journey and contribute to personal transformation. During a pilgrimage, people can spend much time looking at themselves, and be aware of their own consciousness. Transformation can influence individuals and others. 'Learning as a transformational experience, becomes critically aware that personal assumptions made about the world constrain new perspectives' (Murakami 2014). Looking at oneself also represents the life-review process: pilgrimages give a chance to remember and review one's life. For a long time veterans have performed battlefield pilgrimages but recently this has been more as a conceptual basis for understanding pilgrimages, pilgrimage representing a process of achieving beliefs, cultures and religions. Murakami's ethnographic approach to studying the commemorative practice highlights how veterans and participants remember together not only with the use of language, but also with artefacts.

According to Winter (2012) some tourists visit battlefields for leisure activities, education and interests in war history, while others visit battlefields for a commemoration, remembrance, etc. for a personal reason. An individual's personal connection with a site plays a significant role in their visitation behavior, and this has proven useful in visitor management of heritage areas. Tourists have various key motivations to travel to battlefields. Moreover, young people have no knowledge and experience of events and contacts with those who served in the war, so it is important for young generations to visit battlefields and understand what happened in the past. How do they relate to their interests in battlefields of World War I? 'Familial and national connection are not the only connections that people may have with battlefields, however they were selected on the basis of their importance in the formation of social memory of the war over the past century' (Winter 2012). Family site connection is usually for large pilgrimages to pray for the war dead. Pilgrimages are one form of travel, and while their social or traditional practice was motivated by religious reasons, their associations with World War I have typically focused around bereavement. 'Research has found that people can have transformative experiences during their visit to a battlefield and that those without any personal connection can have a deeply emotional experience' (Winter 2012). A person with family connections to a battlefield could be greatly affected by educational and leisure experiences as well.

Museums are the conduit for interpreting histories in battlefields and providing historical materials. To increase visitation of museums, a village started to provide refreshment services and other additional services. According to Winter '[o]ne of the benefits of destination life cycle models is to provide a reminder of the need for monitoring and management of visitation in order that negative impacts for visitors, landscapes, and local people can be minimized and positive impacts maximized'. This paper points out that it is necessary to identify a proper measure for social carrying capacity in terms of aspects of village life, cemetery visitation or the use of facilities.

The purpose of Jenny Macleod's 2013 paper is to examine some aspects of the relationships between the local, regional, national and Imperial layers of identity that are inherent in Britishness by focusing on war commemoration, national museums and war museums. People can create collective memories and develop national identity through commemoration. There are four regions in the United Kingdom – Wales, Scotland, Northern Ireland and England – and each region has its own culture, histories and battlefields. To differentiate from other regional features at museums, national memorials need to explore the way in which different layers of identity are negotiated in this period. By considering the national war memorials to World War I in comparative fashion, the materials in each region show the nature of national identity in Britain and Ireland, and offer the opportunity to explore the relationships between Englishness, Scottishness, Welshness, Irishness and what was once an overarching Britishness. By visiting war commemorations and national museums, people can seek a county's or region's histories and identify their ancestors' roots. In addition, by exploring their own roots, they can understand Englishness, Scottishness, Welshness, Irishness and Britishness, and investigate national identity. As mentioned in the text, people can develop national identity through commemoration, so seemingly each region needs to create commemoration to attract tourists.

Conclusion

As Scates *et al.* observe, 'memory of war is partial and selective… it is produced out of complex relations of public culture and private experience, and… commemorative rhetoric often conceals as much as it recalls' (Scates *et al.* 2012). Commemorative events reinforce what is remembered more than any other process in the present day. The visitor to a wartime commemorative event is part of the construction of heritage in the present day. It is not history that is being made but a construction of the past to suit the present. World War I commemoration is the most topical example for this decade but in fact commemorative events have a more enduring appeal that continues to serve, in the cases of Gallipoli, Fromelles or Dien Bien Phu, to reify the relationship between heritage, landscape and battlefield events. These commemorative events often occur at sites of memory 'spectacular and triumphant, imposing and generally imposed – either by a national authority or by an established interest, but always from above – characteristically hav[ing] the coldness and solemnity of official ceremonies' (Nora 1998). This book includes discussion of epic events such the as the World War I centenary. Yet it also introduces other less well-known themes and events such as the Victorian Trades Hall, the Ni-Vanuatu and Solomon Islander perspectives.

In this volume many of the individual papers contain links with 'events' such as Fromelles, Vimy Ridge and Ypres during World War I, and the John Frum Ceremony in Tanna (a small island in the Pacific) with its origins in the American presence during World War II. Others associate with an event but also investigate thematic approaches: the role of museums and war memory is clear in chapters on Malaysia and the Solomon Islands, and important considerations and analysis of the role of state-sanctioned commemoration runs through the chapters by Vandael *et al* and Logan. The chapter by Stichelbaut, Van Hollebeeke and Bourgeois is about the archaeology of the landscape where the role of the battlefield is central to understanding the commemorative event.

All these offerings highlight how the commemorative events of the centennial have triggered public interest in the theme and ensured that because of the mass tourism there is a need to show this landscape to a large audience. After all, the event of World War I itself triggered the transformation of a landscape that is a source of continuing academic and public interest a century later.

References

Anderson, B. R. O. G. (1983). *Imagined Communities: Reflections on the Origin and Spread of Nationalism* (London: Verso).

Anico, M. and Peralta, E. (2009). *Heritage and Identity: Engagement and Demission in the Contemporary World* (London: Routledge).

Bird, G. R. (2011). 'Tourism, remembrance and the landscape of war', PhD dissertation (University of Brighton).

Cannadine, D. (1981). 'War and death, grief and mourning in modern Britain', in J. Whaley (ed.), *Mirrors of Mortality: Studies in the Social History of Death* (London: Europa Publishing), pp. 187–242.

Connerton, P. (1989). *How Societies Remember* (Cambridge: Cambridge University Press).

Farmer, S. B. (1999). *Martyred Village: Commemorating the 1944 Massacre at Oradour-sur-Glane* (Berkeley; London: University of California Press).

Frost, W. and Laing, J. (2013). *Commemorative Events: Memory, Identities, Conflict* (London: Routledge).

Frost, W., Wheeler, F. and Harvey, M. (2009). 'Commemorative events: sacrifice, identity and dissonance', in A.-K. Jane, R. Martin, F. Alan and L. Adele (eds), *International Perspectives of Festivals and Events* (Oxford: Elsevier), pp. 161–71.

Gegner, M. and Ziino, B. (2012). 'Introduction: the heritage of war: agency, contingency, identity', in M. Gegner and B. Ziino (eds), *Heritage of War* (Abingdon, UK: Routledge), pp. 1–15.

Hau, M. (2013). 'Nationalism and war commemoration – a Latin American exceptionalism?' *Nations and Nationalism, 19*(1), 146–66.

Hobsbawm, E. J. and Ranger, T. O. (1983). *The Invention of Tradition* (Cambridge: Cambridge University Press).

Holyfield, L. and Beacham, C. (2011). 'Memory brokers, shameful pasts, and civil war commemoration'. *Journal of Black Studies, 42*(3), 436–56.

Hoskins, A. (2007). 'Ghost in the machine: television and war memory', in S. Maltby and R Keeble (eds), *Communicating War: Memory, Media and Military* (Bury St Edmunds, UK: Arima Publishing).

Iles, J. (2008). 'Encounters in the fields – tourism to the battlefields of the Western Front'. *Journal of Tourism and Cultural Change*, *6*(2), 138–54.

Koshar, R. (2000). *From Monuments to Traces: Artifacts of German Memory, 1870–1990* (Berkeley, CA: University of California Press).

Lemelin, R. H., Whyte, K. P., Johansen, K., Desbiolles, F. H., Wilson, C. and Hemming, S. (2013). 'Conflicts, battlefields, indigenous peoples and tourism: addressing dissonant heritage in warfare tourism in Australia and North America in the twenty-first century'. *International Journal of Culture, Tourism and Hospitality Research*, *7*(3), 257–71.

Lowenthal, D. (1996). *Possessed by the Past* (New York: Free Press).

Macleod, J. (2013). 'Britishness and commemoration: national memorials to the First World War in Britain and Ireland'. *Journal of Contemporary History*, *48*(4), 647–65.

Marshall, D. (2004). 'Making sense of remembrance'. *Social and Cultural Geography*, *5*(1), 37–54.

Morgan, N. and Dunkley, R. (2011). 'Visiting the trenches: exploring meanings and motivations in battlefield tourism'. *Tourism Management, 32*(4), 860–68.

Murakami, K. (2014). 'Commemoration reconsidered: Second World War veterans' reunion as pilgrimage'. *Memory Studies*, *7*(3), 339–53.

Nora, P. and Kritzman, L. D. (eds) (1998). *Realm of Memory: The Construction of the French Past* (New York; Chichester: Columbia University Press).

Pickering, J. (1997). 'Remembering D-Day: a case history in nostalgia', in J. Pickering and S. Kehde (eds), *Narratives of Nostalgia, Gender, and Nationalism* (Basingstoke: Macmillan), pp. 182–210.

Prost, A. (1998). 'Verdun realms of memory', in P. Nora and L. D. Kritzman (eds), *Realms of Memory: The Construction of the French Past* (New York; Chichester: Columbia University Press), pp. xii, 751.

Scates, B., Frances, R., Reeves, K., Bongiorno, F., Crotty, M., Knapman, G., Seal, G., Becker, A., Reeves, A., Soutphommasane, T., Blackburn, K., Clarke, S. J., Stanley, P., Hoskins, A., Winter, J., Bridge, C., James, L., Wheatley, R., Riches, L., McCosker, A. and Sleight, S. (2012). 'Anzac Day at home and abroad: towards a history of Australia's national day'. *History Compass, 10*, 523–36. doi: 10.1111/j.1478-0542.2012.00862.x.

Seaton, A. V. (2009a). 'Purposeful otherness: approaches to the management of thanatourism', in R. Sharpley and P. Stone (eds), *The Darker Side of Travel: The Theory and Practice of Dark Tourism* (Toronto: Channel View).

Seaton, A. V. (2009b). 'Thanatourism and its discontents: an appraisal of a decade's work with some future issues and directions', in T. Jamal and M. Robinson (eds), *The SAGE Handbook of Tourism Studies* (London: SAGE), pp. 521–42.

Sturken, M. (1997). *Tangled Memories: the Vietnam War, the AIDS Epidemic, and the Politics of Remembering* (Berkeley: University of California Press).

Walton, R. E. (2013). 'Collective memory in contemporary Poland and pre-independence (1918) warfare: an early 21st century foreign traveler's observations concerning Polish battlefield memorials'. *Review of European Studies, 5*(2), 1–12. doi:10.5539/res.v5n2p1. Available at http://search.proquest.com.ezproxy.royalroads.ca/docview/1440186685/fulltextPDF?accountid=8056.

Winter, C. (2011). 'Battlefield visitor motivations: explorations in the Great War town of Ieper, Belgium'. *International Journal of Tourism Research, 13*(2), 164–76.

Winter, C. (2012). 'Commemoration of the Great War on the Somme: exploring personal connections'. *Journal of Tourism and Cultural Change, 10*(3), 248–63.

Winter, C. (2014). 'Tourism to the battlefield memorials in Fromelles'. *Tourism Review International, 17*(3), 211–22.

Winter, J. (2000). 'Public history and the "historial" project 1986–1998', in S. Blowen, M. Demossier and J. Picard (eds), *Recollections of France: Memories, Identities and Heritage in Contemporary France* (New York: Berghahn Books), pp. 52–67.

Winter, J. M. (2006). *Remembering War: The Great War between Memory and History in the Twentieth Century* (New Haven, CT: Yale University Press).

Winter, J. M. (2009). *The Legacy of the Great War: Ninety Years On* (Kansas City, MO: University of Missouri Press; National World War I Museum).

Winter, J. M. and Sivan, E. (1999). *War and Remembrance in the Twentieth Century* (Cambridge; New York: Cambridge University Press).

2 The unquiet grave

Exhuming and reburying the dead of Fromelles

Bruce Scates

On 19 July 2010, a party of soldiers lifted a coffin onto what served as a symbolic gun carriage and began a slow journey to a cemetery less than a kilometre away. The remains were the last to be removed from a mass grave entombing 250 soldiers of the Great War. As the tarnished buttons and bronze shoulder straps told us, most were Australian. But archaeologists also wrested shreds of British uniform from dark earth shadowed by a stretch of woodland. It had taken 17 weeks to carefully excavate all the bodies, many months more to catalogue thousands of relics and belongings and over a year to identify some of these men's descendants. This last coffin, like all that preceded it, would be buried in a cemetery bearing the name of the place where these men were first buried – Pheasant Wood.

The cemetery, like the exhumations, was a long, difficult and costly undertaking. This had been the largest single recovery of human remains from the Great War since the 1920s and it would be the last time the Cross of Sacrifice would be raised on French soil. Heavy clay and the low-lying water table of Flanders had posed problems in terms of drainage. An artificial mound was created, elevating cross, tombstones and coffins alike, lifting them skyward in what some saw as an act of salvation. Four years later a purpose-built museum would adjoin the graveyard, outlining the sequence of the battle, charting the recovery process and displaying some of over 6,000 items recovered from Pheasant Wood. No one knows the real cost of the recovery process, and the creation of the museum and the cemetery, let alone the dedication service – but it must have run to several million pounds. Fromelles was a huge state investment in the commemorative process, and one carefully aligned with the first reburials of soldiers in the immediate aftermath of war. Commonwealth War Graves officials chose an unknown soldier, as the last man to be reburied, a deliberate act mirroring the equality of commemoration set down in the Commission's charter and honouring several reburials still unidentified by DNA testing, known only 'unto God' (Scates, field notes, 19 July 2010).[1]

The choice of 19 July for the dedication service was equally deliberate: this was the anniversary of the bloodbath that claimed these men's lives almost a century ago. Fought over 27 hours, the Battle of Fromelles was a costly, ill-planned diversion near the beginning of the Somme offensive. It was the first time Australians were sent 'over the top' in France and in those two days of fighting the Australian Imperial Force (AIF) suffered over 5,000 casualties. The landing at

Gallipoli seems almost tame by comparison; at Fromelles casualties in a single day exceeded the Australian combined tolls for the Boer, Korean and Vietnam wars. To those versed in the battles of the Great War, Fromelles provides a case study of failed intelligence, tactics, weaponry and strategy. It encapsulated the madness of the Somme in a single action, a potent mix of tragedy, confusion, blind hope and farce.

Fromelles involved a frontal assault on the Aubers Ridge, a slight rise of ground overlooking the flat, bleak fields of Flanders. The stated aim was to prevent the Germans from reinforcing their lines to the south, where fierce fighting along the Somme had already consumed an army. Originally intended as a 'demonstration' or a feint, Fromelles from the outset had no clear or viable strategic objective. Despite a preparatory bombardment by allied guns (including a battery of Australian artillery), German defences remained largely intact, protected by a series of well-sited concrete bunkers. Despite calls from senior officers to cancel the attack, Australian and British troops advanced in broad daylight. Many were killed within minutes of the 'hop over', cut down by machine gun and artillery fire as they stepped out of the sally ports.[2] The trauma of that day is still marked on what remains of their bodies. Forensic archaeologists recorded 'extensive battlefield injuries', broken bones, shattered bodies, 'blast, projectiles and sharp force traumas' (Loe 2010: 32)

The trauma of the missing

The battle at Fromelles was terrible enough. But equally exacting in a way was the toll it took on families back home. The bodies of many of the men killed that day were never recovered. Most lay out in No Man's Land, exposed to the elements, decaying away. That thought was deeply troubling to families raised in what Pat Jalland (2006) has called a Victorian code of death and mourning, a code that placed great store on the decent burial of the dead. Worse still were the false hopes the absence of a body generated. Families were told their men were 'Missing', and many clung to the possibility that they were still alive. Most of the bereaved, like Abbie Mendelsohn, craved some 'definite news' about the fate of husbands, brothers and (in her case) sons. Within hours of hearing of that 'terrible battle', she wrote the first of many letters to the authorities. The 'official telegram' (bluntly announcing Berrol's death) was simply not enough: 'my heart is aching to know how he lost his dear life' (Mendelsohn, A., 1916, in (NAA) B2455).

> I am just heartbroken at this great loss, and my distress has been considerably intensified at not getting any details. Can you help me? I do hope you will be able to find out where my darling hero lies buried. I know nothing at all, and I have not had one night sleep since I received this dreadful news... It is nearly 6 months since my son was killed and so far none of my letters have been returned, neither have parcels... I value every article he possessed and would like to have them to keep forever.
>
> (Mendelsohn, A., 1917, in (NAA) B2455)

In time the details drifted in – though they offered little solace to a mother who had lost 'an ideal son' (Mendelsohn, A., 1916, in (NAA) B2455). The men who fought beside Lt Mendelsohn confirmed his death was instantaneous – and that her boy had died bravely. 'I was with him... when he was hit by a shell', Pte Johnson told a Red Cross worker. 'I saw him just before he died and again after he was dead. He did not seem to suffer' ((AWM) 1DRL/0428). Many of Mendelsohn's belongings were returned to his mother: the personal kit left behind in the trenches at Fromelles, a trunk transported from Marseille, even an identity disc taken from the body by the Germans. A hessian parcel containing an assortment of books, clothing and photographs finally reached the family home in Mossman as late as 1921, a full five years after Berrol's death. 'Such poor little sad articles', Mrs Mendelsohn wrote to Major McLean, 'and my boy had so much which I would love to treasure' (Mendelsohn, A., 21 May 1921, in (NAA) B2455).

And then there was what Mrs Mendelsohn called the 'saddest trial' of all, not knowing what had become of that 'dear boy's' body. On the eve of Anzac Day 1919 she wrote yet again to Major McLean. The officer in charge of Base Records must have dreaded her letters:

> I have waited and waited, in the hope that you might have been able to get some information for me... I have so far received no tidings of his burial place, the only news I have had from the front was that his body was never recovered from the trenches. He was killed in action in France on 20 July 1916, and that is all I know... Each time I have written to you... [I've felt] sure you will do all you can to help me... and I often think that if I knew where my dear son was buried it would be some... consolation.
>
> (Mendelsohn, A., 1919, in (NAA) B2455)

Two years later Mrs Mendelsohn was waiting still. Towards the end of 1921, the authorities dispatched a memorial scroll bearing a grateful message from the King. That only triggered a new spate of enquiries:

> Enclosed please find the receipt for the memorial scroll. I am still waiting, and hoping to hear that the grave of my darling son has been found, but so far have not had that consolation. Could you possibly give me any address I could write to for information and anyone I could enquire from re the above? I would even write to Germany to enquire if they could find out for me if I knew whom to write about it... The heartbreaking thought of not knowing where my darling son lies buried is always with me and it would give me much to know where.
>
> (Mendelsohn, A., 14 September 1921, in (NAA) B2455)

It was the last such letter that Mrs Mendelsohn would write. She died at the age of 80, still 'tormented by not knowing where [Berrol's body] lay' (Mendelsohn, O., 2010 cited in Abitbol 2010). Mrs Mendelsohn's unresolved bereavement mirrored that of a generation.

Finding the lost

Berrol Mendelsohn's remains were not amongst the bleached skeletons brought in from No Man's Land in the immediate aftermath of war. Over 300 men were buried at VC Corner Cemetery within sight of their original trench lines. None could be identified, so the names of all Australian soldiers still missing from the action (Mendelsohn's included) were inscribed in stone on the cemetery wall. Nor, as it turned out, was Mendelsohn recovered in the many isolated burials of 'unknowns'. Unidentified graves are littered in dozens of cemeteries within a ten-mile radius of the battlefield, and any of these men 'known unto God' could well have fallen at Fromelles. But Mendelsohn's fate was different. Unknown to his mother, his body was one of hundreds gathered up by the Germans and hastily interred in those mass graves at Pheasant Wood.

The exhumation of this gravesite was deeply controversial – and in fact the first response of the Australian government was to deny that these graves existed at all. An expert panel was appointed in 2005 to investigate the claim that German forces had buried Australian and British dead in three deep pits dug not long after the battle. The government's default position was that the men had been buried gelsewhere. Those men unacccounted for (like Berrol Mendelsohn) might have been recovered after the war and buried as unknowns. Those pits might have been dug for some other purpose. Despite aerial photographs taken in 1917, despite evidence that bodies had been carted to that very field, despite page after page of verbatim testimony, the Australian government steadfastly refused to initiate a physical search. Then one of the historians appointed to the panel produced compelling new evidence: a letter had come to light confirming that War Graves Units in the 1920s had acknowledged the existence of these mass graves, searched for them but never found them. Faced with the growing weight of archival evidence, besieged by lobby groups and embarrassed by the media, the government capitulated. In 2007, it returned to a task that the authorities had effectively abandoned in 1921 – Australia would resume the search for the missing.[3]

In many ways the government's reluctance is understandable. Opening the graves at Pheasant Wood set an alarming precedent. There are any number of unidentified graves littered across Flanders and the Somme, and no shortage of documentation suggesting where they might be. If this search began, others would be sure to follow. And to what length should we go now to identify these men? In the 1920s enquiries were exhaustive; specially trained units sifted through belongings and remains hoping to put a name to the missing. Today forensic techniques and DNA testing have made that search an exacting – and expensive – science. Then there is what one might call the inequality of commemoration. Mrs Mendelsohn longed for news of the burial place of her son; she would die never knowing. Almost a century on, science now offers the certainty denied the generation that most needed it. Can the great-great-nephew of a soldier lost over a century ago really grieve for a man he never knew? Can *he* claim any kind of 'closure' (Beaumont 2009)? Finally, in commemoration – as in war – there are winners and losers. Australian and British dead recovered from the mass pits of Fromelles were reverently reburied in that purpose-built cemetery. No one has recovered the bodies of Algerian troops also slaughtered in their droves at Fromelles: who cares to put a name to them? The moral, ethical and political questions raised by the exhumation at Fromelles may never be answered – least of all by historians.

Links to the past

What we can investigate is why the recovery of these bodies mattered. One hundred years after the Great War began, why do we place such immense significance on the deaths of these men? Some historians have argued that the commemoration of the Great War – the honouring or recovering of soldiers killed a century ago – serves a conservative political purpose. This, they claim, is a state-fostered remembrance, funded by massive financial investment, cynically manipulated by the mass media and 'manufactured by the prevailing political and commercial imperatives in Australia' (McKenna and Ward 2007, pp 141–51; McKenna 2014, pp 151–68). Few would deny that the state frames the commemorative impulse evidenced at Fromelles. As in the 1920s, it is the state that creates graveyards, recovers the bodies to fill them and orchestrates elaborate rituals like that witnessed during the dedication at Fromelles. The question is whether the commemorative frenzy that attends the centenary of the Great War was driven from above, or is a response to popular demand, or a bit of both. The memory boom that has marked recent times is certainly too complex and too widespread a phenomenon to fall within the jurisdiction of any government agency. And whilst patriotic platitudes abound in the popular press (and in many of the speeches made at official ceremonies), inviting the testimony of family descendants and respecting and recording their personal and emotional investment in history often yield a richer and more nuanced response.

The memory of Fromelles is complex and multi-faceted. Indeed, what we see at Fromelles is not really memory at all. Memory dies with the passing of a witness to an event. A phenomenon called post-memory follows it, a collage of family narratives, physical artefacts and imagined or perceived connections with the past. Perhaps the most distinctive feature of the post-memory of Fromelles is its unresolved character, the way one generation self-consciously takes up the task of mourning for another, the lingering legacies of families like the Mendelsohns.

Such a war memory has a distinctly intergenerational character.[4] The wounds of war, as one of my respondents aptly put it, festered from one decade to another, linking survivors to those who came after them. Graeme's grandfather spent a total of nine days in the front line trenches. His war ended abruptly as he climbed over the parapet at Fromelles and stumbled into No Man's Land. Harry was 37 when he enlisted and sailed off to war, leaving behind a wife and four children. He returned to them two years later with an arm mangled by shrapnel and a mind deeply troubled by the horrors he had seen. Graeme has spent much of his life trying to regain a 'picture' of his grandfather, wresting the truth from 'family mythology', reckoning with personal, archival and anecdotal memory. His recollection of old Harry hardly seems the stuff of romanticised Anzac mythology. Graeme described

a man broken by battle, who drank and smoked far too much, whose body gaped
with wounds, whose lungs were splintered with shrapnel, who coughed his life
away. 'My grandfather', he wrote, 'lost much more than an arm in that war'
(Graeme W., nd)

Children and grandchildren often shared in that survivor's tragedy. Graeme has
visited Fromelles four times now, and each time he has walked the ground where
his grandfather was wounded. 'There's blood in the soil', he wrote to me; it
embodied a sense of his family's abiding loss, a world and 'a history' he now
struggles to reclaim:

> There is little to remind us of Harry's journey. There are the usual photographs
> of him in uniform, some with the slouch hat and some with a peaked cap. He
> received 3 service medals all of which are lost. I still have the [identification]
> tag with his service number 624 stamped on it and the name 'Kitty' scratched
> by him on the back – his wife. I've read about that night of the Battle of
> Fromelles and realise that it was utter carnage and a total waste. A lot of men
> died, and a lot of men, like Harry, not only gave up an arm they gave up their
> futures. Now I want to know more of what he experienced and try to gain
> some sense of [Harry himself].
>
> (Graeme W., 19 July 2006, personal communication)

Gaining 'some sense of him' drives much of the 'memory boom' that attends the
Great War. Here a useful distinction might be made between memory and
remembrance. The former, as Jay Winter has observed, is limited to the individual
with personal experience of the past they are remembering. Remembrance, by
contrast, is a social phenomenon in which individual ideas about the past are
created, reconfigured or passed on. Those with a personal memory of Fromelles
died with the last of the survivors but (as Graeme's account confirms) the children
and grandchildren of those witnesses remain (Winter 2006).

Women are also involved in these acts of 'historical remembrance', breaching
what is often presented as a masculine monopoly of the memory of war. Helen lost
two uncles at Fromelles, Jack, buried at VC Corner, and Tim, whose body was
never found:

> My dad was named after Uncle Jack… so it was very important to visit his
> grave. All our lives we had heard of the Uncles but had always thought they
> died at Gallipoli. A couple of years ago I started researching our family tree
> and found our mistake. In the process of searching around I found people I
> didn't know existed, but in every instance each one had known about our
> Uncles who had died. They became a common denominator, a link we all
> treasured.
>
> (Helen C., 27 July 2006, personal communication)

That term 'link' again. Helen's letter reminds us once more of the process whereby
pilgrims actively reconstitute their history. At one level, as Jay Winter has argued,

this process attempts to situate a family story in a larger national narrative. In that light, it is hardly surprising Helen believed her uncles had died at Gallipoli. The memory boom craves connection with history's metanarratives and the Anzac mythology remains Australia's defining memory of war.[5] But the linkage works in other ways as well. Helen was also conscious that this was a family memory, circulated within a near and distant community of mourners, a common loss all her relations shared. Recovering and revising that memory was made possible by the internet. The digitisation of soldiers' records has placed history within reach of the keyboard, enabling access to knowledge once locked away in the archives. Researchers like Helen read and reread family letters in Red Cross records, they explore graphic accounts of the battle that claimed 'their' soldier and (like the families who mourned him) relive and reassess the circumstances of his death. This is a new and revitalised form of remembrance. It reinvests the history of the Great War with affectivity and sentiment, personalising the past and keeping it within the domain of memory.

The testimony of those distant descendants often has a deeply disturbing character. Like Graeme's and Helen's accounts, Tim's has the character of what psychologists have termed 'a secondary trauma'. His earliest memory of childhood is the unresolved grieving of an ageing aunt and that picture of a great-uncle he never knew:

> I remember her reaction very vividly. It was at our dinner table… and she said to me 'Don't ever be a soldier – you'll… be shot like Uncle Harry'… That's all she or any of her generation knew of [Harry's] fate… it left an indelible mark on my Nan and that emotion I can… remember like it was yesterday.
>
> (Tim W., nd)

Tim sifted through Red Cross records to find some trace of Uncle Harry: 'The poor bugger was shot through the jaw… He must have bled to death suffering a terrible wound. A worse way to die I can't think of. Alone scared and bleeding' (Tim W., nd; Tim W., 25 July 2006, personal communication). And in search of Harry he has visited the battlefield at Fromelles no fewer than four times:

> Walking the ground they fought and died on gives me a little bit of empathy with them. It's important to me… It's no longer 'they' it's 'we' to some extent… I would love to leave a sprig of Gippsland wattle… on the grave of my [great-uncle] if he had one… It's about making tangible links, even if he can't come home, some part of home could come to him.
>
> (Tim W., nd)

There is an evident longing here for a physical focus to memory, a 'tangible link' to complete a cycle of mourning, a place to lay a body to rest. Prior to the recovery of his great-uncle's body, Tim expressed a need to embody and locate his grief in terms remarkably reminiscent of the generation that had actually endured war:

There's nothing there to show that MY people were ever there, even though I know my family should have some sense of ownership of the Fromelles site, there isn't a grave, a memorial, or anything that I can put my hand on and say HARRY WILLIS, DAIRY FARMER FROM ALBERTON FOUGHT AND DIED IN THIS PLACE. So there's always been an emptiness when visiting the place. Maybe that's why I keep going back, maybe next time something will be different.

(Tim W., 25 July 2006, personal communication)

That statement was made in 2006, long before the exhumation process got under way. Now things are different. Harry Willis, like Berrol Mendelsohn, was reco-vered from the anonymity of that mass grave and reburied (with full military honours) in a grave of his own. It was a ceremony Tim attended, along with several hundred others.

Investing meaning in landscape

The dedication service at Fromelles lasted much of the day. The crowd num-bered several thousand: a select group of relatives in the official enclosure, and several tour groups and independent travellers in the paddocks adjoining the site. Proceedings were televised on large screens visible from several angles. The presentation began with readings from letters and diaries (mostly by these men's descendants); it ended with a blast of whistles from every corner of the commemorative precinct: the same shrill call that summoned these men to their deaths.

Both the scale and the structure of the event enabled the author to move freely through the crowd. In addition to the surveys cited above (gathered before the mass graves had been discovered) around 50 interviews were conducted and these ranged from several minutes to half an hour. Family groups were interviewed as well as individuals. Not surprisingly, most of the respondents were Australian, and a large number had some 'family' connection either with Fromelles or another battlefield in France. Most were aged 40 and above, most were of predominantly Anglo-Celtic descent and a large cross-section came from regional Queensland, Victoria and New South Wales.

Some historians have read the new cemetery at Fromelles simply as a political landscape: the reclaiming of the war dead by the state strives to uphold military tradition, and asserts the value of service and sacrifice (McKenna and Ward 2007). But the intimacy of the testimony gathered that day (and in subsequent postal surveys) suggests another reading. Cemeteries, even military cemeteries, create a space for individual memory. Amidst the official process of reburial at Fromelles, there prevailed an insistent individuality, an attempt to 'personalise' the dead. It is not just that a team of forensic scientists laboured to disentangle long co-mingled bodies; nor that over a thousand relatives registered for the DNA sampling Helen offered, determined to give a name to a generation of nameless dead. The personal belongings littered amongst these men (and now on display in the museum) serve to 'regain' some measure of their individuality. These were civilians before they were soldiers – sons, brothers and fathers – not just 'the iconic fallen', or 'anonymous victims' but real human beings. Many of the 'memory objects' recovered are 'heavy with emotional and personal meanings': bibles and prayer books, tattered photographs of loved ones, even a return railway ticket from Perth to Fremantle, kept, one assumes, as a pledge to complete that journey home.[6] One of the first items prised from the soil was a good luck charm from the town of Alberton, Victoria. To Tim, the tarnished pendant seemed like a message from that lost generation, tangible evidence that his great uncle was 'still there'.[7] Archaeologists, a group usually likened to the most dispassionate scientists, openly explore these 'issues of identification, emotion and remembrance'. They speak of offering closure to still grieving families as they sift the yielding earth (Dewilde and Saunders 2009).

The tributes left at Fromelles on the day of dedication inscribed this 'political landscape' with intimate and personal meanings. Poppies, crosses and 'a neatly folded albeit faded Australian flag' are to be expected in a military cemetery (Paul D., nd). But other offerings are far more individual and inventive, re-establishing a broken link with the families and communities these men left behind. As one pilgrim at Fromelles put it, his journey was about 'humanising a number', recovering the memory of men lost long ago, repairing lives 'destroyed... because of war' (anon., 10 July 2010, personal communication). Jessie had three great uncles who served at Fromelles; Sam and Eric died there. The exhumation team found the brothers in the pit 'side by side'; their remains were taken to the new cemetery and laid again alongside each other. In 2010, Jessie – and 15 members of her family – attended the dedication service. She 'took soil from the site of the old [family] home at Hibbard, Port Macquarie and some wattle. These were left on the grave as a bit of Australia and a connection to their home' (Jessie W., nd). Julie was asked to place a pebble from the Macleay River on the grave of her great-uncle, and to do that for a 'distant relative' too ill to make the journey and whom she had never known.

> A lady pressed the stone in my hand with the inscription 'A Macleay River Stone, to rest with you, so far from home'... It was such a beautiful thought and brought tears to our eyes when we laid the stone on our boy's grave. I guess we couldn't bring him home but we were able to bring home to him in some small way.
>
> (Julie W., nd)

Photographs were laid on the freshly dug graves, some laminated to withstand for a time the elements, others intended – like the bodies beneath them – to blend with the soil. One family left a photocopy of a mother's letter pleading (like Abbie Mendelsohn) for news of her son. An old man in his 80s carried a blood-stained crucifix back to France – his father had salvaged it from a ruined church in Pozières, 'wrapped it up in his tunic pocket, and carried it all through the war' (anon., 19 July 2010, personal communication). It was returned to the church where it had first been wrested from the rubble. Many placed photographs of the grandchildren and great-grandchildren these men could never have known by their tombstones; others aged coins from home. All these 'items of intimate significance' fostered a sense of 'meaning and belonging' (Read 1996: 6; Hallem and Hockey 2001), bringing (as Tim and Julie put it) something of home to a man buried oceans away. Adrienne crushed the gum leaves she carried in the earth; just to give him 'the smell of home' (Adrienne D., nd).

Epitaphs too were a way of inscribing individuality, restoring a face to those long decayed remains. Roger's family thought long and hard about the words that they would choose:

> A farmer from Gilgandra
>
> Who gave his all
>
> Never forgotten by his family

> We chose that because one of George's great-nephews still owns and farms the property at Gilgandra that had been George's before he went to war. We felt strongly that we needed to put something on the headstone that gave George an identity as a person and let everyone know the place that George called home... [We wanted] to distinguish that soldier from all the others... The reference to 'never forgotten by his family' related of course to his brother's lifelong desire to know where he was buried.

And on visiting the grave dried wattle – 'a very suitable gift to give a boy from the bush' – was 'scattered in the soil' (Roger, nd; Roger, 19 July 2010, personal communication).

Gestures like these are as much about the local as they are the national; they remind us that remembering war is an event centred on families, neighbourhoods and communities. Indeed, some surveys attest to a very localised landscape of grief. Heather had four great uncles who went to war – two of them were killed at Fromelles. She grew up 'in a small country town [and] there were reminders all around us'. Not just the names passed down the family, or photographs on a mantelpiece but 'the church honour roll, the obelisk at [the] Local Park, and other people's knowledge'. To that inherited knowledge, Heather has added her own, scanning (as Helen did) digitised archival records, 'following up' with long conversations over an extended country family gathering (Heather C., nd). Sue spoke of her family's war in a very similar way. Her uncle Horace had been taken prisoner at Fromelles and the tiny country town he lived in lost 19 men in the war.

> We've got a little obelisk... outside [our] little church in Tugong and that's about all there is in Tugong now – this little church, a couple of houses, but there's nothing else there. There's 69 names there... 19 were killed and the rest came home, but they were within a ten-mile radius... you can imagine... [they] were virtually all neighbours... the whole community was changed.

She was mourning for a whole community wrought asunder by war.

> We're a small community. [I came] to honour the people who went away and
> who were our neighbours and who didn't come home. But also Horace who
> came home… He didn't talk a lot about it, a lot of people didn't apparently.
> (Sue, 19 July 2010, personal communication)

None of those who gathered at Fromelles that day had actually known the men
they honoured. In some cases, stories had been passed down the family, in others
not. Some families (as Sue's testimony suggests) still lived in the communities
these men came from, others had scattered across Australia. Indeed, in several
cases it was DNA testing that led to 'a union of families', alerting relatives to the
existence of distant cousins far away (Jim, 19 July 2010, personal communication).
What one pilgrim called 'digging into history' was an attempt to draw connections,
and fill in the blank spaces on the page (Louise, 19 July 2010, personal communication). Gary remembered 'a photo in my grandparents' home in Rockhampton, but
that's about it'. Although his grandmother died at 94, and 'remembered all sorts of
things', she never spoke of the brother recovered from Pheasant Wood (Gary, 19
July 2010, personal communication). Filling in those silences led families back to
the archives and often some surprising discoveries 'came out of the woodwork'.
Liz had always wondered why her mother's name was 'Wandilla': it was the name
of the troopship that carried her grandfather to war (Stephen and Liz, 19 July 2010,
personal communication). But not all the connections were as laboured or as
tenuous. Ian and Rosemary came to Fromelles to honour an uncle lost in 1916. To
them, a mother's grief was not a story in an archive but something very real.

> I can remember my mother being very affected, for years, I mean we were
> born 25 years after he was killed – and I can remember my mother crying,
> Anzac Day and Remembrance Day – it would have been forty years later… I
> only wish she was here. Because she had no idea – they had very little idea.
> My mother used to go to the Anzac Hostel and go round and talk to the people
> who were ill and injured, and soldiers – returned soldiers – and ask them
> whether they knew anything about her brother.

In a sense, Ian and Rosemary's presence at Fromelles that day was a pilgrimage by
proxy. They ushered a clergyman over to the grave and he spoke of God's
'everlasting love' for a boy ('quite a strong church goer') killed at 17 (Ian and
Rosemary, 19 July 2010, personal communication).

Helen (whose testimony was cited earlier) embarked on a similar pilgrimage
by proxy. In doing so she related a long-dead relative's loss as if it were her own:

> My great-grandmother was devastated by the death and never really recovered.
> She remained broken-hearted until she died. Because she could never visit
> Fromelles, she had the following words put on Jack's headstone: 'Would some
> kind mother as you pass on, stop and pray for my poor son'. This request

haunted me, so I 'had' to visit Fromelles for her and I know it's been the same for other members of the family who have been able to go to France… Even today I find it upsetting that Tim's body was never found

(Helen C., 27 July 2006, personal communication).

Contested terrain

However close or distant families may have been, the next of kin still has the right to choose an epitaph. Determining who was the next of kin was often a challenge for the authorities and so too (with so many direct or indirect descendants) were the words that families chose. Often there was some degree of consensus – families opted to list the name of long-dead parents and brothers, symbolically reuniting the lost with their loved ones. Several chose the haunting refrain of 'Amazing Grace', a hymn that resonated with many families and the recovery process itself: 'I once was lost but now am found'. Sarah's 'whole family' chose those words for a great-great-uncle George Croft. They offered, she said, 'that lovely element of closure' (Sarah, 19 July 2010, personal communication). But the choice of epitaph was also a space for disputation, a forum where (extended) families debated the right expression of grief.

The epitaphs chosen was one of historical facts [Julie lamented], naming Fred's parents with no emotional connections which would have been how it was back in those days [when it] was a sign of weakness to show… too much emotion. I personally would have chosen an epitaph of great emotion reflecting that of a mother torn apart in grief.

(Julie, nd)

Whether she would have been permitted such an epitaph is another matter. In the 1920s, the Imperial War Graves Commission reserved the right to veto any epitaph deemed too long, too 'sentimental' or 'inartistic' (Imperial War Graves Commission 1922; Kenyon 1918). Its successor, the Commonwealth War Graves Commission, claims similar rights today. While all the relatives interviewed and surveyed paid tribute to the Commission's diligence in recovering and honouring their dead, several expressed surprise (even mild indignation) at such intervention. The Commission argued that all epitaphs must be in keeping with those written in the 1920s, imposing a uniformity of remembrance once again. And it should be noted that not all relatives consented to the recovery of the bodies originally buried at Pheasant Wood. *Most* insisted that a burial pit could never be a grave, demanded the dead be laid to rest in consecrated ground and emphasised their duty to past generations. Of all these accounts, Tim's was the most graphic:

Let me illustrate it for you. It's not a pretty picture… There's a digger slumped in a sitting position with his handless arms raised above his chest. Another is in a semi-foetal position with a man tossed over his chest. One man has the remnants of the telephone wire the German troops used to drag him into the pit still wrapped around his limbs. Another still wears the tourniquet some friend attached in a vain attempt to save his life. In pits four and five there are no neat rows, no order, and no dignity... They are a sight of abject horror and it would be nothing less than a travesty to leave these fine men like that.

(*Sydney Morning Herald*, 12 July 2008)

But others expressed a horror that graves at Pheasant Wood should be disturbed; they regarded it best to leave the men where they lay, where other soldiers had placed them, bundled together 'with their mates'. Graeme wondered whether commemoration belied the horror of history. Fromelles for him is haunted earth – what Maria Tumarkin (2006) would call a 'traumascape' – and haunted earth it should remain:

The cemeteries were invariably quiet, peaceful and well-tended. But what surprised me was the sameness of it all. Under each gravestone is a soldier or what is left of a soldier. It seems one dead man is the same as the next, according to the official process of interment. Perhaps it cannot be any other way. But the contrast between the horror, the waste, the confusion of war and the orderliness, the tidiness and the sameness of the cemeteries is stark and provides a somewhat distorted view. It is as though we are saying that leaving our dead here in these beautiful resting places compensates for the horror and stupidity and allow us to repeat it all over again.

(Graeme W., nd)

References

Abitbol, C. (2010). 'Lost Jewish digger identified'. *Jewish News*, 18 March.

Bean, C. E. W. (1922). *Official History of Australia in the War of 1914–1918 – Volume 3, The AIF in France 1916* (Sydney: Angus and Robertson).

Corfield, R. (2000). *Don't Forget Me Cobber* (Melbourne: Robin Corfield and Co).

Dendooven, D. (2009). 'The journey back: on the nature of donations to the In Flanders Field Museum', in N. Saunders and P. Cornish (eds), *Contested Objects: Material Memories of the Great War* (London: Routledge), pp. 60–72.

Dewilde, M. and Saunders, N. (2009). 'Archaeology of the Great War: the Flemish experience', in N. Saunders and P. Cornish (eds), *Contested Objects: Material Memories of the Great War* (London: Routledge), pp. 251–65.

Filippicci, P. (2009). 'Postcards from the past: war, landscape and place in Argonne, France', in N. Saunders and P. Cornish (eds), *Contested Objects: Material Memories of the Great War* (London: Routledge), pp. 220–36.

Hallem, E. and Hockey, J. (2001). *Death Memory and Material Culture* (Oxford: Oxford University Press).

Jalland, P. (2006). *Changing Ways of Death in Twentieth Century Australia: War, medicine and the funeral business* (Sydney: UNSW Press).

Kangisser Cohen, S. (2005). *Child Survivors of the Holocaust in Israel: Finding their Voice* (Brighton: Sussex Academic Press).

Kenyon, F. (1918). *War Graves: How the cemeteries abroad will be designed* (London: HMSO).

Loe, L. (2020). 'Uncovering the fallen', in J. Summers (ed.), *Remembering Fromelles: A new cemetery for a new century* (Maidenhead: CWGC Publishing).

Luckins, T. (2004). *The Gates of Memory: Australian people's experiences and memories of loss and the Great War* (Perth: Curtin University Press).

Lycess, T. and Playle, S. (2013). *Fromelles: the Final Chapters* (Melbourne: Penguin).

McKenna, M. (2014). 'Keeping in step: the Ànzac "resurgence" and military heritage in Australia and New Zealand', in S. Sumatgo and B. Wellings (eds), *National Memory and Great War Commemoration* (Bern: Peter Lang), pp. 151–68.

McKenna, M. and Ward, S. (2007). '"It was really moving mate": the Gallipoli pilgrimage and sentimental nationalism in Australia'. *Australian Historical Studies*, *38*(129), 141–51.

McMullin, R. (2002). *Pompey Elliott* (Melbourne: Scribe).

Read, P. (1996). *Returning to Nothing: the Meaning of Lost Places* Cambridge: Cambridge University Press).

Scates, B. (2010). 'Finding the missing of Fromelles: when soldiers return', in M. Crottty and M. Larsson (eds), *Anzac Legacies: Australians and the Aftermath of War* (North Melbourne: Australian Scholarly Publishing), pp. 212–32.

Scates, B. (2009). 'An Anzac muster: manufacturing memory at Gallipoli', in M. Keren and H. Herwig (eds), *War Memory and Popular Culture: Essays on Modes of Remembrance and Commemoration* (Jefferson, NC; MacFarland), pp. 57–75.

Scates, B. (2006) *Return to Gallipoli, Walking the Battlefields of World War One* (Port Melbourne: Cambridge University Press).

Scates, B. (2002). 'In Gallipoli's shadow: pilgrimage, mourning, memory and the Great War'. *Australian Historical Studies*, *33*(119), 1–21.

Tumarkin, M. (2006). *Traumascapes* (Carlton, VIC: Melbourne University Press).

Winter, J. (2006). *Remembering War: The Great War Between Memory and History in the Twentieth Century* (New Haven, CT: Yale University Press).

Winter, J. (1995). *Sites of Memory, Sites of Mourning: The Great War in European Cultural History* (Cambridge: Cambridge University Press).

Reports/statements

Pollard, A., Barton, P. and Banks, I. (2007). 'Pheasant Wood, Fromelles, evaluation of possible mass graves. Data structure report'. Report commissioned by the Australian Army, July 2007.

Statement by Joan Beaumont at a public forum on war and memory, 18 November 2009, Federation Square, Melbourne; note also the tenor discussion at the Round Table Discussion on the Memory of the Great War, International Congress of Historical Sciences, Sydney, July 2005.

Archives

National Archives of Australia (NAA) B2455, MENDELSOHN, BERROL LAZAR.

Minutes of the Proceedings of the 41st Meeting of the Imperial War Graves Commission... 17 January 1922, NAA: A2909 A453/1/3.

Lt Berrol Mendelsohn, Red Cross Wounded and Missing File, Australian War Memorial (AWM) 1DRL/0428.

Interviews and surveys

Interview, anonymous male 2, Fromelles, 10 July 2010.
Interview, Jessie W., Fromelles, 19 July 2010.
Interview, anonymous male, Fromelles, 19 July 2010.
Interview, Roger, Fromelles, 19 July 2010.
Interview, Sue, Fromelles, 19 July 2010.
Interview, Jim, Fromelles, 19 July 2010.
Interview, Louise, Fromelles, 19 July 2010.
Interview, Gary, Fromelles, 19 July 2010.
Interview, Stephen and Liz, Fromelles, 19 July 2010.
Interview, Ian and Rosemary, Fromelles, 19 July 2010.
Interview, Sarah, Fromelles, 19 July 2010.

Survey completed by Adrienne D. (Malvern VIC).
Survey completed by Jessie W. (Cooma NSW).
Survey completed by Paul D. (Springfield NSW).
Survey completed by Julie W. (Frederickton NSW).
Survey completed by Roger P. (np NSW).
Survey completed by Heather C. (Lane Cove NSW).
Survey completed by Graeme W. (Fairfield VIC).
Survey completed by Tim W. (Tallarook VIC).
Helen C., email correspondence to author dated 27 July 2006.

Notes

1   This article is part of ongoing research into the significance of Fromelles involving Annette Becker (France), Lucy Noakes (UK) and Sally Carlton (NZ). I thank Rae Frances for her comment on this chapter and Catherine Tiernan for transcribing interviews. I am also grateful to the editors of this volume, Keir Reeves and Laura James.
2   The best account of the battle remains Bean 1922; see also Corfield 2000 and McMullin 2002, ch. 9.
3   For an account of the deliberations of the committee see Scates 2010, pp. 212–32; also opinion piece, *Sydney Morning Herald,* 12 July 2008. For the perspective of those lobbying the government see Lycess and Playle 2013.
4   The intergenerational character of trauma is discussed by holocaust scholars and (in an Australian context) by Joy Damousi; see also Kangisser Cohen 2005 and the survey completed by Graeme W. (Fairfield VIC). This survey was gathered in the course of ARC-funded research into pilgrimages to the cemeteries of the Great War. For a discussion of methodology see Scates 2006, introduction and Scates 2002.
5   See Winter 1995, ch. 4; Scates 2006, ch. 4; Scates 2009; this discussion also draws on Filippicci 2009, pp. 220–50.
6   For the emotional and intellectual purchase of these conflict objects see Dendooven 2009, p. 70; descriptions of the objects recovered from Fromelles can be accessed on the Commonwealth War Graves Commission's website.
7   For an extended discussion of the anthropological concept of 'memory objects' see Scates 2009, ch. 1, also Tanja Luckins' important contribution to this field (Luckins 2004). The recovery of the pendant is discussed in Pollard, Barton and Banks 2007.

3   Māori chivalry during a British defeat

150 years of remembering Gate *Pā*

Lloyd Carpenter

Battles are remembered and commemorated for different reasons; some, like Gettysburg and the Somme, are noted for casualty figures and others, like Waterloo and D-Day, as turning points while a few are remembered for bravery againt impossible odds like Bannockburn, Rorke's Drift and the Kokoda Trail. Popular imagination celebrates foolhardy bravery, like the Light Brigade's charge at Balaklava and Custer's stand at Little Big Horn, but one unique battle at Gate *Pā* on 29 April 1864 stands out for the chivalric code of conduct under which it was fought.

Gate *Pā* was fought on Pukehinahina ridge as part of the New Zealand Land Wars, in what would become the town of Tauranga. Historian James Belich comments:

> The New Zealand Wars of 1845–72 were a series of conflicts involving the British, Imperial and colonial, and the Māori tribes of the North Island. They were not, as is sometimes suggested, storms in a teacup or gentlemanly bouts of fisticuffs, but bitter and bloody struggles, as important to New Zealand as were the Civil Wars to England and the United States.
>
> (Belich 1988: 15)

At Gate *Pā*, the Māori defenders looked after the wounded British soldiers and marines who fell among their entrenchments and this has motivated memorialisation of the battle ever since. The events that led to the fight on 29 April 1864 reflect and influence the long and difficult journey to the modern bicultural nation of New Zealand, which began with equality under a treaty.

The 1840 Treaty of Waitangi – promises and breaches

New Zealand's colonial history is unique. Britain's 1840 Treaty of Waitangi with the indigenous Māori tribes of New Zealand is an expression of this uniqueness and is also a cause of it. The vast blood-letting that followed European traders' introduction of muskets into Māori intertribal warfare in the 1820s (Stenhouse 2005; Wright 2011; Walker 2004), settler-farmer and Australian 'land sharks' engaging in questionable land purchases from Māori during the 1830s (Ward 1997; Tonk 1986), threatened corporate colonisation through the New Zealand Company in 1838

(Burns 1989), and pressure from concerned missionaries (Stenhouse 2005; Orange 2011) all combined to form this document. The Treaty promised partnership between the Crown and the Māori, and pledged that Māori land would stay in collective tribal ownership as long as that was desired (Williams 1941; Orange 2011). Despite such laudable aspirations, in 1845 concerns from (Northland) Ngapuhi chiefs Hone Heke and Te Ruki Kawiti relating to breaches of the treaty erupted into battles at Kororāreka (O'Malley 2007) and against Kawiti's brilliantly designed fortified *pā* at Puketutu, Ohaeawai and Ruapekapeka, with Ohaeawai a bloody defeat for the British (Golson 1957; Wright 2006; Cowan 1922; Kawiti 1953).

Conflict erupted anew in the 1860s, when demands by settlers for farmland met Waikato Māori's desire to retain their lands, unified under the *kingitanga*/Māori King movement (Gorst 1864; Fox 1866; Rosenfeld 2010; Banner 2000; Ballara 1982). Under popular, political and economic pressure to free up Māori land for settlement, Governor Thomas Gore Brown's disregard for legal niceties at Waitara caused his government to blunder into warfare in the Taranaki in 1860–1 (Dalton 1966). Two years after this settled, Gore Brown's successor, the Machiavellian George Grey, sent an army into the heart of the Waikato, ostensibly under his edict that Waikato Māori support for the *kingitanga* amounted to treason against the Queen. Grey's actions were designed to provoke a response that would allow him to utilise the recent New Zealand Settlements Act (1863) to confiscate land from Māori who resisted him (Sewell 1864; Gorst 1864; Dalton 1966; Rutherford 1961). This forced the confrontation Grey wanted and war erupted, costing hundreds of lives and leading to thousands of acres of Waikato land being confiscated (Gilling 2009, pp 13–30).

War comes to Tauranga

Grey's 1863–4 Waikato campaign concluded with a decisive Māori defeat at Ōrākau, a battle immortalised by Rewi Maniapoto's defiant 'Ka whawhai tonu ahau ki a koe, ake, ake, ake' [I shall fight you for ever, and ever, and ever] with which he and the beleaguered Māori defenders greeted invitations to surrender (Fitzgerald 1864a; Pugsley 1997). Waikato settled, Grey turned his attention towards Tauranga, the port that had supplied the Waikato Māori with a steady trickle of arms, *matériel* and men from the Bay of Plenty and the East Coast (Fox 1866; Cowan 1922; Bohan 2005). The government dispatched 700 troops under Colonel Carey to Tauranga in January 1864, followed in March by the 68th Durham Light Infantry under Colonel Meurant and the 43rd Monmouthshire Infantry under Colonel Booth. These were joined in April by a 'flying column' from the 12th, 50th, 70th, 65th and 14th regiments, together with General Duncan Cameron, the respected leader of the Highland Brigade in the Crimea (Belich 2012) and the man credited with the cessation of hostilities in Taranaki in 1863 (Dalton 1966), to lead them all. The newly arrived troops threw up defensive redoubts around the Tauranga mission settlement of Te Papa (Keenan 2009). Remnants of these redoubts may still be seen in historic reserves near the port.

Having tried to remain neutral throughout the Waikato conflict – despite allowing some young warriors to join that fight – Bay of Plenty Ngaiterangi and Ngāti Ranginui tribes were incensed by the 'invasion' of British troops (Alexander 1873) and high above the lower Wairoa River, at the fortified *pā* of Poteriwhi, the tribal leaders met under chief Rawiri Puhirake to decide that, if there must be war, it would be fought under a code defining rules of warfare. These 'laws for regulating the fight' declared that any European going about unarmed should be unmolested, that no Māori would commit murder, and that any wounded falling into their hands would be respected (*Daily Southern Cross,* 29 June 1864: 4; Mair 1926), in an almost-to-the-letter forerunner of the 1864 'Convention for the Amelioration of the Condition of the Wounded in Armies in the Field', which underpinned formation of the International Red Cross in 1865 (Keith 2010). On 28 March 1864 Rawiri instructed his lieutenant, the Otaki Mission-trained lay missionary Hēnare Wiremu Taratoa, to write and dispatch a copy of this code, together with a formal challenge, to Lt-Col Greer (Alexander 1873). The bemused Greer (who had taken over from Carey) did not know how to respond to a letter that concluded 'A challenge for a fight between us is declared; the day of fighting, Friday, the 1st of April, is fixed' (*New Zealand Herald*, 6 April 1864: 5; Keenan 2009) and replied with a letter of his own, requiring all Tauranga Māori to surrender their guns (Cowan 1922).

In early April Rawiri led Ngaiterangi and their allies to a strong position on Pukehinahina ridge, where he commissioned veteran warrior Pene Taka Tuaia to build a fortified *pā* on the narrow spur (Walker 2004). This location presented a clear challenge: if the British were to attack, they must do so onto Māori land. It was known as 'Gate *Pā*' because Pukehinahina was the location of the ditch, fence and gate that marked the boundary between the church-owned land of the Te Papa Mission and the Māori-owned land of the interior (Keenan 2009).

Pene Taka Tuaia's design at Gate *Pā* would lead to the defeat of the British army and his genius is one of several reasons that the battle is remembered. A leader of the Ngati Rangi *hapū* [sub-tribe] of Ngaiterangi (Matheson 2012) and veteran of the Northern War of the 1840s, Pene Taka fought beside 'loyal' Māori warriors siding with the government against 'rebel' leaders Hone Heke and Kawiti (Fides, cited in Simon 2012). When hostilities concluded at Ruapekapeka, he lived with and learned from the Ngapuhi chiefs. Pene Taka would put Kawiti's expertise to deadly use; his fortification at Pukehinahina was later described in stiffly worded admiration by General Cameron:

> It was constructed on a neck of land about 500 yards [457 metres] wide, the slopes of which fell off into a swamp on either side. On the highest point of this neck they had constructed an oblong redoubt, well palisaded and surrounded by a post and rail fence, a formidable obstacle to an assaulting column and difficult to destroy with artillery.
>
> (Cameron to Grey, 5 May 1864, enclosure 41, Further Papers
> Relative to the Native Insurrection AJHR: 61)

Figure 3.1 'Hēnare Wiremu Taratoa at the Gate *Pā*' by Horatio Robley, c. 1868.
Source: Reproduced with the permission of The Adams Collection, Tauranga Heritage Collection.

Gilbert Mair, working with letters from Lt Robley (who fought at Gate *Pā* with the 68th DLI), official surveys and interviews with veterans, added:

> the main redoubt… stretched about 87 yards [80m] along a rise with a smaller redoubt some 22 yards [20m] from the main redoubt… The main redoubt (where the Naval Brigade was to attack) was some 22 yards [18m] in depth. It consisted of parapets, rifle pits and a triple line of trenches covered with timbers through which the Maori could fire. There were also covered dugouts and underground shelters.

(Mair 1926: 24)

In a comment revealing the deceptively simple design, Ensign Spencer Nicholl of the 43rd Monmouthshires noted before the fight 'the Pah *[sic]* from the outside looks a most insignificant place' (Nicholl cited in Macdonald 2014).

Battle

General Cameron and his staff arrived on 21 April and five days later 600 naval men and marines disembarked from transport ships *Miranda*, *Curacoa*, *Esk* and *Harrier*, with a 110-pounder and two 40-pounder Armstrong guns from the *Esk*, to which were added fourteen guns removed from other ships to be dug into embankments in sight of Rawiri's men (Mair 1926).

On the morning of 28 April, the 1,700 men of Cameron's force made their way to within 1,200m of Pukehinahina. The 68th under Greer filed across mudflats to take up a position at the rear of the *pā*. Facing the British were warriors from Ngaiterangi, Ngati Ranginui and Ngati Pukenga, reinforced by contingents from Waitaha and Whakatohea from the east coast, plus Ngati Rangiwewehi of Te Arawa (Rotorua) and others from Ngati Koheriki from the Hauraki area, for a total of around 230 warriors (*Bay of Plenty Times* Gate *Pā* Commemorative Issue, 4 April 2014: 11). Entrenchments and dispositions complete, the batteries opened fire on Pukehinahina for around an hour, with desultory rifle exchanges between defenders and attackers, and no apparent loss of life.

On the morning of the 29th, the artillery renewed and increased its fire. Four batteries made up of the three Armstrongs, two 40-pounder and two 6-pounder cannon, two 24-pounder howitzers, two 8-inch mortars and six Coehorn mortars let loose, moving Belich to comment:

> the concentration of British artillery was of considerable power even in absolute terms. When it is considered that these guns fired unhampered by enemy artillery from a distance of 350 to 800 yards at a target of less than 3,000 square yards, their power appears awesome.
>
> (Belich 1988: 182)

He calculated that, in eight hours, 'the British fired roughly twenty times the weight of shell per square yard... as they did into the Somme battlefield during the initial bombardment of 24 June–1 July 1916' (Belich 1988: 295). Ngaiterangi Chief Hori Ngatai would later recall: 'When we gazed at those sons of thunder, launched forward in their might, can you wonder that the cooked potatoes seemed to have lost their sweetness and many a one of us seemed to forget his hunger?' (Mair 1926: 25). The 68th heard Rawiri's voice repeatedly calling 'Ko te manawa-rere, ko te manawa-rere, kia u, kia u!' [Trembling hearts, trembling hearts, be firm, be firm!] (Cowan 1922: 426) as the cannons fired.

After eight hours of intense shelling, a breach was judged to be practical and an attacking party of 300 men, half Naval Brigade under the HMS *Harrier*'s Cdr Hay, half 43rd under Col Booth, charged in to the *pā*. Once they were in the trenches the trap in Pene Taka's design was sprung, and volleys fired from the depths of covered

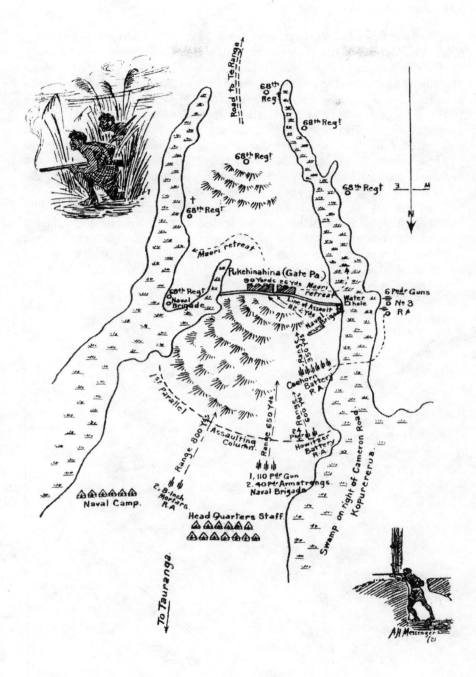

Figure 3.2 'Plan of the Attack on the Gate *Pā* (29th April, 1864)' by A. H. Messenger, 1921 for James Cowan, *The New Zealand Wars and the Pioneering Period* (Wellington; Government Printer, 1922): 424.

dugouts and firing holes brought down most of the attacking officers and many men. Vicious hand-to-hand combat then followed as the defenders rose, Mrs Heni te Kiri-karamu describing '…navy cutlass met long-handled tomahawk – *tupara* [shotgun] was clubbed to counter bayonet and rifle. Skulls were cloven – Maoris were bayoneted – Ngai-te-Rangi tomahawks bit into *pākehā* limbs' (Cowan 1922: 429). With over a third of the attacking force dead or wounded, the British retreated. The 43rd had lost 20 killed, including Col Booth and 5 other officers, and 12 wounded; the 68th had 4 killed and 16 wounded, while the Naval Brigade lost 13 killed, nearly all officers, with 26 wounded. Māori losses were around 25, most of whom were killed by the 68th regiment piquet line when the warriors took the opportunity at nightfall to progressively abandon their *pā*.

The next day the British occupied the abandoned fortification, finding badly wounded from both sides of the fight, and looked with wonder at the entrenchment design and construction that had caused such slaughter. Ensign Nicholl wrote, '[t]hose who went in this morning for the first time say that they never saw such a place in their life, and that you might as well drive a lot of men into a sheep pen and shoot them down as let them assault a place like that' (Nicholl cited in Macdonald 2014).

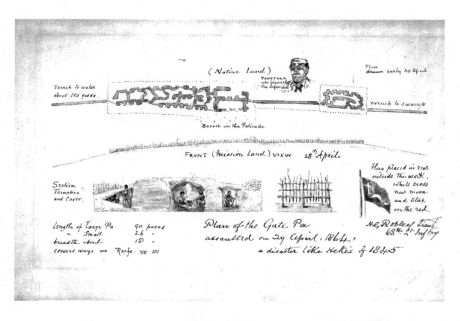

Figure 3.2 'Plan of the Gate *Pā* assaulted on 29 April, 1864, a disaster like Heke's of 1845' by Horatio Robley, 1864.

Source: Reproduced with the permission of the Trustees of the former Durham Light Infantry and the DLI Museum. Accession number DURLI: 420.

Chivalry

It was as Colonel Booth and the other wounded who had endured the night lying in the trenches were recovered, that it emerged that this was a fight like no other. From his hospital bed, the dying Booth told regimental surgeon Dr William Manley and others that he and other wounded soldiers near him in the *pā* had been given water by their Māori 'enemies'. Manley later received the Victoria Cross for his actions at Gate *Pā* (Harper and Richardson 2006).

The legend and memorialisation of Gate *Pā* had begun. Buddy Mikaere [Ngati Tamarawaho], organiser of the 2014 commemorations, adds 'the British clearly saw Gate *Pā* as a defeat, but in the shock of defeat, a legend about the chivalrous conduct of the Māori participants was born. So much so, that in subsequent years the aftermath of the battle was thought by *Pākehā* in particular to be worthy of remembrance, even celebration' (*Bay of Plenty Times* Gate *Pā* Commemorative Issue, 4 April 2014: 10).

Which of the Māori defenders ministered to the wounded is debated, with some claiming Henare Taratoa (including many Ngaiterangi I consulted), others Te Ipu, while many more (including Mair and Cowan) are convinced it was Heni Te Kiri Karamu, who after 30 years wrote several letters to substantiate her claim (Oliver 2014; Helliwell 2013). Whoever it was – and, given the code under which the battle was fought, it is not inconceivable that each of those named helped one or more of their wounded foes – word of these chivalrous actions spread.

Newspaper reports about Gate *Pā* and Te Ranga in 1864 are suffused with wonder at the idea of fighting a war by a code, and a précis of these reports published for each anniversary of the battle reinforced this. When the first widely published books on the subject of the New Zealand Wars came out early in the twentieth century, much was made of the code. The most significant was written by the veteran of the later stages of the wars and the leader of the famed 'loyalist' Māori Flying Column, Captain Gilbert Mair. His narrative is based on interviews with veterans from both sides, especially his own and those of Hori Ngatai and Ngati Raukawa chief Hitiri Te Paerata. Mair's ability to speak the Māori language means that, despite some in-built bias from fighting similar 'rebels' in later campaigns, his is the first narrative after the official reports by Cameron, Greer and Governor Grey to attempt a comprehensive history of the battle. Mair's work was reprinted as an appendix in James Cowan's popular 1922 two-volume *The New Zealand Wars and the Pioneering Period*. This guaranteed that generations of New Zealanders would discover the Māori warriors who had risked their lives to help their enemy.

Te Ranga

The victory over the British at Gate *Pā* was avenged two months later, when one of Greer's patrols found Puhirake's warriors, reinforced by allies from Ngāti Rangiwewehi, Ngāti Pikiao and Ngāti Porou, building a new fortification at Te Ranga, inland from Pukehinahina. With incomplete defences on a poor site, the British used their strategic advantage and quickly attacked. The result was one of the bloodiest slaughters of the New Zealand campaigns, where many Māori were bayoneted and those who fled were picked off by soldiers wielding modern rifles firing *minié* bullets. Over 100 Māori were killed and 37 wounded were taken prisoner. The British lost 13 killed and 39 wounded. Among those killed and later buried in the trenches where they fell were chiefs Rawiri Puhirake and Henare Taratoa. At Te Ranga British officers found on Taratoa's body the 'Orders of the day' for fighting, which began with a prayer and ended with Romans 12:20, 'Ki te mate kai tou hoariri, whangainga; ki te mate wai ia, whakainumia' (If thine enemy hunger, feed him; if he thirst, give him drink).

Te Ranga led the remaining Tauranga chiefs under Hori Ngatai to sue for peace, and large areas of land were confiscated, surveyed and allocated to military settlers, who built the nucleus of the new town of Tauranga. This was not done without criticism; in 1864, James Fitzgerald, editor of Christchurch's *Press* declared:

> But this we know – there will be men in after times whose pens will narrate the causes and outcomings of this contest, and who will seek, in the objects of the war, the key to its disasters. They will say it was not a war for safety or for law, or for truth or liberty, but it was a war dictated by avarice and prosecuted for spoliation.
>
> (Fitzgerald, *The Press*, 16 April 1864: 2)

Land loss

Gate *Pā* saw an official policy of *raupatu* [land confiscation] after the battles, which, when combined with questionable land transactions over the years, created a sense among Māori that the treaty had not been honoured. In the 40 years leading up to 2014, this narrative has changed, since through the Waitangi Tribunal the Māori have successfully fought for and secured some measure of redress and financial settlement to reconcile the past breaches of the treaty. This meant that any modern celebrations would reflect the country's bicultural relationship under the treaty and as such would be an expression of both Pākehā and Māori voices.

Buddy Mikaere [Ngati Tamarawaho], Tauranga historian and director of the Pukehinahina Trust that organised the 150th anniversary commemorations, commented to the *Bay of Plenty Times:*

> From the Māori perspective there are much stronger reasons for remembering the battle [than helping the wounded]. There is still grief for the death and loss of brave and revered ancestors, but the grief and sense of loss is now more focused on land loss... The Native Settlements Act (1863)... legitimised the confiscation of almost 50,000 acres of their most productive lands as punishment for rebellion.
>
> (*Bay of Plenty Times* Gate *Pā* Commemorative Issue,
> 4 April 2014: 10)

Memorializing compassion in battle

Formal memorialising of chivalry at Gate *Pā* began with magnanimity when, ten years after the battle, local Māori leaders and settlers (including veterans) combined to organise the disinterment of Rawiri Puhirake's body from the Te Ranga site, re-burying him beside the grave of Col Booth in the Otamataha/Mission Cemetery as a mark of respect (Rorke 2012). In June 1914, as part of the 50th anniversary of the battles, an imposing, locally funded memorial to Rawiri was unveiled by Col Logan, ADC, Officer in Command of the Auckland Military District, in the presence of a large crowd of locals, including Māori. In his speech, Logan said

> Rawiri... insisted that the prisoners of war should be treated with mercy, and at Gate *Pā* he himself saw to it that his orders were carried out... and to-day we are met to do honour to the memory of a great chief, a great general, and a noble Christian gentleman.
>
> (*Evening Post*, 22 June 1914: 3)

The same memorial has Henare Wiremu Taratoa's name engraved and is marked by a distinctive marble relief showing Rawiri organising Taratoa to bring a calabash of water to the fallen Booth.

Figure 3.4 Laying wreaths on Rawiri Puhirake's tomb, Otamataha/Mission Cemetery, 29 April 2014.

Source: Photographer Lee Switzer, Tauranga. Reproduced with the photographer's permission.

Within two years of the jubilee, the descriptor 'Descendants of the Warriors of Gate *Pā*' was used to laud Māori soldiers who had fought alongside their New Zealand and British counterparts (who included the Durham Light Infantry) at the battles of Gallipoli (*Hawera and Normanby Star*, 7 January 1916: 8). 'Gate *Pā* warriors' became the epistemological touchstone to describe Māori *élan*, selflessness and fighting ability, in a way that battles of the Waikato at Ōrākau and Rangiriri or the earlier fight at Ohaewai, apparently did not do.

Logan's words and those engraved on Rawiri's tomb are perpetuated in the Tauranga Historical Society's plaque on the monument erected to mark the centennial of the battle at the battlefield reserve, which reads:

> On 29th April 1864 the battle of Gate *Pā* was fought on this site. This plaque commemorates the chivalry displayed by both Māori and Pākehā, which has helped unite the two races. Kua iwi kotahi tatou [we two are now one people].

This has been described by New Zealand Ministry of Culture and Heritage historians Chris Maclean and Jock Phillips as perpetuating 'pākehā myths and biases' (1990) in the popular memorialisation of the battle, although there has been no move to revise either in subsequent commemorations.

Centennial

The centennial celebrations were a remarkably formal affair, largely organised by the local Historical Society, rather than in partnership with Tauranga Māori. They included C. Kingsley Smith's drama *The Oval Table* about nine officers of the 43rd on the night before battle dining at The Elms (only one survived the day), a service to unveil the new monument at the Gate *Pā* site, followed by a reception for invited guests at St George's Church hall and a ball to follow. The next day saw a day of sports and performances ('marching, bands etc.,... football matches, Pakeha v Maori') and in the evening, 'Maori Entertainment, arranged by the Maori Cultural and Promotions Committee in Sportscentre, Memorial Park' (Adams 1964). Stilted and careful, this bears no resemblance to the events of 50 years later.

Sesquicentennial

For the sesquicentennial anniversary on 29 April 2014, commemorative events built up to the main events, including an art exhibition, a school speech competition, poetry readings and popular lectures by historians Des Tata of Ngai Tamarawaho (a *hapū* of Ngaiterangi) and Lt-Col Cliff Simons of the New Zealand Army's Defence Headquarters. On Saturday 26 April, the Waikato-based Armed Constabulary reenactment group fired three cannon salutes from Armstrong cannons and Coehorn mortars at 11am, 1pm and 3pm in the Tauranga Domain.

On 28 April, 150 years after the British troops had marched out of the redoubts at Te Papa, an Art Exhibition opened at St George's Church Hall and the New Zealand Army Band held a lunchtime concert at The Strand Park, where the music

'Battle of Gate *Pā*', written for the commemoration by Wt-Off Dwayne Bloom-field, had its debut. The day concluded with the Gate *Pā* Commemoration Dinner at Trinity Wharf, with guest speakers Willy Apiata VC and the British Army's Assistant Chief of the General Staff, Maj Gen David Cullen.

The commemorations of 29 April started at 6am in a rain-soaked dawn with solemn *karakia* (prayers) at the battle site. Dressed in black and carrying fresh-cut green branches as a sign of mourning, Māori elders led the remembrance of the fallen. Prayers in *te reo Māori* [Māori language] and English reminded all present that the place and soil itself was *tapu* [sacred] and the entire site was imbued with the *wairua* [spirit] of those who fought, those who died and those who later made peace. Flags were raised to symbolise reconciliation between Māori and Pākehā, then eight newly-erected *pou whenua* ['land posts', used to mark significant sites or boundaries] on the edge of the Gate *Pā* Reserve were unveiled and blessed. The crowd moved to the old Otamataha *pā*/Mission Cemetery site, where a formal military memorial service was held, followed by morning tea at the nearby Trinity Wharf. The major art exhibition at Greerton Hall was blessed and opened at 10am and the crowd moved back to the Gate *Pā* reserve to join in the noon *pōwhiri* (formal welcome) for the *kingitanga* representatives and the Māori King, Te Arikinui Tuheitia Kiingi Paki.

Two hours later, a commemorative march led visitors from Tauranga Girls' College (near one of the artillery emplacements in the battle) to the reserve, where there was a traditional *wero*, or challenge. This latter was in the form of a massed *haka* [war dance], with more than 1,000 men, women and children performing the new *haka* especially composed for the occasion by Rewiti Te Mete and Tauranga City Councillor Awanui Black. This vast *haka*, New Zealand's unique form of challenge, defiance, celebration, commemoration and ritual, was a means of 'bringing together Tauranga *Moana iwi* and *hapū* as well as those tribes who experienced similar battles in their tribal areas'; the *haka*, or *peruperu* 'represented solidarity and retells the stories from the perspective of local Māori' (Awanui Black, personal communication, 7 January 2015). This was no mere cultural performance; the massed *haka* 'provided a cultural role for the young people, renewed the pan-*iwi* unity of 1864 and commemorated the challenge laid down to the invading troops; it gave *mana* (respect) to the occasion and determinably provided something memorable and spectacular to be remembered for the next 100 years' (Buddy Mikaere, personal communication, 6 January 2015). The unison of the performance – a key element for any *haka* – was attributed to the months of work by Josh Te Kani, who organised practices across the region.

Those in the *haka* party wore European woollen blankets, trousers and cotton shirts as some warriors had in 1864, while others wore traditional flax *maro* or *piupiu* [kilt] and *tātua* [belt]; all wore hairstyles, *pounamu* earings, *hei-tiki* pendants, facial paint and/or pen-drawn *moko* [facial tattoos] in the style of their ancestors. Some carried *pū* [muskets] or *tupara* [double-barreled shotguns], many with wooden stocks elaborately carved, while others carried *rakau* [traditional wooden, whalebone or stone] weapons such as *taiaha*, *tewhatewha*, *kotiate*, *tao*, *mere*, *waihaika* and *pou whenua*. The *haka* party came down the road in tight

Figure 3.5 *Wero* [challenge] by Tauranga Māori *haka* party to New Zealand Governor-General Jerry Mataparae, Gate *Pā* Domain, 29 April 2014.

Source: Photographer Lee Switzer, Tauranga. Reproduced with the photographer's permission.

formation, then poured en masse into the reserve, where the traditional ritual of challenge and counterchallenge played out. The effect of 1,000 people stomping, leaping and chanting this traditional *haka*, written especially for them for that day, and moving in tight-knit, enthusiastic unison as they had practiced for months, can only be imagined.

As well as the singing of *waiata* [songs], the afternoon ceremony, which was called a 'Reconciliation Service' rather than a commemoration, was addressed by New Zealand's Governor-General, Sir Jerry Mataparae, who said

> Today, we share the sorrow of those whose ancestors or predecessors in the armed forces lost their lives here – we mourn them and we celebrate their example… In coming here today, we also acknowledge the New Zealand Wars as an integral part of this nation's story. Remembering what happened here and paying homage to those who lost their lives gives us a better understanding of our shared past so that we can work together more effectively for a better future… The spirit underpinning today's commemorations and the progress of recent efforts to right these historical wrongs reflects the courage and compassion of the men and women who fought here 150 years ago.
>
> (Governor-General of New Zealand Te Kānawa Tianara o Aotearoa 2014)

The landscape of Gate *Pā*

Gate *Pā* is now the name of a bustling suburb, with a large shopping centre, schools and sports grounds. The Pukehinahina *Pā* site, designated the 'Gate *Pā* Domain' is in a well-tended, shady, public park, bounded to the north by a hardware store and to the south by St. George's Anglican Church. To the east is a vestigial swamp of the type that aided in the fortification, while to the west is Cameron Road, and westward from the road is the Gate *Pā* bowling club greens and premises, built on the western part of the original fortifications and possibly over the original burial sites for the Māori killed in the battle.

Figure 3.6   Tauranga Māori *haka* party, Gate *Pā* Domain, 29 April 2014.
Source: Photographer Lee Switzer, Tauranga. Reproduced with the photographer's permission.

The landscape has changed. Photographs from the 1960s show a bare, green, grassy sward, with no memorials or structures to note that the site was important in any way, except for two concrete memorial posts that had 'expended British shells and Maori shotguns' embedded in them (*New Zealand Herald,* 28 August 1937: 12). This reserve was very nearly turned back into a fortified *Pā* for tourist visits; in the mid-1920s the Bay of Plenty Development League and the Tauranga

Chamber of Commerce were concerned that 'the site of the historical Gate *Pā* battle had been allowed to practically go into oblivion', proposing that 'the church be removed to the new [neighbouring] site and thus enable the work of [trench] restoration to be carried out' (*Evening Post,* 15 January 1926: 6).

This proposal was still mooted a decade later, when only World War II dislodged the idea (*Auckland Star,* 16 September 1937: 6).

Entrance to the Gate *Pā* reserve is from Cameron Road, through a carved *tomokanga* [archway welcoming people to a sacred place] erected in 2007. This depicts Tūmatauenga [God of War] and Rongo-mā-Tane [God of Peace] on the uprights, while the *maihi* [barge boards] symbolise the *hokioi* [the Haast Eagle or 'Spirit Messenger of the Gods' (Simmons 1986: 15)]. When this *tomokanga* was completed, carver James Tapiata noted that it was 'the first Māori symbolism going onto the site' since the battle (Udy 2007). Passing beneath the *tomokanga*, visitors walk past eight elaborately carved ceremonial *pou*, erected in a project overseen by Peri Kohu of Ngai Tamarawaho for the 2014 commemorations. Each *pou* was completed by a different *marae* and each represents a different person or group associated with the battle, from one showing General Duncan Cameron, to ones representing the Ngāti Ranginui and Ngāti Pūkenga *iwi*, and another simply called Matepū [we will die by the gun], representing the decision to go to war.

Through the *tomokanga*, a sealed pathway meanders between mature trees, taking visitors from Cameron Road to Church Street via a series of professionally designed, carefully written and fully illustrated interpretation panels erected in 2010, designed to progressively tells the story of the battle and its aftermath. The panels emphasise the separate Māori and Pākehā narratives at Gate *Pā*, but the text

Figure 3.7 Gate *Pā tomokanga* and commemorative *pou*, Gate *Pā* Domain, 17 December 2014.

Source: Photographer Lloyd Carpenter. Reproduced with the photographer's permission.

on each is English, with almost no Māori language. The grounds are neatly tended grass, with occasional humps and hollows that hint at either the earthworks of the fortification, or the army redoubt that was built to replace it a few days after the battle.

At the highest point of the reserve is a flagpole and commemorative platform, built of concrete for 1964 and replaced with timber to become a ceremonial *marae atea* [place of the welcome ceremony, or *pōwhiri*] for 2014. For the commemorations, the flagpole had the New Zealand flag, the naval ensign and the Pukehinahina/Gate *Pā* flag on it. The red Gate *Pā* flag with its white symbols of a cross, four-pointed star and a crescent in the centre (see Figure 3.8), is the flag which with the British flag is on the New Zealand Wars memorial at the Auckland War Memorial Museum. The National Museum Te Papa Tongarewa in Wellington also hoisted this flag for the duration of the commemorations.

Central to the platform and immediately in front of the flagpole is the commemorative block from 1964. Behind it is a picket fence marking the church property boundary with a lychgate allowing admittance to the church grounds, the latter designed by the Rev Cyril Stevens, first vicar of St George's, as a symbol of the gate of 'Gate Pa' (St George's Church, nd). Beside the platform is the remnant of two totara trees carved into intricate *pou* for the ceremonies in 2014. The left is a memorial to Christian *tohunga* (spiritual leader) Ihakara Koikoi, who was slain by

Figure 3.8 Gate *Pā marae atea*, memorial *pou*, flagpole, 1864 monument and St George's Church and lychgate.

Source: Photographer Lloyd Carpenter. Reproduced with the photographer's permission.

a shell burst as he prayed for a blessing on all present. There are 39 crosses also carved into three teardrops to represent the British soldiers who were killed during the battle or later died of their wounds. The right *pou* represents the traditional *tohunga* Te Wano, who was killed by a cannon shot whilst giving a *karakia* (prayer) for victory. This *pou* also has two gourds to represent the code of conduct (Peri Reweti Kohu, quoted in McCauley 2014a).

St George's church is the second erected on the site and is built over the eastern part of the original *pā* fortifications. Its entranceway is a memorial to the Māori fallen, especially those who were buried in an unmarked grave. The church reflects one of its original purposes, with a sign erected across the door into the main chapel inviting 'All who enter here be reconciled'. Beside this is a plaque from the first church, beginning with the verse from Romans 12:20 found on Taratoa's body, then the text 'To Commemorate the chivalry based on the Christian faith of those who defended the Gate *Pā* April 29th. 1864'. The bell in the separate tower came from HMS *Acheron* in 1967, presented to the church in memory of the men of the navy who were killed in the battle.

The most spectacular of the church memorials is a stained glass window of Heni Te Kirikaramu designed by Rita Haagh, installed in 1993 and dedicated 'for her womanly compassion to Lt.Col. H. J. P. Booth and others at Gate *Pā*...' This window has an older twin in England: when Bishop Selwyn concluded 25 years of New Zealand ministry to take up the Bishopric of Lichfield in 1867, local soldiers and their families sent funds with him, which he spent to erect stained glass windows in the Bishop's private chapel adjoining the palace at Lichfield to honour the fallen. One has special meaning; it depicts David pouring out the water fetched for him by three soldiers from the well at Bethlehem (1 Chronicles 11:15–19) and commemorates Selwyn's former student Taratoa's act of mercy at Gate *Pā* (Dixon 2012).

Names on the landscape

Gate *Pā* is central to Tauranga's narrative. Locals have spent 150 years describing how the battle 'enabled' the thriving city to develop, and it is built on and around the Gate *Pā* battlefield landscape. The path traversed by advancing British troops is now Cameron Road, named after General Cameron and running from the British camp site near the mission house 'The Elms', through the middle of Gate *Pā* towards Te Runga. The centrality of Gate *Pā* is confirmed on the Tauranga City Council's website: 'the Battle was a pivotal moment in the founding of our city' (Tauranga City Council 2015).

As well as Cameron Road, the rest of Tauranga echoes with names memorialising the British at Gate *Pā*; Lt-Col Greer is remembered in Greerton and Greerton Road, Pye's Pa, Manley Grove and Mitchell Street are all named for British servicemen, while the Naval ships *Esk*, *Harrier* and *Miranda* each have a street named after them, and Durham and Monmouth Streets commemorate the two main army units. HMS *Esk's* commander was killed leading the attack, and is recalled in Tauranga's Hamilton Street and the Waikato city of Hamilton (Byrnes

2002). Only Ngaiterangi chief Hori Ngatai has Otumoetai's Ngatai Street named after him; there is no Taratoa Street, Pene Taka Avenue or Puhiraki Road to commemorate the Māori leaders at Gate *Pā*.

The future

Among the many speeches and *waiata* (songs) at the reconciliation service at the Gate *Pā* Reserve in 2014 was the inaugural Battle of Gate *Pā* address by Justice Joe Williams, a direct descendant of Māori defenders at Pukehinahina. His talk addressed the past and the future, summing up what it is hoped that the commemorations of Gate *Pā*/Pukehinahina and Te Ranga meant for New Zealand in 2014:

> the battle... was described as the worst defeat suffered by the professional British army at the hands of tribal irregulars – no more than 'a horde of half naked, half armed savages', according to one report at the time. Extraordinarily, Māori stuck to their promised Christian code of behaviour... defenders... crept out from the *pā* to take water to wounded British soldiers still lying in the battle field... Māori won the battle but lost the war. And they have suffered the economic, social, cultural, and political consequences of that fact... the Crown now acknowledges that *it* was the aggressor in Tauranga – not Māori – and *it* broke the promises solemnly made at Waitangi in 1840. Reparations have been made or are in the process of being made... But we must celebrate the lessons we have learned. The fact is, we Māori and Pākehā New Zealanders... are utterly interdependent now.
>
> (Williams quoted in McCauley 2014b)

A popular *whakatauki* [proverb] among Bay of Plenty Māori sums up the overall attitude to this battle and the others related to it for the people of Tauranga and New Zealand: Pupuritia ngā taonga a ngā tīpuna [hold on to the treasures of the past].

References

Adams, E. L. (ed.) (1964). 'Commemoration activities 28 April – 3 May, Gate *Pā* centennial souvenir'. *Journal of the Tauranga Historical Society Inc., 19*, 34–5.

Alexander, J. E. D. W. (1873). *Bush Fighting – Illustrated by Remarkable Actions and Incidents of the Maori War in New Zealand* (London: Sampson Low, Marston, Low and Searle).

Ballara, A. (1982). 'The pursuit of mana? A re-evaluation of the process of land alienation by Maoris, 1840–1890'. *Journal of the Polynesian Society, 91*(4), 519–41.

Banner, S. (2000). 'Conquest by contract: wealth transfer and land market structure in colonial New Zealand'. *Law & Society Review, 34*(1), 47–96.

Belich, J. (2012). 'Cameron, Duncan Alexander', from the *Dictionary of New Zealand Biography. Te Ara – the Encyclopedia of New Zealand*. Available from: www.TeAra.govt.nz/en/biographies/1c2/cameron-duncan-alexander [30 October 2012].

Belich, J. (1988). *The New Zealand Wars* (Auckland: Penguin).

Bohan, E. 2005 *Climates of War – New Zealand in Conflict 1859–69* (Christchurch: Hazard).

Burns, P. (1989). *Fatal Success: A History of the New Zealand Company* (Auckland: Heinemann Reed).

Byrnes, G. (2002). 'A dead sheet covered with meaningless words? Place names and the cultural colonization of Tauranga'. *New Zealand Journal of History, 36*(1), 18–35.

Cowan, J. (1922). *The New Zealand Wars and the Pioneering Period, Vol. 1* (Wellington: Government Printer).

Dalton, B. J. (1967). *War and Politics in New Zealand, 1855–1870* (Sydney: Sydney University Press).

Dalton, B. J. (1966). 'A new look at the Maori Wars of the Sixties'. *Historical Studies Australia and New Zealand, 12*(46), 230–47.

Dixon, N. (2012). 'Taratoa, Henare Wiremu', from the *Dictionary of New Zealand Biography. Te Ara – the Encyclopedia of New Zealand.* Available from: www.TeAra.govt.nz/en/biographies/1t15/taratoa-henare-wiremu [30 October 2012].

Fitzgerald, J. (1864a). 'The native war'. *The Press*, 13 May, 2.

Fitzgerald, J. (1864b). 'Ake! Ake! Ake!' *The Press,* 16 April, 2.

Fox, W. (1866). *The War in New Zealand* (London: Smith, Elder & Co).

Gilling, B. (2009). 'Raupatu: the punitive confiscation of Māori land in the 1860s', in R. Boast and R. S. Hill (eds), *Raupatu: the Confiscation of Māori Land* (Wellington: Victoria University Press), pp. 13–30.

Golson, J. (1957). 'Field archaeology in New Zealand'. *Journal of the Polynesian Society, 66*(1), 101–106.

Gorst, J. E. (1864). *The Maori King; Or, The Story of Our Quarrel With the Natives of New Zealand* (London: MacMillan).

Governor-General of New Zealand Te Kānawa Tianara o Aotearoa (2014). 'Battle of Gate *Pā* commemorations'. Available from: https://gg.govt.nz/content/battle-gate-pa-commemorations [29 April 2014].

Harper, G. and Richardson, C. (2006). *In the Face of the Enemy – the Complete History of the Victoria Cross and New Zealand* (Auckland: HarperCollins).

Helliwell, G. (2013). 'Battle of Gate *Pā* scene revisted'. *Bay of Plenty Times*, 21 January, available from: www.nzherald.co.nz/bay-of-plenty-times/news/article.cfm?c_id=150 3343&objectid=11088048 [11 June 2015].

Kawiti, K. T. R. M. (1953). 'The storming of Hone Heke's *Pā*'. *Journal of the Polynesian Society, 62*(1), 85–7.

Keenan, D. (2009). *Wars Without End* (Auckland: Penguin).

Keith, K. J. (2010). *Tutti fratelli*? Perspectives and challenges for international humanitarian law. *Victoria University of Wellington Law Review, 41*, 123–34.

Macdonald, C. (2014). 'Looking down the barrel of history', blog, History Department, Victoria University of Wellington. Available from: http://lookingdownthebarrelofhistory.weebly.com/ [October 2014].

Maclean, C. and Phillips, J. (1990). *The Sorrow and the Pride: New Zealand War Memorials* (Wellington: GP Books).

Mair, G. (1926). *The Story of Gate Pa, April 29th, 1864* (Tauranga: Bay of Plenty Times Ltd).

Matheson, A. (2012). 'Tuaia, Pene Taka', from the *Dictionary of New Zealand Biography. Te Ara – the Encyclopedia of New Zealand.* Available from: www.TeAra.govt.nz/en/biographies/1t107/tuaia-pene-taka [30 October 2012].

McCauley, D. (2014a). 'Tōtara tree pou'. Available from: http://tauranga.kete.net.nz/battles_of_gate_pa_and_te_ranga_1864/topics/show/2070-totara-tree-pou-2014-by-debbie-mccauley [June 2014].

McCauley, D. (2014b). 'Tauranga Library "Kete" blog, speeches, the Inaugural Gate *Pā* address' (29 April 2014) by Justice Joe Williams. Available from: http://tauranga.kete. net.nz/battles_of_gate_pa_and_te-ranga_1864/topics/show/2017-the-inaugural-gate-pa-address-29-april-2014-by-justice-joe-williams [June 2014].

Oliver, S. (2014). 'Te Kiri Karamu, Heni', from the *Dictionary of New Zealand Biography. Te Ara – the Encyclopedia of New Zealand.* Available from: www.TeAra.govt.nz/en/biographies/1t43/te-kiri-karamu-heni [4 March 2014].

O'Malley, V. (2007). 'English law and the Māori response: a case study from the Runanga System in Northland, 1861–65'. *Journal of the Polynesian Society*, *116*(1), 7–34.

Orange, C. (2011). *The Treaty of Waitangi* (Wellington: Bridget Williams).

Pugsley, C. (1997). 'Walking the Waikato Wars: the siege of Orakau'. *New Zealand Defence Quarterly*, *18*, 32–6.

Rorke, J. (2012). 'Puhirake, Rawiri', from the *Dictionary of New Zealand Biography. Te Ara – the Encyclopedia of New Zealand.* Available from: www.TeAra.govt.nz/en/biographies/1p30/puhirake-rawiri [30 October 2012].

Rosenfeld, J. E. (2010). *Island Broken in Two Halves: Land and Renewal Movements Among the Maori of New Zealand* (University Park: Pennsylvania State University Press).

Rutherford, J. (1961). *Sir George Grey, 1812–1898: A Study in Colonial Government* (London: Cassell and Company).

St George's Church (nd). *Historic St George's Anglican Church Gate Pā* (Tauranga: St George's Church).

Sewell H. (1864). *A Letter from Henry Sewell, Esq., Late Attourney-General of New Zealand, to the Right Hon. Lord Lyttelton* (London: MacMillan).

Simon, C. R. (2012). 'Military intelligence in the New Zealand Wars, 1845–1864', PhD thesis (Palmerston North, NZ: Massey University).

Simmons, D. R. (1986). 'Iconography of New Zealand Maori religion', in *Iconography of Religions,* II/I, (Leiden: E.J. Brill).

Stenhouse, J. (2005). 'Imperialism, atheism, and race: Charles Southwell, old corruption, and the Maori'. *Journal of British Studies*, *44*(4) (October 2005).

Tauranga City Council (2015). 'Council A–Z, Gate *Pā* Commemorations'. Available from: https://www.tauranga.govt.nz/council-a-z/gate-pa-commemorations.aspx [January 2015].

Tonk, R. V. (1986). 'The first New Zealand Land Commissions 1840–1845', MA thesis, (Canterbury, NZ: University of Canterbury).

Udy, C. (2007). 'Carving push crowns Gate *Pā* battle site'. *Bay of Plenty Times*, 30 April, 4.

Walker, R. (2004). *Ka Whawhai Tonu Matou, Struggle Without End* (Auckland: Penguin).

Ward, A. (1997). 'National overview Vol. II'. *Waitangi Tribunal Rangahaua Whanui Series*, Waitangi Tribunal (Wellington: GP Publications).

Williams, T. (1941). 'James Stephen and British intervention in New Zealand, 1838–40'. *Journal of Modern History*, *13*(1), 19–35.

Wright, M. (2011). *Guns and Utu* (Auckland: Penguin).

Wright, M. (2006). *Two Peoples, One Land – The New Zealand Wars* (Auckland: Reed).

4 Landscape, soundscape and youth

Memorable moments at the 90th commemoration of the Battle of Vimy Ridge, 2007

Geoffrey R. Bird

> I am standing with 20,000 Canadians and French locals, bathed in a warm sun that silhouettes one of the most striking sites of memory on the Western Front: the Canadian Memorial at Vimy Ridge. We are marking 90 years since the iconic Canadian victory as well as the official rededication of the newly refurbished memorial by Queen Elizabeth, attended by the Prime Ministers of Canada and France. Some 3,500 Canadian youth, aged 15–18 years old, are also attending. The crowd's energy is palpable. I feel an odd mix of excitement of 'being here', pride as a Canadian, yet an overriding somberness of one commemorating the fallen. As an academic, I am striving to understand what is happening in terms of remembrance: We are standing where thousands were killed and wounded and yet this place, with the green grass and forest, blue sky and white marbled memorial, is entrancingly beautiful.
>
> (Bird, field notes, 9 April 2007)

The aim of this chapter is to examine how people, specifically young Canadians, are affected by engaging in an act of remembrance, a battlefield event at a site of memory. The purpose is the interplay of sense of place, meaning and recollections after attending a commemorative event associated with a mythic World War I battle. As Winter (2006) notes, acts of remembrance evolve from one generation to the next. A commemorative event organized by the state is also one where political messages may surface, potentially a highly emotional performance that can serve as ritual to foster or maintain identity for an imagined community (see Anderson 1983). Focusing on what is memorable for youth at a commemoration allows us to gain insight into what resonates with a generation who, for the most part, have no experience of war and who have not interacted directly with veterans of World War I.

This chapter draws upon the results of pre- and post-trip online surveys – a method adapted from Jennings and Weiler (2006) – that asked Canadian youth about their expectations of and experiences at the Canadian National Historic Site of Vimy Ridge near Arras, France. The site has particular significance in Canadian mythic narrative as the principal national war memorial of World War I and a place often described as where Canada became a nation. The sample is drawn from a group of 3,500 15–18-year-old students who literally took centre-stage in the commemorative service on a sunny afternoon on April 9, 2007, symbolically embodying the 'commitment to remember' by future generations.

An assumption I make here is that what youth remember, what they find memorable, from attending a commemorative event shapes at least in part how they understand and contextualize war in the modern age. This chapter is therefore an examination of the collision of debates with regard to why, what, and how to remember World War I. Some examples of recent arguments help to unpack the nature of this discourse. For some, there is the ongoing concern that Canada's military history is being forgotten. A survey conducted in 2007 found that only 30 per cent of Canadians knew of the Battle of Vimy Ridge (Vimy Foundation website). The concern regularly surfaces. In 2014, historian Jack Granatstein (2014) wrote an editorial arguing that the Canadian Government was 'botching' the World War I centenary. In contrast, another perspective argues that the government, the military and other stakeholders are not only celebrating war history in a mythic, nation-building light, but they do so to legitimize contemporary policies that support war and a strong military (see Fournier *et al.* 2012; Richler 2012; Frenette 2014). The debate as to why, what and how to commemorate World War I is not unique to Canada. With the 100th anniversary, commemoration plans and public debates in Australia (see Department of Veterans' Affairs 2010) and the United Kingdom (see Jones 2014; Mycock 2014) fall along a spectrum from recommending guidelines on how best to commemorate the war to questioning why the war is worth remembering at all.

Related to the politics of remembrance is the role played by tourism and pilgrimage to commemorative events. We can characterize the relationship between remembrance and tourism by a range of conflicting and beneficial traits. Large commemorations may be loosely described as pilgrimage by some, particularly when it involves veterans and next of kin (see Lloyd 1998). These journeys can also be viewed as an extension of what Jay Winter (2006) describes as the business of remembrance, involving tour operators, bus companies, and hotels that profit from the event. However, touring a battlefield, including commemorating at one, can be a very profound and transformative experience, and certainly more resonant than reading a textbook in a classroom.

Coming into play in this act of remembrance is the interaction with the landscape; the sense of place leads to emotional insights that result from what many describe as 'walking in the footsteps' of soldiers. I will limit the focus to the co-construction of meaning as conceptualized by Chronis in his research on visitors to Gettysburg Battlefield National Park (2005). He argues that meaning is drawn from the landscape, artifacts, and mediated narrative that collectively create a storyscape. The visitor filters and shapes meaning through their experience and values as well as the broader contemporary context of world events. In this way, I argue that touring and also participating in commemoration at a battlefield, as an act of remembrance, are opportunities to gain emotional and even transformative insight that is more resonant than other commemorative experiences.

The main storyscape for this research is the stunning memorial (see Figure 4.1), the cratered terrain that stretches throughout the park, as well as the nearby cemeteries and trenches that are also mentioned by students. In addition to landscape, the aural sensory experience, such as music at the ceremony, silence and birdsong, offers another experiential dimension as soundscape. Collectively, these elements can be understood as the sense of place of this landscape of war. Underlying sense of place is the opportunity of the experiential element of 'walking in their footsteps', literally to touch the memorial and to imagine a proximity to history, war and death. These experiences are what resonated most with youth who attended the commemoration and toured the site.

In large part, this chapter focuses on the voice of youth in their interpretation of the Vimy commemoration. Youth are indeed at an early stage of life's learning and we can therefore anticipate a certain naïveté in their views. Yet significant expectation is directed at youth as the next generation to 'carry the torch' of remembrance. Implicit in acts of remembrance involving youth is learning about war and its significance. As Fournier *et al.* (2012) note, people learn how to engage in remembrance in part by their interaction with the education system. The authors argue that the broader remembrance narrative involves a simplified discourse about good and evil, and a purified version of history. Their research is particularly useful here as it offers insight into learning objectives and plans that government curriculum directs. This chapter takes further the concept of learning as an act of

Figure 4.1 Vimy commemoration and rededication of the Memorial, 9 April 2007.

remembrance, offering insight into the experiential element of touring a battlefield and experiencing a commemoration. As one respondent explained,

> ... seeing the Battlefield [sic] in real life is so much more[;] you can smell the air, feel the cold gross wet muck in the trenches, be able to go in the tunnels, it's just that much more of an experience. Plus it's a lot easier to imagine what might have happened when you are standing right there.

Co-construction of meaning by youth is not free from messages of sentimentality toward war, or even blatant misunderstanding. Nonetheless, in the evolution of learning, I argue that visiting a battlefield provides a unique form of experiential learning that can be emotionally impactful, if not transformative, of one's worldview (see Bird 2013). Whereas memorials and commemorative messages may attempt to guide a way of thinking about war, there is no certainty of a particular outcome in an individual's belief or values.

Certainly, from a learning perspective there are challenges in touring battle-fields. Freeman (2014) speaks of 'cemetery overload' for British students who visit site after site in two- to four-day trips to the Western Front. For Canadians and other Commonwealth nations, the chance to travel to Europe is even more of an obstacle, given the cost and distance. But for those lucky enough to go, a tour may involve a ten-day to two-week experience, perhaps longer, covering a range of topics in addition to war history. Indeed, the post-trip survey did find students responding with stories of memorable times in Rome and Paris, but touring Canadian heritage sites of the two world wars was the priority of the itinerary.

Several questions warrant attention in future research with regard to commemo-ration as a battlefield event, as well as the pedagogy of remembrance as experiential learning. Certainly, this chapter does not have space to consider broader pedagogical issues with regard to topics such as experiential learning as well as contextualizing the broader, life-changing travel. Although I include my own observations in this chapter, another topic for research might be to examine meaning-making of various age groups to reveal how meaning varies by generation, maturity and life experience. Examining the narrative of speeches offered by prime ministers and other heads of state may also be useful in assessing the ways in which the war memory is employed in the contemporary political setting. As this chapter is guided by what youth found memorable, the reader will not be surprised that the speeches made by Her Majesty Queen Elizabeth and the Prime Ministers of Canada and France did not get any mention, although seeing these individuals did generate memorable moments for some. However, these speeches should not be simply dismissed as tropes of the nation thankful and proud of its fallen soldiers. Brinkley's (2003) analysis of President Reagan's 1984 speech at the D-Day commemorations shows how these orations can mark a significant moment in a nation's political direction if not its philosophical stance in the contemporary global context.

This chapter draws on a range of methods in an effort to give voice to meaning-making at a battlefield event. In addition to pre- and post-trip surveys of youth, I use my own observations from attending the event. Given the emotional nature of commemoration, the desire for privacy may hinder people's survey responses. Furthermore, probing may represent an unethical intrusion by the researcher, particularly when surveying youth. Although I am older by 20 years, my own observations *in situ* have some use here, as Dunkley (2007) might agree. They provide another voice to expose the emotionality of the moment and perhaps a contrast to the youth perspective. However imperfect, reflexivity does assist in building deeper insight into the experience of what is memorable, particularly at sites associated with death (see Seaton 1997; 2000; 2002).

To account for my positionality, what Everett (2010: 170) describes as '... where our personal biography directly informs how we react when we investigate', I served in the military for eight years. I have also participated in peace marches, thereby making the influence of military experience somewhat unclear. However, it does indicate that I have some knowledge of the military but not of war itself. I also draw upon previous experiences visiting Vimy, specifically working as a heritage interpreter at the park during the summer of 1990. Witnessing daily the power of place to evoke reaction in visitors led to life-long research interest (see also Lemelin and Johansen 2014).

The pre-trip survey involved getting permission from school districts and teachers to distribute the survey. Approximately 300 students received the survey link, and 200 respondents participated to varying degrees of detail and completeness. Of these, 67 per cent were female, 90 per cent of those who responded were 18 years old or younger, the rest being teachers or parent guardians accompanying the group. Nearly 14 per cent indicated that they had an ancestor who had fought in World War I. The post-trip survey included 87 respondents. There was no plan to collate pre- and post-trip responses by individual. Instead, analysis focused more generally on perceptions and insights of respondents.

In order to contextualize the commemoration and commentary by youth, I present the Battle of Vimy Ridge and its place in national mythology including recent debates regarding the Vimy effect. I will examine the significance of the landscape of war and the significance of place in the performance of remembering and how youth interpret and reflect on the value of 'being there'. Next, I will explore the aural experience of the commemoration, both natural and man-made, as an emotional trigger and galvanizing element for the memorable nature of the experience.

History, myth and the Vimy effect

I have always wanted to see this memorial up close. It strikes me as something that all Canadians should do before they die – as Canadian as driving across the country, or visiting every province and territory, or learning French.

(youth survey response)

There is no question that Vimy has a unique status in Canada's identity. Its mythic significance is reflected in the mandate of an organization called the Vimy

Foundation, formed in 2007: 'To preserve and promote Canada's World War I legacy as symbolized with the victory at Vimy Ridge in April 1917, a milestone where Canada came of age and was then recognized on the world stage' (Vimy Foundation website). In 2012, an image of the Vimy Memorial was placed on the twenty dollar note, emblematic of the profile of Vimy over other battles and, controversially, other aspects of Canadian history (see Frenette 2014).

Like other dominions and colonies of Britain, Canada was automatically involved as soon as Britain declared war in August 1914. For a nation barely 50 years in the making, the losses were staggering. Roughly 425,000 Canadians served overseas, a commitment made even more notable by a relatively small population of 7.8 million people (Cook 2008). Of the 345,000 who made it to France, more than 60,000 Canadians were killed during the war with more dying from injury in the immediate post-war years; 174,000 were wounded and countless others mentally scarred by the war. Cook (2008: 611–13) calculates that these losses indicate that roughly 6.5 to 7 of every 10 Canadians on the Western Front were either killed or wounded.

Vimy can be studied both as military history and as cultural memory, two perspectives that are often braided and oversimplified to form a mythic national narrative. Interestingly, Hayes, Iarocci, and Bechthold (2007) offer a comprehensive reassessment of Vimy's place in military history and how the nation-building myth has evolved. From an historical perspective, the attack on Vimy Ridge was a diversion within the larger Spring Offensive involving British and French troops. Vimy had long been a focus of attacks by British and French forces resulting in a heavy loss of life. The ridge was important because it commanded the coal fields of the Douai Plain. Several books present the battle in detail (see Berton 1986; Hayes, Iarocci and Bechthold 2007; Cook 2008). In brutally short and simple terms, months of preparation, coupled with new strategies and tactics, led to the Canadian victory. The battle was also symbolically significant as it was the first time all Canadian troops fought together under one (primarily Canadian) command. Over 10,000 Canadians were killed or wounded over the three days of battle. Whereas Vimy was a notable military success for the Canadian Corps, the larger Allied Offensive failed. German regimental accounts outline this period along the Western Front as being a victory for them or at least a draw, given their success in other parts of the line.

Despite the debate as to the significance of the battle within the larger history of the war, the cultural memory of Vimy quickly evolved to represent the 'coming of age' of Canada. Certainly, Vance (2007) notes the profile of Vimy Ridge as one of the Great War's most popular battles, a point fuelled by assertions such as that of Goodspeed (1969: 91) when he argues 'undoubtedly, the capture of Vimy Ridge has been the greatest British victory of war up to that time." Vance also points to the symbolic religious connection noted, or created, in the media of the time, that the advance took place on Easter Monday, thereby entwining the birth of the nation with celebrating the resurrection of Christ. Such a coincidence only helped to fuel the popularity of Vimy.

Nine decades later, in 2007, thousands of Canadians made plans to attend the commemoration. In the pre-trip survey, there was a great level of consistency in responses to the question 'is remembering the Battle of Vimy Ridge important to Canada today? Why?" Many comments were similar in pointing out central components of the Vimy narrative, as evident here:

> It is important today because Canada was born on April 9th; it was symbolic because it was the first time the whole Canadian Corps fought together. This meant that Canada as a nation could work together to achieve victory in the face of great adversity and previous failure by the British and French.

> It is important because Canadians fought together, English and French. It helped Canada to achieve international status. It showed the genius of Canadian military leadership. It showed that we were more than just a colony.

These responses parallel what Hillier (2010) means when he uses the term 'Vimy effect'. After serving as the Chief of Defence for the Canadian Armed Forces from 2005 to 2008, Hillier wrote a book on leadership (2010), offering 'points of wisdom for today's leaders' by drawing upon his experience in the military. He used the term Vimy effect to articulate a vision for the present-day military, an 'inspiration [coming] from how the [Vimy] fight was won, not necessarily what it achieved' (ibid. 101). Recognizing the gravitas of Vimy in the mindsight of the military and Canadians, Hillier unpacked its significance in terms of three broad traits, namely a unified and visible leadership, valuing and supporting soldiers, and the military becoming a learning organization. As he concludes,

> Thus, our vision [for the Canadian Forces] ('We are after the Vimy effect') summed up in six words a rich background, history, significance and under-standing by all who heard it. This vision did not represent pages of bureaucratise, doublespeak and political correctness. It was a rallying cry to the greatness that our nation had once experienced and could again. It... resonated with everyone in uniform (ibid. 109–10).

In speeches to business leaders, Hillier argued that the Vimy effect goes beyond the military context, evoking a quintessentially Canadian character: innovative, tough and resolute. These are standards which, as Canadians, we should learn from and strive to emulate. However, Hillier's perspective is contradicted later in this chapter by Richler's interpretation of the term Vimy effect.

Another tone in the youth responses regarding why Vimy is important to remember was the predictable national pride. At times, the tone was akin to the bragging rights of a sports team or pride by way of some uniquely Canadian genetic trait. The following exemplars attest to a common tone in responses:

> YES! because it was the first time Canada proved itself as an independent to the britts *[sic]* and the world! WOOT GO CANADA!!!!!!!!!!

Yes it is, very important, we would not be who we are without those brave soldiers. 'They said it was impossible… we did it'. I wish I could have met the man who said those words so that I could thank him for giving my country an identity, so that I could tell him that I will never forget.

… [I]t should be more important to Canada because we were the only ones capable of taking the ridge which should fill us with pride in knowing that when we are needed we get the job done, Properly *[sic]*.

The use of the pronoun 'we' reflects the sense of ownership within the imagined community, that what defines Vimy as a victory is what defines 'my' Canadian identity. In contrast, Noah Richler (2012) views the Vimy effect polemically. He redefines Vimy effect as the twenty-first century manipulation of a war myth to catalyze patriotism in support for future wars. Richler argues

[w]hen Canadians tell the story of the Battle of Vimy Ridge as a creation myth, they tell it in a manner that prompts complicity rather than outrage. Rather than telling a story that became the emblem of the many that the Canadian Expeditionary Force fought in some manner that might compel today's Canadian to protest against such absurd, senseless slaughter, it suggests that war is a permanent condition and how to prepare for its return (p.57).

Richler (2012) views the telling of Canada's story of World War I as a barometer of the changing profile that the Canadian Armed Forces, and Canada's military history as a whole, has taken over the past 15 years. In his view, Canada is moving away from its post- World War II stance of peacekeeping and has embraced a conservative and militaristic stance. The media, politicians, teachers, clerics, artists, and academics invented and continuously shape the myth. At times, these gatekeepers are in collaboration, at other times unaware of their efforts that support the needs of this pro-war worldview. Certainly, Richler's interpretation of the Vimy effect represents the dynamic and political nature of war remembrance and commemoration. What is of interest here is how visiting Vimy impacts on student perceptions and the extent to which what is memorable reflects complacency toward the realities of war in lieu of a pro-war form of national pride.

The next two sections present post-trip survey responses. First, I examine what was memorable in touring the battlefields, cemeteries and war memorials. Second, I explore the actual commemoration from the experience of youth.

Memories from the landscape of war

This section presents qualitative results and analysis with regard to the general experience of visiting battlefields and cemeteries and then comments specific to the Vimy Ridge Memorial. Given the pre-trip comments in the previous section, along with arguments of propagandizing war history to contemporary ends by Richler, Frenette and others, it would be incorrect to characterize students as blind to at least attempting to contemplate the trauma of war. From the responses received, reflecting upon the war's violence and the death of soldiers was made clearer by visiting cemeteries and battlefields. As one student explained,

> I used to be the kind of person that would just read a book, or a movie and think I 'got' it. But you never really 'get' it until you live it. Knowing that you are standing on one of the most famous, and important battlefields in the world is about the most breathtaking experiences of your lifetime. Seeing the shell holes in the ground all around you is like nothing you could picture in a book. And even if it's in a movie, it doesn't do it any justice. To live it is to actually understand it.

This statement reflects the power of visiting a battlefield as a form of resonant remembrance, learning about that war that is transformative (Bird 2011). We may question the extent to which war is fully understood in the manicured setting of a memorial park free from the noise, horror, and carnage, but there is nevertheless a deeper reflection and an opportunity to evolve the conversation of war and peace for a young person (see Freeman 2014). Students also spoke about their experience reflecting on death and war, as illustrated below:

> Standing behind the grave of a fallen soldier was a very humbling experience. It was dreadful to think that this man died and they do not know who he is. It made me realize how lucky I am to live a life that is not endangered by war.

> It is important because when your *[sic]* there you can sense the people[,] you can sense all the horrible things that went on there.

> One of my most powerful memories about Vimy Ridge was being utterly shocked at how the earth had been destroyed by the battle.

These contemplations present another form of meaning-making that takes place in a battlefield which is separate from thoughts associated with national identity: reflections on humanity, death, and war's destruction. Vimy is a 100-hectare park provide by the Government of France as a Canadian memorial site for eternity. In this way, these comments embody the polysemic nature of the landscape of war (Seaton 2009a), that meanings co-constructed can lead to a range of reflections that inform social identity, anti-war sentiment, a pro-war stance, or a range of other reactions. The war memorial at Vimy is the most significant symbol that is interpreted by students.

Vimy is a 100-hectare park provided by the Government of France as a Canadian memorial site for perpetuity. Attracting over 300,000 visitors a year, the memorial park is distinguished by cratered terrain, the remains of a trench and tunnel system, and an interpretive center staffed by Canadian guides. However, the evidence of war is muted by the tranquil beauty of pine and maples trees which cover much of the battlefield.

The creation of the memorial at Vimy Ridge fulfills three roles:

- to recognize the victory that occurred in April 1917
- to serve as the main national memorial overseas for those who died in World War I and
- to memorialize the 11,285 Canadian soldiers killed in France and with no known grave.

As the national memorial, Vimy receives particular attention because of Sir Walter Allward's expressive design. Constructed between 1922 and 1936, a marble base, or crypt, establishes a dramatic platform at the top of the ridge upon which two towers rise 85 metres. Vimy is quite distinct from other major memorials on the Western Front in terms of its imagery and symbolism. For example, carved figures represent the virtues of Truth, Faith, Justice, Charity, Knowledge, and Peace which together 'sing the Hymn of Peace' as Allward described. In the middle is the 'Passing of the Torch', echoing the imagery offered in the poem 'In Flanders Fields' by the Canadian John McCrae. A nine-metre female figure represents Canada 'mourning over her fallen sons'.

Many survey respondents indicated that simply 'being able to touch the monument', as one student noted, was the most memorable part of their experience. As other students described,

> When I stood on top of the monument, and looked around, it was the first time I ever felt REALLY proud to be a Canadian.

> My most powerful memory was firstly, when the sun was passing directly behind the monument, lighting up the entire background with an almost heavenly light...

> I think that the memorial beautifuly *[sic]* represents Canada and the sacrifice of all the Canadians who died for Canada.

> There was something about [the Vimy Memorial] that just amazed me and gave me a special feeling inside every time i *[sic]* looked at it.

As the major Canadian memorial overseas and possessing a particularly evocative design, Vimy dominates attention. The number of visitors easily overshadows the sum of visitors to the other national memorials in Belgium and France such as Sanctuary Wood, Courcelette, Dury, and Bourlon Wood. This outcome was prophesied by General Sir Arthur Currie, Commander of the Canadian Corps, in 1922 when he said:

> [If] they place the large memorial at Vimy it will confirm for all time the impression which exists in the minds of the majority of the people of Canada that Vimy was the greatest battle fought by the Canadians in France. In my

mind this is very far from being a fact.

(Currie cited in Cook 2008: 625)

In its defense, one may argue that Vimy provides a gateway to learn about other aspects of Canada's war effort. But few sites match the dramatic setting of Vimy Ridge. There is a natural beauty in this landscape of war, defying the imagery of death and carnage, entrancing the hearts and minds of visitors and Canadians in particular.

The next section presents the 2007 commemoration at Vimy Ridge. Of focus here is what made the event memorable for students, coupled with my own field notes of what occurred that day.

Battlefield event: 2007 commemoration at Vimy Ridge

The Queen and the Prime Ministers of Canada and of France arrive and the formalities of the commemoration begin... Then, there is the music, evoking emotions that take me by surprise. First, standing on the memorial, the fanfare trumpeters play. Then, a Metis woman plays a haunting Lament on the violin. Finally, a song is passed from the performers, to a bag piper, to a male choir, to a children's choir. The lyrics are simple:

> Dreaming of home, I feel so alone
>
> I am dreaming of home

There is an emotional power at this moment, in this place. For all the significance of the battle and its importance to Canada that the dignitaries each try to convey, the emotional pull of the landscape and its message of the horror of war is revealed by the lyrics about the loneliness of a soldier, far away from home and loved ones. The event is orchestrated to perfection as the last note turns to silence just as four jets thunder past. Amazing. The performance is complete.

(Bird 2007)

This excerpt offers a snapshot of the afternoon commemoration of April 9, 2007 (see Figure 4.2). For Casey (1987: 216), a commemoration involves two components: A formal eulogy and participation in a liturgical service. This 'intensified remembering' involves ritual and a narrative text and leads to what is described as 'a cult enacted' (Connerton 1989: 70). As a cult enacted, individuals participate in a ritual of commemoration and feel a sense of belonging. For Connerton (1989: 53), the symbolism and meaning of commemorative practices is where 'myth and ritual diverge' as the voices of the state and religion, veterans and the community at large come together to formally remember.

Indeed, a central element in the commemorative event is ritualized traditions. Set in the context of the commemoration, sound had a profound impact in engaging youth and the audience as a whole. For authors such as Wyle (2009) and Foreman

Figure 4.2 Commemoration in the shadow of the Vimy Ridge War Memorial, 9 April 2007.

(2014: 2) 'distances, loss, and absences' is what constitutes the soundscape for remembrance, commemoration and memorialisation.

As Marshall (2004: 40) explains, 'state sanctioned remembrance has been characterized by a specific, and for the most part, unchanging series of sounds used at every scale, ranging from music to its counterpoint silence'. Marshall describes commemoration as a ritual engagement of the senses: The music, the footfalls of soldiers and veterans, mirroring almost the sound of marching to war, singing, the Last Post, national anthems and prayer; the language of ritual also combines the collective 'we', and appropriate poses are also seen as part of the ritual: Salutes, the bowing of heads in prayer, the lowering of flags by flag bearers. All of these observations point to the sensual aspect of ritual commemoration that emphasizes the sense of memorialized place and time. The Vimy commemoration reflects all of these ritual traits.

In asking youth what was most memorable about the commemoration, the aural aspect stood out for many. Sound is particularly significant because as a medium it is a forum of interpretation – by way of offering a sound to represent a feeling – that evokes an emotional response and connection. Set in the context of the commemoration, sound had a profound impact in engaging youth and the audience as a whole.

However, in the case of producing the musical score for a commemorative event, in addition to following rituals and traditions, the other dimension of the commemoration is to create a mood, by way of the 'right' music, to support an appropriate and respectful ambiance to elicit reflection. The concern with managing the music selection parallels Seaton's focus on managing the aura of death assoc-iated with a site of memory. As he explains, 'evoking and conserving its auratic impacts are the central tasks of management' (2009a: 75). In this regard, the aural experience at a commemoration is carefully staged yet nevertheless exposed to dissonant intrusion. For example, when a student started to play his trumpet while waiting for the commemoration to start, he was quickly silenced by organizers.

Two pieces of music were mentioned in the survey responses as being memorable. A young Metis violinist, Ms Sierra Noble, played a haunting piece entitled 'The Metis Prayer, The Warrior's Lament'. The other piece was 'I'm Dreaming of Home', a hymn written for the movie *Joyeux Noël* (2005) that was sung by a military choir, then a children's choir, and finally by Inuit singer, Ms Susan Aglukark. As one student commented, 'This song really seemed to touch me in my heart and has left a significant impact'. Transcending national identity the music speaks about humanity. The hymn draws imagery of the loneliness of a soldier, presenting a concept universally understood by the audience. Another student explains, '[t]he song was very powerful and it made me realize that the men who fought in the war were very sad and alone from being so far away from home'.

In addition to music was the power of silence, described by one student as 'bone-chilling', that occurred during the service. As one respondent commented, '[d]uring the ceremony it was completely silent and all I could hear were birds singing. It didn't seem possible that the place where I was would have been destroyed by bullets and a place where people were killed only ninety years ago'.

For Marshall, silence is part of the commemorative soundscape, formalizing a time for reflection within the ceremony itself, most notably in the two-minute silence, traditionally commenced and concluded by the sounding of the Last Post. The meanings evoked by various sounds and silences exemplify how a soundscape can illicit an historical sensation, or a sense of the past (see Benschop 2009). In the context of what was experienced and then later recalled by youth, the soundscape of the commemoration evoked a range of memorable and powerful meanings including thoughts of absence and loss.

Conclusion

What then is the significance of these memorable moments at a commemoration in how war is understood and remembered? Analyzing the symbolism drawn from the memorial, the landscape of war, and the soundscape of commemoration provide insight into the ways in which 'being there' inform not only our understanding of the past but how youth connect and draw meaning from the experience. This focus enables us to better understand how visiting a battlefield is framed and understood and to gain insight into the role that commemoration and a mediated, memori-alized act of remembrance plays in shaping learning. But to what extent does it help to understand perspectives about war?

I learned of the death of six Canadian soldiers fighting in Afghanistan the day following the Vimy commemoration. I wrote in my journal on April 10 and again on the 11th:

> The news stuns me. What have I gained from yesterday's experience to help me understand the news of today? I struggle to consider the meaning of these two events, attempting to judge my thoughts and filter them into some sort of description, but words fail me. At this moment, I can only feel despondence for the loss of six soldiers in a faraway land.

> April 11: I am reflecting on the experience of the past few days. I recite the lyrics that were so powerful, and the image of the memorial standing on the Ridge, basking in the sun, comes to my mind. I review the photographs and sound recordings that I have made. It is the music that stays with me. The death of the six soldiers in Afghanistan is still hard to contemplate. I also reflect on the 3,500 Canadians killed in the three days of fighting in 1917. Is it the past that informs my reaction and understanding of today's events, or is the present informing my emotion, memory and imagination of a battle that occurred 90 years ago?

> (Bird, 10 and 11 April 2007)

The energy and patriotism exhibited at the Vimy commemoration had little leverage in rationalizing the death in Afghanistan. As Chief of Defense, Hillier himself learned of the deaths of the soldiers while he was in France for the Vimy ceremony. Awaiting details before making a public announcement, he describes 'the depths of despair' he felt at the news (2010: 87), in contrast to those around him who were in the full swing of commemorative events and parades.

As a term, the 'Vimy effect' gained profile in the years following the 2007 commemoration. Hillier and Richler represent a debate of two contrasting worldviews that exemplify the politics of remembrance. From what was recalled by youth, Richler's polemic loses ground in the context of commemoration in the Vimy landscape. With its pock-marked fields reflecting the tumult of war, its cemeteries and powerful memorial coupled with the commemorative event and its soundscape, youth reflect in ways that inform a sense of national identity. But they also they imagine about the suffering of those who fought and died. While some of the responses of youth may reflect an uncritical or sentimental tone or even a disconcerting form of patriotism, the responses also show that youth are engaged in deeper thoughts about standing in the footsteps of soldiers and grappling with thoughts about war and death. Their path of understanding and negotiating the war's role in humankind continues, as it does for the rest of us.

During the three days of battle in April 1917, the Canadian Corps suffered over 10,600 dead and wounded. More horrifying is that many were of those killed were never recovered. As Cpl Fred Maiden of Calgary's 10th Battalion explained, '[w]e tried to identify some of the boys... But we couldn't do it. See, the boys were blown to pieces, lots of them' (Dancocks 1990: 115). Today, standing on the lush

green slope of Vimy Ridge we are presented with an impossible leap of the imagination through time and space to fully comprehend the plight of those who fought.
The purpose of commemoration is to make the attempt.

References

Anderson, B. (1983). *Imagined Communities: Reflections on the Origin and Spread of Nationalism* (London: Verso).
Benschop, R. (2009). 'All the names: Soundscapes, recording technology, and the historical sensation'. *Sound Souvenirs: Audio Technologies, Memory and Cultural Practices* (Amsterdam: Amsterdam University Press), pp. 182–198.
Berton, P. (1986). *Vimy* (Toronto: McClelland & Stewart).
Bird, G. R. (2013). 'Place identities in the Normandy landscape of war: touring the Canadian sites of memory', in L. White and E. Frew, *Dark Tourism and Place Identity: Managing and Interpreting Dark Places* (New York: Routledge), pp. 167–86.
Bird, G. R. (2011). 'Tourism, remembrance and the landscape of war', PhD thesis, University of Brighton, UK. British Library.
Bird, G. R. (2007). 'Field notes of Vimy commemoration'. Unpublished.
Brinkley, D. (2005). *The Boys of Pointe du Hoc: Ronald Reagan, D-Day, and the US Army 2nd Ranger Battalion* (1st edn) (New York: W. Morrow).
Casey, E. S. (1987). *Remembering: a Phenomenological Study* (Bloomington, IN: Indiana University Press).
Chronis, A. (2005). 'Co-constructing heritage at the Gettysburg Storyscape'. *Annals of Tourism Research, 32*(2), 386–406.
Connerton, P. (1989). *How Societies Remember* (Cambridge: Cambridge University Press).
Cook, T. (2008). *Shock Troops: Canadians fighting the Great War 1917–1918, Vol. 2* (Toronto: Penguin).
Dancocks, D. G. (1990). *Gallant Canadians: The story of the Tenth Canadian Infantry Battalion, 1914–1919* (Toronto: Penguin).
Department of Veterans' Affairs Australia (2010). *'A century of service' community research*. Government of Australia, Project no. 41509.
Dunkley, R. A. (2007). 'Re-peopling tourism: a "hot approach" to studying than a tourist experiences', in I. Ateljevic, A. Pritchard and N. Morgan (eds), *The Critical Turn in Tourism Studies: Innovative Research Methods* (Oxford: Elsevier), pp. 371–85.
Everett, S. (2010). 'Lessons from the field: reflecting on a tourism research journey around the "celtic" periphery'. *Current Issues in Tourism, 13*(2), 161–75.
Foreman, I. (2014). 'Spectral soundscapes: exploring spaces of remembrance through sound'. *Interference, 4*, 1–11.
Fournier, G., Loughridge, J., MacDonald, K., Sperduti, V., Tsimicalis, E. and Tabir, N. (2012). 'Learning to commemorate: challenging prescribed collective memories of war'. *Social Alternatives, 31*(2), 41–5.
Freeman, J. (2014). 'Remembering the First World War: using a battlefield tour of the Western Front to help pupils take a more critical approach to what they encounter'. *Teaching History 155*, 45–52.
Frenette, Y. (2014), 'Conscripting Canada's past: the Harper Government and the politics of memory'. *Canadian Journal of History, 49*(1), 49–65.
Goodspeed, D. J. (1969). *The Road past Vimy: The Canadian Corps 1914–1918* (Toronto: MacMillan).

Granatstein, J. (2014). 'Why is Canada botching the Great War centenary?' Editorial, *Globe and Mail*, 21 April, A11.

Hayes, G., Iarocci, A. and Bechthold, M. (2007). *Vimy Ridge: A Canadian reassessment* (Waterloo, ONT: Wildred Laurier University).

Hillier, R. (2010). *Leadership: 50 points of Wisdom for Today's Leaders* (Toronto: Harper-Collins).

Jennings, G. and Weiler, B. (2006). 'Mediating meaning: perspectives on brokering quality tourist experiences', in G. Jennings and G. Nickerson (eds) *Quality Tourism Experiences* (Boston, Lincs: Butterworth-Heinemann), pp. 57–78.

Jones, H. (2014). 'Goodbye to all that?: Memory and meaning in the commemoration of the First World War'. *Juncture*, *20*(4), 287–91.

Lemelin, R.H. and Johansen, K. (2014). 'The Canadian National Vimy Memorial: remembrance, dissonance and resonance'. *International Journal of Culture, Tourism and Hospitality Research*, *8*(2), 203–18.

Lloyd, D. (1998). *Battlefield Tourism: Pilgrimage and the Commemoration of the Great War in Britain, Australia and Canada, 1919–1939* (Oxford: Berg).

Marshall, D. (2004). 'Making sense of remembrance'. *Social and Cultural Geography*, *I*(1), 37–54.

McCready, A. L. (2010). '"Tie a yellow ribbon" round public discourse, national identity and the war: neoliberal militarization and the yellow ribbon campaign in Canada'. *TOPIA: Canadian Journal of Cultural Studies*, *23/24*, 28–51.

Mycock, A. (2014). 'The First World War centenary in the UK: "a truly national commemoration?"', *The Round Table*, *103*(2), 153–63.

Richler, N. (2012). *What we talk about when we talk about war* (Frederickton, NB: Goose Press).

Scates, B. (2008). 'Memorializing Gallipoli: manufacturing memory at Anzac'. *Public History Review*, *15*, 47–59.

Seaton, A. V. (2009a). 'Purposeful otherness: approaches to the management of thana-tourism', in R. Sharpley and P. Stone (eds), *The Darker Side of Travel: the Theory and Practice of Dark Tourism* (Toronto: Channel View), pp. 75–108.

Seaton, A. V. (2009b). 'Thanatourism and its discontents: an appraisal of a decade's work with some future issues and directions', in T. Jamal and M. Robinson (eds), *The SAGE Handbook of Tourism Studies* (London: SAGE), pp. 521–42.

Seaton, A. V. (2002). 'Observing conducted tours: the ethnographic context in tourist research'. *Journal of Vacation Marketing, 8*(4), 309.

Seaton, A. V. (2000). '"Another weekend away looking for dead bodies...": battlefield tourism on the Somme and in Flanders'. *Tourism Recreation Research*, *25*(3), 63–77.

Seaton, A. V. (1997). 'Unobtrusive observational measures as a qualitative extension of visitor surveys at festivals and events'. *Journal of Travel Research* Spring, pp. 25–30.

Vance, J. (2007). 'Battle verse: poetry and nationalism after Vimy Ridge', in G. Hayes, A. Iarocci and M. Bechthold (eds), *Vimy Ridge: A Canadian reassessment.* (Waterloo, ONT: Wildred Laurier University), pp. 265–79.

Vimy Foundation website: www.vimyfoundation.ca/mission [2 February 2015]

White, G. (2000). 'Emotional remembering: the pragmatics of national memory'. *American Anthropological Association*, *27*(4), 505–29.

Winter, J. M. (2006). *Remembering War: the Great War between Memory and History in the Twentieth Century* (New Haven, CT: Yale University Press).

5   Comines-Warneton 1914–2014

A landscape approach

Birger Stichelbaut,[1] *Yannick Van Hollebeeke*[2] *and Jean Bourgeois*[2]

Introduction

In Belgium, the centenary of World War I has been accompanied by a renewed and increased interest in the history, heritage and archaeology of the Great War. In both the Flemish and the Walloon regions of the country there is an obvious and urgent need for scientific data for the interpretation and study of the former war landscape. This has been reinforced in particular with the – political – wish to nominate the heritage of the former Western Front in Belgium and France as a UNESCO World Heritage site. The overall interest in World War I and its legacy, the centenary and the huge number of visitors from all over the world are all evidence that this WWI heritage cannot be neglected.

One of the initial and most basic steps in heritage management involves the identification and recording of heritage (Cleere 2000: 11). Without strong management, little by little cultural sites will be lost and ultimately will disappear forever. Yet when it comes to World War I, most of the effort and interest focuses on the recording and study of cemeteries, monuments, bunkers and scars on the landscape, such as huge mine craters. As a field of study, archaeological heritage remains largely untouched.

To meet the need for scientific research into the material remains of World War I, we propose an aerial archaeological approach aided by Geographical Information Systems (GIS) to assess this specific war heritage in Belgium's Walloon region. (There are three main regions in Belgium: the Flemish, the Walloon and the Brussels-Capital regions, each with its own heritage agencies and legislation.) Historical aerial photographs can be used in a non-invasive way to study the war landscape, especially in combination with archaeological field surveys using mobile GIS applications. This chapter outlines the methodology used and discusses the results of this approach in the Walloon community of Comines-Warneton. The research area forms an interesting case study because it is an administratively well-defined and closed research area. Comines-Warneton, the only Walloon municipality falling within the front area, is located between Flanders and France and its heritage comes under the legal authority of the Walloon region.

The main research question posed by the project – which was kindly funded by the Walloon Government – was to identify the heritage of World War I in Comines-Warneton and to give an idea of its diversity, density and distribution.

World War I heritage in Belgium

Although the war ended almost 100 years ago, not all traces of it have vanished from the landscape. The cultural heritage of the Great War is very diverse. It consists not only of the very visible and present commemorative landscape of monuments and cemeteries, but also includes large stretches of landscape that were transformed by the industrialised scale and intensity of warfare during 1914–18 and resulted in a landscape of war. Besides the front area, the hinterland is also part of this landscape, where the logistics of the belligerents were deployed. Now that the last survivors of the Great War have passed away, the landscape remains as the last witness to this bloody episode.

The 'evidence' is diverse: from subtle traces, such as overgrown shelters, to the enormous craters blown in the landscape by the underground war and the endless rows of white tombstones dominating the countryside as palpable reminders of the enormous loss of human life. In certain fields and woods – although rare now – some original trenches are still preserved as shallow earthworks. Perhaps the greatest aspect of this heritage is also the least tangible although certainly not the least important. Buried beneath the surface are thousands of kilometres of trenches, many bunkers and shelters, and the remains of thousands of soldiers still lie buried in Flanders fields.

The archaeology of conflict as a scientific discipline started out from what was called 'Battlefield Archaeology'. This sub-discipline within archaeology deals with battlefields from different periods and, by extension, those of World War I, providing scientific information that cannot be obtained merely from documentary sources (Freeman and Pollard 2001: 1; Sutherland 2005: 2). The first time a battlefield was investigated using archaeological methods was at Little Big Horn, where Native Americans fought against General Custer's men near Montana in the USA. The archaeological study of battlefields in the United Kingdom witnessed its first large battlefield archaeology project in 1996, at the 15th century Towton battlefield in North Yorkshire. On this site, various archaeological techniques were used to unlock the data concealed in the battlefield in the form of material remains ranging from small objects to mass graves dating from the period of the battle (Sutherland 2005: 15).

However, according to Saunders, this perspective on the archaeology of recent conflicts such as World War I is actually too narrow and is doomed to disappear (Saunders 2013: 11). Modern conflict archaeology strives to compile knowledge of all aspects of sub-recent conflicts, addressing other academic disciplines, too. It no longer relies solely on things found in the former battlefields, but on a lot more. The conflict is approached as a multifaceted phenomenon that leaves behind it a large diversity of features. These remnants may carry different meanings, each attributed by different individuals or communities of people who come into contact with it, which can change over time (Saunders 2010: 33). In short, in recent years battlefield archaeology has evolved from a narrow field of research – often site-directed – to an interdisciplinary and multifaceted archaeological study of the material culture and landscape of World War I.

The management of World War I heritage in Belgium – both in the Walloon and the Flemish regions – is still in its infancy. This war was an industrialised conflict,

Figure 5.1 A British aerial photograph taken on 2 May 1917 shows the extent of the trench
fortifications and the interrelation with the physical landscape.
Source: © Imperial War Museum (IWM) Box Collection, Box 76 44 7B 36C.

which is also reflected in the density of the buried heritage. Compared with older
archaeological periods – for instance, there are only a few Roman and medieval
sites known within the research area – the quantity of identified features has created
specific problems with which the heritage agencies in Belgium and France are still
struggling. This is reflected in the Flemish government's attitude towards the

possible UNESCO nomination as a world heritage site. Although there was an excavation scheme instigated by the Flemish Organisation for Immovable Heritage to validate the presence of buried war heritage, this is currently being neglected and the focus remains solely on cemeteries and monuments (Vandael 2014). Ironically, none of the 18 selected sites actually dates from the war period and, moreover, there is no mention of the archaeological heritage at all.

Historical prospection versus archaeological prospection

The most pressing questions probably concern establishing what this heritage consists of, how well it has been preserved, and how objective criteria can be developed to decide which sites should be protected or excavated. In our opinion, this problem can be partially addressed by means of a solid – processual and quantitative – methodology. Using aerial photography, conceptually there are two different approaches possible to record the heritage of war.

A first approach – which can be described as historical prospection – uses aerial photographs (Stichelbaut 2011) that are contemporary with the research period. These historical photographs – not only of World War I but also of more recent events, i.e. World War II (Hegarty and Newsome 2007), the Cold War (Fowler 2008), etc. – provide an unprecedented visual record of war. From this we can reconstruct in detail the past landscape on more than one scale (at both landscape and site level), since they offer the huge advantage of showing the conflict landscape during its formation. This is a unique situation in archaeology – for the first time, the remote-sensing data used to study the heritage is actually contemporary with the archaeological period. By studying World War I using aerial photographs it is possible to reach conclusions about the density, diversity and distribution of features within the war landscape. However, on the other hand, this only indicates where possible archaeological sites could be located. The aerial photographs do not give additional information on taphonomic processes (i.e. differences in battlefield clearance in the post-war period, destructive deep ploughing, etc.) or on the differential preservation of the heritage.

The second approach is most commonly used in archaeology and applies fieldwalking and high-tech prospection techniques to identify buried archaeological remains by means of geophysical prospection (Masters and Stichelbaut 2009; Saey *et al.* 2013), Light Detection and Ranging technology (Lidar) (Stal *et al.* 2010) or the use of oblique aerial photographs for the detection of buried sites. The huge advantage of this approach is that many sites can be detected on a landscape level of research, and large areas can be covered, although the information is biased by the limitations of the techniques. For instance, modern-day archaeological aerial photography works better on sandy soils than on the heavy clay soils in the Ypres Salient, not all the subtle features can be detected with geophysics and some techniques (i.e. Electromagnetic Induction survey (EMI), magnetometry, Ground-Penetrating Radar (GPR), and others) work better on different soil types, etc. Some of these issues can be overcome by a multi-method approach combining both historical and archaeological prospection (Saey *et al.* 2013).

Figure 5.2 Comparison of an historical aerial photograph (British aerial photograph taken
on 5 February 1918) with the corresponding cropmark site of a World War I
trench in Comines-Warneton. The vegetation mark in the crops gives a clue to
the preservation of the trench beneath the surface. On the other hand, the absence
of cropmarks elsewhere does not mean there is no preserved heritage. It simply
means that no circumstances – soil moisture, suitable vegetation, etc. – were
favourable for aerial archaeology.

Source: British aerial photograph: © IWM Box Collection, Box 205 110 X3BA 28U.

Research area

The municipality of Comines-Warneton has been chosen as a case study as it
provides an opportunity to study a part of the Western Front as a closed adminis-
trative entity under one set of legislation. Project goals were to understand the
heritage in the area of the village from a landscape archaeological point of view.
Comines-Warneton is located south of the Ypres Salient in a quiet sector of the
front on the southern part of the notorious Messines Ridge. Ploegsteert, the western
part of the town, was called 'Plugstreet' by the Commonwealth soldiers who
resided there during the greater part of the war. After the British troops lost the
strategic Messines Ridge to the Germans on 1 November 1914 (Edmonds 1925, pp
303–12), the front area stabilised for two-and-a-half years and trench systems
developed on each side of a narrow no-man's-land. In 1916, preparations were
made to launch an Allied offensive on the Messines Ridge: 21 deep offensive mines

were dug beneath key German positions. Early in the morning of 7 June, the Battle of Messines began. Nineteen deep mines – four of which lie within the research area – were detonated and a large-scale infantry attack followed immediately. The German first line of defence crumbled and troops from Australia and New Zealand pushed the German defenders back some three kilometres. However, all this captured terrain was lost again in April 1918, when the Germans launched their Spring Offensive.

Data acquisition and methodology

One of the objectives of this chapter is to offer an insight into the use of historical aerial photographs for assessing war heritage. From the end of 1915 onwards, photo-reconnaissance units were sent out along the Western Front on a regular basis to record the outline of the enemy's defences (Carlier 1921). These photographs, collected over a period of four years, survived in large quantities in Europe, the USA and even Australia. Aerial photographs of the study area were retrieved from the Imperial War Museum, the Belgian Royal Army Museum, the Australian War Memorial in the Flanders Fields Museum and the Bayerisches Hauptstaatsarchiv (Stichelbaut and Bourgeois 2009). The area in our case study was covered by 1,628 vertical aerial photographs taken between 4 February 1915 and 9 October 1918. All these photographs were georectified in a GIS. Further, all visible traces on the photographs were interpreted, dated and mapped to a digital layer in the GIS. By doing this, the exact location of each trace could be identified, as well as its length, width and surface area. This GIS layer is projected on to a modern orthophoto providing the opportunity to conduct a quick assessment of the preservation of the relics visible in the aerial photographs from World War I.

Second, an extensive field survey was carried out in order to locate relics (i.e. pillboxes, tunnel entrances and preserved trenches) that are preserved above the surface. This survey was supported in the field with georectified trench maps and aerial photographs on a GPS-enabled tablet PC. In short, aerial photographs are not useful only for desktop analysis of the landscape of war, but are also more than useful when operating in the field. Their use provides an opportunity to locate possibly preserved relics easily and to access direct feedback concerning the historical and landscape context of any remains discovered in the field.

Third, geophysical prospection techniques have been used within the research area to verify and validate the presence of archaeological remains beneath the surface. A first survey had already been carried out in 2009 when a large gradiometer survey was focused on the Allied-German front line at Saint-Yvon – a small hamlet within the study area of Comines-Warneton (Masters and Stichelbaut 2009). The research indicated that the majority of trenches that were visible on the aerial photographs could also be detected in the geophysical dataset, indicating the presence of large numbers of preserved trenches and some pillboxes. More geophysical prospection is currently under way.

Site-oriented approach

Historical aerial photography can provide information at two different scales of research. Comparative research into the time series of aerial photographs gives a visual record of war in many individual sites. An example of one such site is 'The Birdcage'. Between the hamlets of Le Pelerin and Le Gheer, the Germans built the notorious position called by British troops 'The Birdcage' on account of the large quantities of barbed wire in front of the trenches (Spagnoly 1997: 26). The small protruding salient was surrounded on three sides by British trenches, which was an unenviable and dangerous situation. Between June and September 1915, this sector was the stage for an underground war in which the British and Germans sought to undermine each other's lines. A chronological series of aerial photographs illustrates the sequence of the mine explosions and gives a useful insight into the early stages of the underground war in the Ypres Salient (Stichelbaut and Chielens 2013: 86–7).

In the Bois de la Hutte, the combination of aerial photo-interpretation and a GPS-aided field survey enabled the rediscovery of the entrance to a deep dugout system. The topography of the Mont de la Hutte provided an ideal sheltered position to excavate a deep, extensive system of galleries in which two full battalions (up to 2,000 soldiers) could be safely accommodated. The official name of the system was the 'Hill 63 dugouts', although the soldiers called the complex 'The Catacombs' or 'Wallangara' (Spagnoly 1997: 74). Careful examination of the aerial photographs led to the discovery of a number of possible entrances to the tunnel network. The field survey revealed the location of the – now collapsed – entrances as three small depressions.

Landscape scale of research

The use of a large number of aerial photographs in combination with a GIS allows the information that is visible on individual photographs to be compiled on a landscape scale. The study area of Comines-Warneton has been covered by 1,628 vertical aerial photographs. All these images have been geolocated, interpreted in detail and subsequently mapped to produce a GIS inventory of up to 13,681 individual war features. These include all visible features such as trenches, pillboxes, barracks, ammunition dumps, narrow-gauge railways, fortified shell holes, buried communication cables, etc. A detailed analysis and description of all feature categories would occupy many pages, so in this chapter we will focus on the trenches and pillboxes.

The Western Front stretched for more than 700 kilometres from the North Sea in Belgium to the French-Swiss border at Pfetterhouse. Trenches can be considered emblematic of the horrors and futility of the years of stalemate during the war. Although the geographical scope speaks for itself and, as such, hints at the industrial scale of events, this becomes even more impressive when the attention is redirected to our research area. In this small sector of the front alone, 478km of trenches have been recorded within an area of just 61km². Of these, 199km are fire trenches, while the majority (278km) are communication trenches oriented at straight angles leading towards the front line. In addition, 619 features were

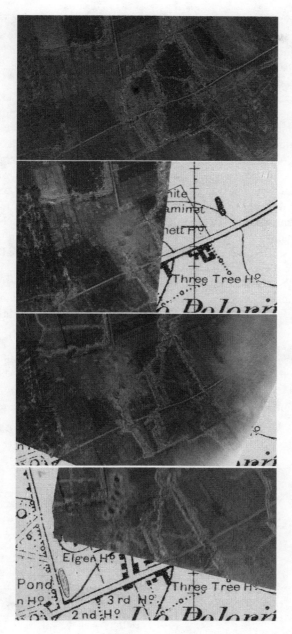

Figure 5.3 By analysing a series of aerial photographs taken over a period of time the chronology of the mine explosions can be recaptured. These aerial photographs were taken (from top to bottom) on 24 May, 7 June, 12 July and 10 September 1915.

Source: (From top to bottom) © IWM Box Collection, Box 23 349 C 28U, Box C 467 28U, Box C 567 28U and Box 22 298 BB 28U.

identified as bunkers, a large majority of which are of German origin (450 German and 169 Allied). Unlike the trenches, however, we should urge caution about considering the numbers as absolute because most of bunkers and shelters were camouflaged so that they would not show up on aerial photographs.

The spatial distribution of the trenches (see Figure 5.4) reveals that the greatest density is located in a zone 3.5km wide between two major shifts in the front line. The landscape in this small area is veined with Allied and German trenches, constructed during different phases of the war. First there are Allied and German trenches dating between November 1914 and the start of the Battle of Messines on 7 June 1917. At the end of 1914, the field fortifications were nothing more than disorganised and unconnected trenches. By the eve of the Battle of Messines an elaborate trench network had been dug on both sides of No Man's Land. To a certain extent the trenches were standardised and fixed types (i.e. fire trenches with square and semi-circular traverses or typical communication trenches with either zigzag or sinuous traces). Following the Allied victory in the Battle of Messines, the front line shifted almost 2.5km eastwards and the newly gained territory soon became covered with a new network of Allied trenches, often including new types of trench – i.e. many Allied trenches had trapezoid and island traverses. During the German Spring Offensive, this territory was lost and the front line moved to just west of the research area. The spatial distribution of the bunkers shows a different pattern. Most are identified at the front prior to the Battle of Messines, which was also the longest stable period. The remaining German bunkers are distributed towards the rear to form an in-depth defence, which was in line with the German military doctrine of 1917 and 1918 (Chef des Generalstabes des Feldheeres 1918).

A comparison of this GIS dataset with the results of the field prospection is interesting from an academic point of view but it is also daunting to see how few features have actually been preserved. During the survey, trenches were only

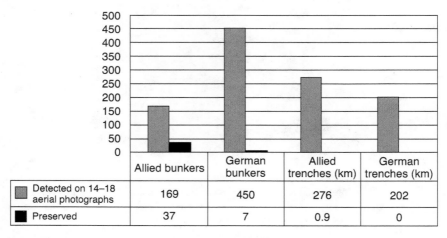

Figure 5.4 Comparison of recorded and preserved trenches and bunkers.

identified above the surface in three locations. They were visible as depressions 40–50cm deep and measured 961m long in total, which represents just 0.2 per cent of what was originally dug during the war in the research area. On the other hand, geophysical research has indicated that many – and in certain cases most – of the trenches recorded in aerial photographs are to a certain extent still preserved beneath the surface (Saey *et al.* 2013; Masters and Stichelbaut 2009). The numbers for the concrete bunkers are somewhat more positive: of the 619 bunkers identified in the aerial photographs, 44 have been located on the ground.

From the distribution map of preserved features in Comines-Warneton (see Figure 5.5) it is immediately obvious that there is a differential preservation of features within the study area. In the years immediately after the war, the battle-fields were cleared of war debris, trenches were backfilled, local populations returned to the destroyed villages and fields were restored for agriculture. This reconstruction eradicated many of the traces of World War I. However, in some

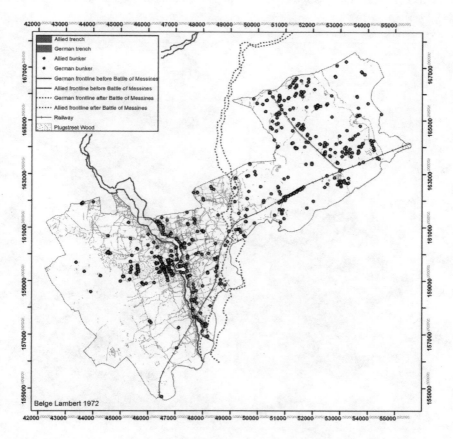

Figure 5.5 Distribution map of trenches and bunkers identified on historical aerial photographs.

Source: (© Authors).

places this reconstruction was less intense because the relics of war did not interfere with the pursuit of everyday life. Two examples of this are the Bois de La Hutte and the Bois du Gheer, two small woods that became known as 'Plugstreet Wood' during the war. These woods were heavily fortified with large numbers of concrete pillboxes (see Figure 5.5). After the war, the woods were maintained and, consequently, many of the war features were preserved. Because of this unique conservation, Plugstreet Wood can now be considered as an important heritage and relic landscape.

Future perspectives and conclusions

It is clear that by combining historical aerial photographs with archaeological prospection techniques we can reach a conclusion about the nature, preservation and historical context of the war heritage in Belgium, both above and below the surface. In fact, the possible volume of preserved archaeological heritage is huge.

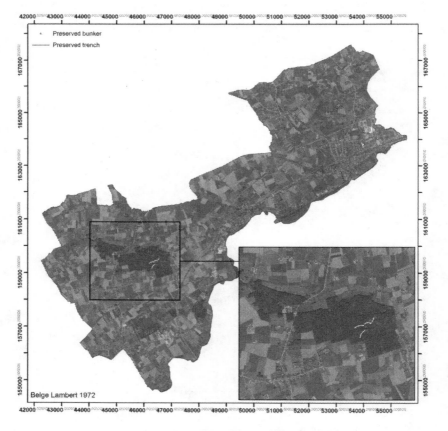

Figure 5.6 Distribution map of preserved trenches and bunkers.
Source: (© Authors and GDI-Vlaanderen).

If World War I remains are considered as archaeology, then the former Western Front in Belgium and France could well be seen as one of the largest continuous archaeological sites in the world, stretching for hundreds of kilometres between Nieuwpoort on the North Sea coastline in Belgium and the Franco-Swiss border. It also points to the need to decide whether it is appropriate to preserve certain parts and how to unlock the sites and their information.

The aerial photographic research indicates that only a small part of the traces of war can still be seen in the present-day landscape, yet there is a huge potential for the buried archaeology of World War I. At the moment, we can only hint at some of the choices that have to be made by the responsible government agencies in Belgium. Important and urgent questions for the future include: how should an industrialised war landscape with thousands of sites be dealt with? Which sites are the most important? What will be the criteria to decide whether or not scientific value gained from excavation of a World War I site justifies the economic cost? Beside the purely scientific research questions there are also ethical issues, because even now tens of thousands of fallen soldiers are still 'missing' and buried in Flanders Fields.

For the time being these questions must remain open without definitive answers. Yet we believe there is potential for a GIS-aided approach in which the possible heritage of the Great War can be assessed based on a combination of criteria. Such criteria include: density of features, uniqueness of certain types of feature, historical importance of the area, proximity to the front line, duration of occupation, current land use (i.e. trenches that were located in a forest during World War I and remain within that forest are more likely to be well preserved than features located in deeply ploughed fields, etc.).

With the demise of the generation who lived through World War I, the heritage is increasingly vested in the places where the war once raged, rather than in its people. Modern visual analysis of military aerial photography from the war is an essential instrument for bringing to light the former front region as a 'last witness' to this conflict.

References

Barton, P., Doyle, P. and Vandewalle, J. (2005). *Beneath Flanders Fields. Tunnels en Mijnen 1914–1918* (Zonnebeke: Johan Vandewalle).

Carlier, A. (1921). *La Photographie Aérienne pendant la Guerre* (Paris: Librairie Delagrave).

Chef des Generalstabes des Feldheeres (1918). *Allgemeines über Stellungsbau* (Berlin: Druckerei des Chef des Generalstabes des Feldheeres).

Cleere, H. (2000). 'Introduction: the rationale of archaeological heritage management', in H. Cleere (ed.), *Archaeological Heritage Management in the Modern World* (Milton: Routledge), pp. 1–17.

Edmonds, J. (1925). *History of the Great War. Military Operations: France and Belgium, 1914. Volume II: Antwerp, La Bassée, Armentières, Messines and Ypres, October–November 1914* (London: Macmillan).

Fowler, M. J. F. (2008). 'The application of declassified KH-7 GAMBIT satellite photographs to studies of Cold War material culture: a case study from the former Soviet Union', *Antiquity, 82*, 714–32.

Freeman, P. and Pollard, A. (eds) (2001). 'Fields of conflict: progress and prospect in battlefield archaeology', BAR (British Archaeological Reports) International Series 958, (Oxford: Archaeopress).

Hegarty, C. and Newsome, S. (2007). *Suffolk's Defended Shore: Coastal Fortifications from the Air* (Swindon: English Heritage).

Masters, P. and Stichelbaut, B. (2009). 'From the air to beneath the soil – revealing and mapping Great War trenches at Ploegsteert (Comines-Warneton), Belgium', *Archaeological Prospection, 16*(4), 279–85.

Saey, T., Stichelbaut, B., Bourgeois, J., Van Eetvelde, V. and Van Meirvenne, M. (2013). 'An interdisciplinary non-invasive approach to landscape archaeology of the Great War', *Archaeological Prospection, 20*(1), 39–44.

Saunders, N. (ed.) (2013). *Beyond the Dead Horizon. Studies in Modern Conflict Archaeology* (Oxford: Oxbow Books).

Saunders, N. (2010). *Killing Time: Archaeology and the First World War* (Stroud: Sutton Publishing).

Spagnoly, N. (1997). *A Walk around Plugstreet: south Ypres sector 1914–1918* (London: Cooper).

Stal, C., Bourgeois, J., De Maeyer, P., De Mulder G., De Wulf, A., Goossens, R., Nuttens, T. and Stichelbaut, B. (2010). 'Kemmelberg (Belgium) case study: comparison of DTM analysis methods for the detection of relics from the First World War', in *Remote Sensing for Science, Education, and Natural and Cultural Heritage: proceedings of the EARSeL Symposium 2010* (Paris: EARSeL), pp. 65–72.

Stichelbaut, B. (2011). 'The first thirty kilometres of the Western Front 1914–1918: an aerial archaeological approach with historical remote sensing data', *Journal of Archaeological Prospection, 18*(1), 57–66.

Stichelbaut, B. (2006). 'The application of First World War aerial photography to archaeology: the Belgian images', *Antiquity, 80*, 161–72.

Stichelbaut, B. and Bourgeois, J. (2009). 'The overlooked aerial imagery of World War One: a unique source for conflict and landscape archaeology', *Photogrammetrie – Fernerkundung – Geoinformation, 3*, 231–40.

Stichelbaut, B. and Chielens, P. (2013). *In Flanders Fields. The Great War Seen from the Air, 1914–1918* (Brussels: Mercatorfonds and Yale University Press).

Sutherland, T. (2005). *Battlefield Archaeology – A Guide to the Archaeology of Conflict* (Bradford: BAJR).

Vandael, L. (2014). 'Het erfgoed van de Eerste Wereldoorlog als UNESCO Werelderfgoed: uitgangspunten, preselectie en vervolgtraject', oral presentation at Contactdag 'Het Erfgoed van de Eerste Wereldoorlog als UNESCO-Werelderfgoed', AOE, Diksmuide.

Notes

1   Department of Archaeology Ghent University/In Flanders Fields Museum – Ypres
2   Department of Archaeology Ghent University

6 Celebrating peace and commemorating war in the city of Ieper

Caroline Winter

Introduction

The original 'event' on a battlefield is an armed conflict of some kind. In the aftermath, individuals, families, societies and nations attempt to remember and commemorate the dead and wounded, to ease the grief of the bereaved and to make sense of or justify the conflict. They may also choose to forget the war or to change the perspective on some aspects. A range of processes can be invoked to remember a war, particularly through the writing of its history and the processes involved in creating creation of a social memory (Halbwachs 1992; J. Winter 1995). Historians are tasked with recording an objective account of war using verifiable documents and other evidence, in an effort to record the 'facts'. Social memories aim to make sense of the past to satisfy the needs of a particular group, and they are drawn from, but not wholly limited to historical events (Halbwachs 1992). It was once considered that the processes of history and social memory are entirely distinct, but some recent thought suggests that they are linked in ways that are mutually supportive (J. Winter 2010; Ziino 2010). Many memories can therefore be created, but social memory refers to those that are widespread and supported throughout a society. Later generations may elect to modify, re-shape or shift the priorities – including forgetting some events and people (Schwartz 1982; Shaw 2009). In 1915, for example, there were many large battles at Loos, Aubers and Neuve-Chapelle in northern France but, for various reasons, they have been almost forgotten, while the battles on the Somme and in the Ypres Salient are widely known (Reed 2014). This chapter discusses some of the events held in the city of Ieper, Belgium, in relation to the performance of social memory relating to the Great War of 1914–18 and to contemporary life in the city.

The city of Ieper (Ypres) is well known today as the centre for some of the most horrific battles of World War I in the area known as the Ypres Salient. Conflict was continuous in the Salient for four years, but some battles were officially named in acknowledgement of their magnitude and destructive force. The First Battle of Ypres was fought during October/November of 1914, the Second Battle during April/May 1915 and the Third Battle of Ypres (better known as Passchendaele) was fought from 31 July to 10 November 1917. It is this latter campaign that is perhaps best known, for its futility, the terrible conditions in which the men fought and the high number of casualties, estimated at 275,000 British and 200,000

German (Prior and Wilson 2002). In April 1915, to the north of Ypres, the Germans released the first poisonous gas, a weapon that both sides would use to terrorise each other for the rest of the war. Other battles fought in the region included the Battle of Messines in June 1917, during which 19 great mines were detonated by the British on the Messines Ridge, and the Fourth Battle of Ypres in April and in September/October of 1918 (Great War 1914–18 2014). As many as 50 nations fought on the Flanders battlefields, but the dominant forces in the Ypres Salient were from Germany and Britain (including her 'dominions', Australia, Canada, New Zealand, South Africa and India) (Government of Flanders 2012; Prior and Wilson 2002).

Remembrance events conducted in Ieper make a particularly strong contribution to the social memory of the Great War through the city's urban landscape and its relationship with the battlefields. This chapter considers two remembrance events, the annual Ypres Memorial Tattoo and the nightly Last Post ceremony at the Menin Gate, that are designed to recall the memories of the war. It also describes some funfairs that are held at various times in the main square, and seeks to identify how these different types of event can each claim a place within the same urban area.

Landscape

Ieper's urban landscape: the Cloth Hall and the Grote Markt

Before 1914 Ieper was a wealthy city, known for its large textile industry, and along with other Flemish cities such as Bruges and Ghent it was an important centre for merchants from England, France and Germany. Because of its position and wealth Flanders had been attacked many times over the centuries, and controlled variously by France, Austria, Spain and the Netherlands. Since 1830 Ieper has been part of Belgium, and in 1914 the city's population was about 18,000 (Michelin Tyre Company 1994). Ieper's wealth was reflected in its built heritage, particularly the massive Cloth Hall, St Martin's Cathedral and many other buildings surrounding the central square (the Grote Markt). The original Cloth Hall was constructed in the 14th century and it operated as a warehouse and market place for the textiles produced in the surrounding areas – ironically, the building was used as a safe place to store the cloth until it was sold. The belfry was used to store the town archives and the records of the guilds that used the building as a meeting room, and at the southern end, abutting the Cloth Hall, was the Nieuwerk, completed in 1624 which served as the town hall. St Martin's Cathedral, which was begun in the 13th century, had been extended and renovated over the centuries, and by 1914 it was a magnificent part of Ieper's heritage. The buildings were beautiful in their own right but they also held many valuable artworks: paintings, statuary, stained glass windows and murals (Michelin Tyre Company 1994).

By November of 1914, after attack by incendiary and explosive shells, the buildings of the Grote Markt and most of Ieper lay in ruins. After the war, the Michelin guide (1994) described Ypres in the 1920s as:

a city of incomparable splendour in the Middle Ages, and of which nothing now remains but a heap of ruins. Of the last precious traces of this ancient prosperity, the rich and splendid buildings which filled the mind with wonder – the immense Cloth Hall, the beautiful cathedral, the churches, the sumptuous mansions, the sculptured houses – the German guns have spared nothing. History furnishes few examples of such grandeur followed by destruction so swift and so complete. Ypres is now but a memory.

(Michelin Tyre Company 1994: 69)

Ieper was of such symbolic importance to the British, that in 1918 Winston Churchill declared his wish that the whole of the city be retained in its ruined state as a war memorial. Local citizens disagreed with his idea, however, and rebuilt the city, insisting that it be constructed as it was before the war. The Menin Gate, a new war memorial, was inaugurated in 1927 but the reconstruction of the massive Cloth Hall took much longer and was completed in 1967 (see Figure 6.1). The market square (the Grote Markt) along with its beautiful buildings, the Menin Gate with the Cloth Hall, now form a central place for the city's visitors and for remembrance activity. The Cloth Hall now houses the In Flanders Fields Museum and the Office de Toerisme. The spires of the Cloth Hall and St Martin's Cathedral can be seen from some of the battlefields, such as Hill 60 and the Canadian Memorial at Sanctuary Wood several kilometres away, and thus 'mark' the city, not only in a physical sense, but also in a social sense, to indicate to visitors the link between the city and the battlefields. A stylised silhouette of the Cloth Hall, the Menin Gate and the Cathedral is used to indicate the Heritage Footpath around the city. The city of Ieper is contiguous with the battlefields of the Ypres Salient, and so the dead are to an extent present – or at least they can be conceived as being located reasonably nearby. The large number of cemeteries that were built during and after the war to hold the dead dominate the Flanders landscape around Ieper.

The urban space around the Grote Markt, with the Cloth Hall at one end and the Menin Gate at the other, are strong markers for the Great War, and as such the activities performed in this area are also symbolic, albeit in different ways. In her study of Trafalgar Square in London, Sumatojo (2009) argues that urban space is not benign, but plays a role in the ongoing construction of national identity, first by its use as a platform to disseminate messages about the nation, and second through media representations of events conducted on the site. Importantly, the 'the built environment of the square physically framed the events, helping to link them to aspects of the national past. The square's physical elements were central to the representation of the events, and were used to contextualise them historically, referencing a version of British history to draw a link between the past and the present' (Sumatojo 2009: 424).

The battlefield landscape

One of the most basic forms of remembering war is the acknowledgement given by official (military or state) organisations. The importance of a conflict is

Figure 6.1 Cloth Hall at night.
Source: C. Winter.

determined by many factors, including its duration, the number of casualties, its location and its magnitude (Dupuy 1987). During World War I, for example, the role of identifying and naming the various operations (including 'battles', 'actions' and 'incidents') was undertaken by the British Battles Nomenclature Committee. This formal acknowledgement provides a certain status for a military event that can influence the extent to which it will be remembered, not the least of which is its listing on regimental colours and on war memorials. The battlefield landscape is integral to the history, as well the social and individual memories of World War I, and is viewed by many as the bearer of these memories (Gough 2004). World War I battles were usually named for the specific, geographically defined locations in which they were fought – the Battle of Menin Road for example. The unique feature of the burials at that time was that the dead were buried as close as possible to where they fell and, because of this, the cemeteries also were very often named for their location, (such as Menin Road South Military Cemetery, in figure 6.2), thus intimately linking the dead with the landscape, not only through their physicality but also in name (Longworth 2003).

The bodies of thousands of men, from all armies, remain 'missing': some lie in individual graves marked 'Known Unto God' (British), 'Inconnu' (French) or 'Mort pour la Belgique' (Belgian), some lie in mass graves and others have not been recovered at all. Unknown German soldiers are usually buried in communal graves, with inscriptions that vary, but tend to simply state the number of soldiers entombed. For example, the researcher has observed headstones that read 'zwei unbekannte deutsche soldaten' (two unknown German soldiers), and 'in einem gemeinsamen grabe ruhen hier 91 deutsche soldaten' (here in a common grave rest 91 German soldiers), which includes both named and unknown men. The entombment of these soldiers has therefore rendered the battle landscape as sacred ground for many people, and especially for nations and families (Foote 1997; Laqueur 1994; Tuan 1976). The linkage of family, nation, war and death is deeply and intimately embedded in the landscape of the Salient, and these memories are maintained by regular commemorative events held on the battlefields and in Ieper.

The Government of Flanders (2012) states that the landscape is not only integral to the war itself, but is now:

> the most important last witness, even more so than all these material relics. This landscape did, in effect, create the conditions and circumstances, wherein the First World War's savage combat raged. Therefore, major landscape units such as battlefields, sight lines, defence lines, and landscapes where (archaeological) relics may be found in mutual coherence, receive great attention in this heritage project.
>
> (Government of Flanders 2012: 33)

Military cemeteries and memorials

The cemeteries built for the British dead by the then Imperial War Graves Commission (now the Commonwealth War Graves Commission (CWGC)) are the most visible and numerous, with over 100 in Flanders, 75 of which are located in the city zone (Toerisme Ieper 2014). The two largest are Tyne Cot (11,960 graves) and Lijssenthoek (10,875 graves) and they attract thousands of visitors (CWGC 2014a). The Belgian cemetery nearest to Ieper is at the Forest of Houthulst north of Poelkapelle, although some men are buried in CWGC cemeteries much closer to Ieper (Holt and Holt 2011). The American Battle Monuments Commission is responsible for graves of United States servicemen, and the graves are marked by white marble crosses in a park setting similar to the CWGC cemeteries. The largest American cemetery is located on the Meuse-Argonne in France (14,246 burials) with one cemetery in Belgium (the Flanders Field American Cemetery) located at Waregem, which holds 368 burials (American Battle Monuments Commission nd). Some large French cemeteries are located close to Ieper at St Charles de Potyze, the Ossuary at Kemmelberg with plots of French graves at Oostvleteren, Woesten Churchyard and Lijssenthoek CWGC cemetery (Holt and Holt 2011). French graves also are marked by individual white crosses. The German graves are cared for by the Volksbund Deutsche Kriegsgräberfürsorge e. V. (VDK) organization, which has as its purpose 'Gedenken und Frieden' – remembrance and peace (VDK 2014). In Belgium there are only four German cemeteries and they were built after the war as 'concentration' cemeteries in which the bodies were recovered from smaller sites and the battlefields and reinterred (Van Alstein 2011). These cemeteries hold large numbers of men: 47,864 are buried at Menen German cemetery, over 44,000 at Langemark, 25,644 at Vladslo and 8,241 at Heeglede. German deaths in Flanders are estimated at 210,000 with 83,000 missing (VDK 2014). The German cemeteries have a different appearance from those of the other nations: the black metal crosses, large oak trees, the absence of flowers and the fact that several men are usually buried beneath each marker, create 'a strong feeling of grief for the dead' (Holt and Holt 2011: 263).

Figure 6.2 Menin Road South Cemetery.
Source: C. Winter.

The missing

The 'missing' are named on many memorials at various locations in the Salient, and again, those built by the British are the most dominant in the area. The Menin Gate is a massive stone monument that spans the roadway linking the city centre to the former battlefields, and it is located a short walking distance from the Grote Markt. It was designed by Sir Reginald Blomfield, to record the names of 54,404 men of the British armies (including those from Australia, Canada, India and South Africa) who died and remain missing from battles in Flanders (CWGC 2014b). There are three other memorials to the British missing in Belgium: the walls at Tyne Cot cemetery record a further 34,952 names and New Zealand memorials are located at Buttes New British cemetery and Messines Ridge British cemetery (CWGC, 2014b). At the inauguration ceremony of the Menin Gate in 1927, Field Marshal Lord Plumer, in an effort to comfort the relatives of the men whose final burial place was not known, but who were named on the memorial, said to them: 'He is not missing, he is here'. As Heffernan (1995) notes, remembrance activities in Britain (and other countries that fought the war) are performed in the absence of those who are being remembered. Even so, remembrance is implicitly dependent on the existence of these places of battle, and in the knowledge that the graves and memorials exist and are cared for (Ziino 2007). The Menin Gate thus links the battlefields with the urban landscape of memory through naming the missing, whose bodies remain on the battlefields.

Marking the landscape

In order for a battle site to be remembered, a number of social processes must be enacted and reinforced on a regular basis. Foote (1997: 7) argues that sites of violence are often 'sanctified', meaning that the events that occurred there 'are seen to hold some lasting positive meaning that people wish to remember – a lesson in heroism or perhaps a sacrifice for community'. Various theories conceptualise processes through which a geographic site can be distinguished and MacCannell's (1999) five-stage 'sight sacralization' process of 'marking' (that is, of creating a system of signs) is well known. It has been applied to the Gallipoli battlefield by Slade (2003) and to Waterloo by Seaton (1999), who found that, of the five stages (naming, framing, elevating, enshrining and mechanical reproduction), only naming and mechanical reproduction are essential. These processes help visitors to recognise sites of significance, and to then 'read' the memories encoded within them. As MacCannell (1999) argued, in the absence of information or evidence such as barbed wire and artillery, a visitor is often unable to interpret a battlefield, and requires a 'marker' or 'sign' to 'signify' a meaning. Clearly air and sea battles present very difficult sites for most people to locate and visit, let alone interpret. Most of the Great War battlefields were cleared of 'evidence' very quickly after the war, and once they had been returned to agricultural use very little remained for anyone other than a very well informed visitor to interpret. In the Ypres Salient, there are several 'markers' that assist visitors to interpret the past. On the battle-fields, the cemeteries now serve as markers, not only to individual soldiers buried within them, but also to particular battles and to the war overall (Laqueur 1994). The reconstructed city of Ieper itself can also be regarded as a marker to the military operations in the Ypres Salient, especially 'Passchendaele', and for World War I, while the Cloth Hall and the Menin Gate mark the city.

Seaton (1999: 153) notes that the MacCannell's (1999) process of sacralization is 'a shifting process affected by the relationships among groups, interacting within a changing force field of production and consumption'. Furthermore, it is delimited not just 'by the social power of representation vested in the attraction sponsor, but by the situated motives and perspectives of those to whose gaze a sight is offered, both of which may change over time' (p.154). To help sustain memories over time, sites that are marked as being sacred host ritualised ceremonies, forming a set of highly stylised and standardised behaviours conducted at particular times (Edensor 2000; Mayo 1988). The Ypres Memorial Tattoo, and particularly the Last Post ceremony at the Menin Gate, are two events that seek to remind visitors of the war through wreath laying, bugle calls, military performances and attendance at memorials. It has been shown that tourists play a central role in the processes though which a battle is remembered (Seaton 1999; Smith 1996; Slade 2003).

Ieper and tourism

After the war, a large industry developed in Ieper to provide lodging and travel facilities for visitors, and efforts were made by organisations such as the British Legion and the Michelin guides to avoid any kind of luxurious style, in keeping with an image of respectful pilgrimage (Connelly 2009; Iles 2008; Malvern 2001). Contemporary research indicates that there remains an underlying theme of pilgrimage in World War I tourism, but leisure activities are also acknowledged as an important component in the visitor experience (Clarke and Eastgate 2011; Holt and Holt 2011; Iles 2008). Many other types of people now visit battlefields such as those in Flanders, to satisfy a range of motivations including researching family history, leisure experiences, education, military training and curiosity (Baldwin and Sharpley 2009; Lloyd 1998). Notably, the Flemish Government wishes to increase the visibility of the area during the centenary period by encouraging peace tourism to the city and to create 'amongst the present and future generations in Flanders an awareness of themes such as tolerance, intercultural dialogue, and international understanding' (Government of Flanders, 2012: 7).

In 2008, annual visitors to the Westhoek region were estimated to number 326,900 and the total had risen to approximately 415,500 by 2013, with most (73 per cent) being interested in the history of World War I. The proportion of visitors by nationality was Belgian 44.1 per cent, British 37.2 per cent, Dutch 11.3 per cent and other 7.4 per cent (Vandaele and Monballyu 2008; Westtoer nd). Of the total visitors, 44.4 per cent were individuals, 44.2 per cent schoolchildren and 11.4 per cent on tours. A very high proportion of British were schoolchildren (98,200, or 63.5 per cent) compared with 31.6 per cent of Belgians and 35.5 per cent of other nationalities. Total income from the 415,000 visitors was €39,684,405, with most coming from accommodation, meals and shopping (Westtoer nd). Early reports indicate that the centenary will bring even more visitors to the area, with 2014 visitors numbering 789,500 (*Flanders News* 2015).

Remembrance and commemoration in Ieper

Ieper provides a centre around which remembrance of the war in the Salient is performed, and many ceremonies and remembrance activities are conducted annually in and around Ieper at times and places of significance. Examples include the beginning and ending of major battles such as Passchendaele, remembrance of military regiments and the 1914 Christmas truce, and a monthly commemorative service is held each month at the Ploegsteert memorial to the missing organised by the Comité du Memorial de Ploegsteert. In addition to the regular activities, there are also many ad hoc events of varying sizes and form, including concerts, poetry readings, art displays, walks, lectures and exhibitions and formal ceremonies at the war memorials. Many people come to the battlefields in groups, much like the pilgrimages in the early post-war years, to visit the cemeteries and memorials, and it is not unusual, for example, to see a small group set up in the Grote Markt and perform a short musical arrangement. Ceremonies are also conducted at military cemeteries on the occasions on which a previously 'missing' soldier has been recovered and interred in a grave.

There are several war museums in Ieper and the surrounding area that present the war in different ways, the largest of which is the In Flanders Fields Museum (IFFM), located in the Cloth Hall (along with the Tourism Office/Visitor Centre). Van Alstein (2011: 16) comments that the museum promotes a globalised perspective on the war that 'transcends outdated national narratives of allies and enemies' and recognises that 'war is primarily a reality experienced by people – soldiers and civilians alike'. In this respect the museum features a number of local and individual stories and experiences, including those of how local citizens interpreted the war. The museum thus illuminates the experience of the city and its people, in addition to the military operations on the battlefield.

The *Ypres 2014* guidebook lists several events in Ieper relating specifically to the centenary of World War I, and these include exhibitions in museums, a carillon festival, a special walking day, an international philately event, a 'Käthe Kollwitz Peace run', a four-day remembrance march (Albert on the Somme to Ieper), concerts, a project to illuminate the names of war dead on three towers and another to illuminate the 1914 front line with torches. Also listed are the Ypres Memorial Tattoo (28 September) and the nightly Menin Gate Last Post ceremonies (Toerisme Ieper 2014: 3, 4).

Three events in Ieper

The Menin Gate and the Last Post ceremony

At the Menin Gate each night since 1928, the road has been closed to traffic, and members of the local fire brigade have sounded the Last Post at 8pm in honour of the men named on the walls of the memorial (Last Post Association nd; and see figure 6.3). The ceremony itself is quite short (about ten minutes), involving the Last Post bugle call, recitation of 'The Ode', and a one-minute silence followed by the Reveille bugle call. As ritual, this act of remembrance is performed not only by the buglers, but by the audience who stand in silence, repeat the line at the end of the Ode ('we will remember them') and act as witnesses to the ceremony. The Menin Gate ceremony can be extended up to a half hour or more, by wreath laying and short musical performances by community groups such as schools, remembrance and veterans' associations and people representing their home towns and a range of different groups. The Last Post ceremony is one of the more sombre remembrance activities on the Western Front and it is representative of many similar rituals performed across the battlefields. This ceremony has become one of the defining events of Ieper with sometimes several hundred people attending during the summer months.

While the Menin Gate is a dominant British memorial in Ieper, it does not present as a nationalistic monument: the large memorials such as those built by Canada, Australia and the UK were not designed to be victorious, but a way to console the bereaved and to acknowledge the deaths of men whose bodies could not be located (Inglis 2005). As Stephens (2009: 17) argues, too, 'the names and the architecture of the Menin Gate provide a narrative on the cost of war'. While the walls list the names of the British missing, they also serve as a reminder of the men missing from Germany, on the other side of the trench line.

The ceremony at the Menin Gate is a deeply symbolic and solemn ritual of remembrance, and although its origins lie in military tradition, it is performed by civilians in honour of the war dead. It also forms a symbolic burial for men whose final resting place is not known, and after the war it provided a physical site at which relatives could allay some of their grief. The Gate is a vehicle thoroughfare during the day – as it was before and during the war, through which the 'missing' passed on their way to the battlefields (Stephens 2009). The range of other activities under the Gate is far less limited than that permitted in the Grote Markt, and when combined with the daily ceremony, this helps to sustain the position of the memorial as a sacred space (Mayo 1988).

The Ypres Memorial Tattoo

A 'tattoo' originates in the military tradition of drummers recalling soldiers to their barracks at night (Taps Bugler: Jari Villanueva 2010), but today a tattoo combines ceremonial displays of music and dance for the entertainment of the public. A very well-known event is the Royal Edinburgh Military Tattoo that has been performed at Edinburgh Castle for the past 65 years. In 2014, its theme was about 'our home, friends and family', to celebrate a 'global gathering' of many nations across the British Commonwealth in displays of music and dance. It is promoted as having a 'unique ability to bring together thousands of people for this annual celebration of music and entertainment… and the public's appetite for pomp and ceremony shows no sign of diminishing' (Royal Edinburgh Tattoo 2013).

Figure 6.3 The Menin Gate.
Source: C. Winter.

The inaugural Ypres Memorial Tattoo was performed in September 2011 to 'keep alive the memory of the soldiers who fought in the Ypres Salient in order to restore the freedom of the city and the independence of our country' (Ypres Memorial Tattoo 2014: 4). It is organised by the Last Post Association and the Ypres Surrey Pipes and Drums, and performed in the Grote Markt in front of the Cloth Hall. The event is ticketed with approximately 1,500 seats at a cost of €15 each (for 2014). The area is closed off with temporary fencing, but it is clearly very popular, and many people can be seen listening to the music from outside the enclosure, and standing on almost anything available to get a view. The 2014 event comprised performances by several military bands, folk singers and two dance groups, and the programme brochure included the words of popular old songs 'Auld Lang Syne', 'It's a Long Way to Tipperary' and 'Will Ye Go To Flanders' – and the audience sang along. The program began at 4pm and included the Last Post ceremony at the Menin Gate at 8pm as the final item. Of the 12 bands, 2 were British, the Irish Guards (formed in 1900) and the Dundee Boys Brigade Pipe Band (formed in 1914). The other ten bands included three with Belgian traditions (the Royal Symphonic Bands, Ypriana; Ons Verlagen; and the Belgian Royal Chapel Local Police Antwerp Band). The other seven bands were Belgian and had adopted the Scottish traditions of wearing tartan kilts and playing bagpipes. Figure 6.4 shows one of the bands in front of the Cloth Hall.

Figure 6.4 Ypres Military Tattoo in front of the Cloth Hall, 2014.
Source: C. Winter.

The tattoo, like others of its kind, combines a militaristic style of precision, in marching, formal costumes (uniforms) and music, but is designed primarily to entertain the public. It also presents a very anglicised performance, particularly evidenced by the presence of the Irish Guards, the Scottish dress and musical instruments of the Belgian bands and the 'sing-along' programme.

Funfairs

While war remembrance may be dominant in Ieper, it does not inform all of the activity in the city. The *Ypres Guide* (2014) lists many non-war events and activities including a cat fair, a cycle race, street theatre, an annual flower market, a three-day walking event as part of the peace festival, 'beach' volleyball', several fairs and music festivals, a street run and an ice rink in the square (Toerisme Ieper 2014). The very large Bellewaerde children's theme park. which, ironically, is located close to Chateau Wood, is also popular. Saturday morning markets are held in the Grote Markt, and there is a weekly live music performance in St Martin's Place. Cycling is also very popular in Ieper and the Westtoer research found that approximately 15 per cent of visitors are not interested in the war but in other leisure activities.

The funfairs are similar to those conducted in many countries, thus having an almost universal appearance and themes, consisting of games, carousel rides, the sale of toys and sweets, mainly for the entertainment of children (see Figure 6.5). At times, musical performances for adults are also held as part of some of the fairs. While the cartoon-like imagery, bright flashing lights and entertainments are a somewhat uneasy fit with the thirteenth-century architecture of the buildings, especially the Cloth Hall, they perhaps better reflect the more ancient purposes of the square – for trade and entertainment in a time of peace. The eclectic and apparently disordered style of the fairs challenges the rigidity of the Tattoo and the Menin Gate ceremony, which seek to communicate more sombre notions of remembrance and national identity. The fairs however, are an expression of peace, both before and after the war, and of life rather than death.

Conclusions

It is through behaviours and performance that memories are realised and passed on to new generations (Halbwachs 1992), and attendance and participation by tourists is an important part of the process. The Last Post ceremony is a daily ritual that is performed under the Menin Gate, which, with the attendance of tourists, helps to retain the sense of sacredness to the memory of thousands of men whose final resting place is unknown (Foote 1997; Mayo 1988). By comparison the Grote Markt, which is a 'designated' place (Foote 1997), allows a much wider range of activities than the Menin Gate, including the military and nationalistic sentiments of the Tattoo and the leisured fantasy of the fairs. At the same time, the whole of the city of Ieper is 'marked' as a wartime city, and so the performance of both the Tattoo and the Last Post hold additional significance because of the space in which they are performed.

Figure 6.5 Funfair in Grote Markt, Ieper.
Source: C. Winter.

The buildings surrounding the Grote Markt establish a sense of historical continuity between the present and the city's origins extending back hundreds of years before the war: the Cloth Hall and St Martin's Cathedral form important icons for the city. On the other hand, some could argue that the reconstructed buildings challenge the notion of authenticity, echoing Hobsbawm's and Trevor-Roper's (2012) notion of 'invented tradition'. It is, however, the resurrection of the original city as a modern-day phoenix that is part of Ieper's attraction, where the meaning of the structures is informed by the local culture and, more recently, by remembrance of World War I. As Franklin observes,

> [w]hat happens in tourism sites is not circumscribed by the site itself or the interpretations of its object or the manner by which tourists are organised in and through the site. Instead heritage is an artefact of the interaction of a multiplicity of tourist subjectivities constituted away from the tourist site and the particular configuration of objects on that site.
>
> (Franklin 2003: 206)

It is something of an irony that funfairs are conducted in a city centre that is well known for its connections with the most horrific and destructive battles of the war.

The bright colours and contemporary designs of the rides and games at first seem to be an uneasy fit with the remembrance of war, but they also form a reminder that the city is more than a war memorial (in spite of Churchill's wishes). The market days and fairs reflect the functions for which the Cloth Hall and the Grote Markt were originally designed, for industry, trade and daily interactions of the citizens and the city's visitors. Research has found that tourists come back to places like bars and restaurants at the end of the day, and appreciate some leisure time after the emotional experiences of the battlefields (Clarke and Eastgate 2011). These activities are a reflection of Ieper as a city of peace and as a place in which local Belgian people live and work.

There is an element of entertainment to even the most sacred rituals, and indeed, most religious, military and legal rituals are performed using elaborate costumes, grand buildings and symbolic music. That is, they are designed as spectacle in order to communicate images of power or other important social messages in a way that resonates with members of society. The Tattoo in particular, while military in origin, is primarily concerned with the presentation of a spectacle for the entertainment of civilians, and at the same time it also imparts notions of British identity. The Last Post ceremony, as well, presents an impressive and emotional spectacle, held under the massive monument, beneath thousands of names of the missing and, as several have observed, those in attendance give life to the memorial (J. Winter 1995).

As Van Alstein (2011) observes, British remembrance is the most visible and dominant tradition in Ieper, as reflected in the high proportion of British visitors, particularly schoolchildren, as well as the large and distinctive number of military cemeteries and memorials, including the Menin Gate. This is partly a consequence of the British operations in the Salient during the war, and also that German remembrance has not become evident in the area (Van Alstein 2011). The Ypres Tattoo presents a highly anglicised performance in the city centre, including the reference to 'Ypres', the name by which the British referred to the city during the war, rather than its Belgian name, Ieper. It can also be seen as an expression and performance of British national identity, in which the audience participates by watching and singing along. As Franklin (2003: 179) observes, 'nationalism and culture had to be performed, they were not simply a set of ideas that could be read about or taught simply by visiting national sites'. The performance also supports Sumatojo's (2009) study of the active role of urban space in constructing national identity, and Ieper remains substantially 'marked' by its British wartime efforts.

These events were selected to illustrate the diversity of activity that is currently sustained in Ieper, and that although recent history has focused on World War I, the city has a much longer past that links its citizens to their lives in the present day. Tourists move freely within this urban landscape: from the leisurely restaurants to the seriousness of the Menin Gate, from the militaristic and nationalistic Tattoo, to the In Flanders Fields Museum with its globalised view of the war and to the games of the fairs. For some reason, in Ieper all of these activities seem to 'work', providing a rich commemorative urban landscape that reminds us of the horrors of war and the pleasures of peace.

References

American Battle Monuments Commission (nd). 'Flanders Field American Cemetery and Memorial', brochure (Garches, France: ABMC).

Baldwin, F. and Sharpley, R. (2009). 'Battlefield tourism: bringing organised violence back to life', in R. Sharpley and P. Stone (eds), *The Darker Side of Travel: the Theory and Practice of Dark Tourism* (Clevedon: Channel View), pp. 186–206.

Clarke, P. and Eastgate, A. (2011). 'Cultural capital, life course perspectives and Western Front battlefield tours'. *Journal of Tourism and Cultural Change*, *9*(1), 31–44.

Commonwealth War Graves Commission (2014a). 'Cemetery details, Tyne Cot cemetery'. Available from: www.cwgc.org/find-a-cemetery/cemetery/53300/TYNE COT CEME-TERY [5 January 2015].

Commonwealth War Graves Commission (2014b). 'Cemetery details. Ypres (Menin Gate) Memorial'. Available from: www.cwgc.org/find-a-cemetery/cemetery/91800/YPRES (MENIN GATE) MEMORIAL [23 December 2014].

Connelly, M. (2009). 'The Ypres League and the commemoration of the Ypres Salient 1914–1940'. *War in History*, *16*(1), 51–76.

Dupuy, T. N. (1987). *Understanding War: History and Theory of Conflict* (New York: Paragon House Publishers).

Edensor, T. (2000). 'Staging tourism: tourists as performers'. *Annals of Tourism Research*, *27*(2), 322–44.

Flanders News (2015). 'Number of Great War tourists exceeds all expectations'. Available from: http://deredactie.be/cm/vrtnieuws.english/News/1.2206490 [13 January 2015].

Foote, K. E. (1997). *Shadowed Ground: America's Landscapes of Violence and Tragedy* (Austin: University of Texas Press).

Franklin, A. (2003). *Tourism: An Introduction* (London: Sage).

Gough, P. (2004). 'Sites in the imagination: the Beaumont Hamel Newfoundland Memorial on the Somme'. *Cultural Geographies*, *11*(3), 235–58.

Government of Flanders (2012). *The Great War Centenary in Flanders 2014–18*. Catalogue number D/2011/3241/265. Project Office – The Great War Centenary (2014–18), Brussels, Belgium.

Great War 1914–18 (2014). 'The Ypres Salient Battlefields, Belgium'. Available from: www.greatwar.co.uk/ypres-salient/index.htm [8 December 2014].

Halbwachs, M. (1992). *On Collective Memory* (Chicago: University of Chicago Press).

Heffernan, M. (1995). 'For ever England: the Western Front and the politics of remembrance in Britain'. *Ecumene*, *2*(3), 293–323.

Hobsbawm, E. and Trevor-Roper H. (2012). *The Invention of Tradition* (Cambridge: Cambridge University Press).

Holt, T. and Holt, V. (2011). *Major and Mrs Holt's Battlefield Guide to Ypres Salient and Passchendaele* (Barnsley: Pen and Sword Military).

Iles, J. (2008). Encounters in the fields – tourism to the battlefields of the Western Front. *Journal of Tourism and Cultural Change, 6*(2), 138–54.

Inglis, K. (2005). *Sacred Places: War Memorials in the Australian Landscape* (Melbourne: The Miegunyah Press).

Laqueur, T. (1994). 'Memory and naming in the Great War', in J. R. Gillis (ed.), *Commemorations: the Politics of National Identity* (Princeton, NJ: Princeton University Press), pp. 150–67.

Last Post Association (nd). 'Ieper', brochure.

Lloyd, D. (1998). *Battlefield Tourism: Pilgrimage and the Commemoration of the Great War in Britain, Australia and Canada* (Oxford: Berg).

Longworth, P. (2003). *The Unending Vigil: the History of the Commonwealth War Graves Commission* (Barnsley: Pen and Sword).

MacCannell, D. (1999). *The Tourist* (London: Sage).

Malvern, S. (2001). 'War tourism: "Englishness", art, and the First World War'. *Oxford Art Journal*, *24*(1), 45–66.

Mayo, J. M. (1988). 'War memorials as political memory'. *Geographical Review*, *78*(1), 62–75.

Michelin Tyre Company (1994). *Ypres and the Battles of Ypres*. Illustrated Michelin guides to the Battle-fields (1914–1918) (Easingwold, Yorks: G.H. Smith and Son).

Prior, R. and Wilson, T. (2002). *Passchendaele: the Untold Story* (New Haven, CT: Yale University Press).

Reed, P. (2014). 'The forgotten front'. Available from the Old Front Line website: http://battlefields1418.50megs.com/front2.htm [5 January 2015].

Royal Edinburgh Military Tattoo (2013). 'History of the Tattoo'. Available from: www.edintattoo.co.uk/beyond-the-ramparts/history-of-the-tattoo [5 January 2015].

Schwartz, B. (1982). 'The social context of commemoration: a study in collective memory'. *Social Forces*, *61*(2), 374–402.

Seaton, A. V. (1999). 'War and thanatourism: Waterloo 1815–1914'. *Annals of Tourism Research*, *26*(1), 130–58.

Shaw, R. (2009). 'Afterword: violence and the generation of memory', in N. Argenti and K. Schramm (eds), *Remembering Violence: Anthropological Perspectives on Intergenerational Transmission* (New York: Berghahn Books), pp. 251–60.

Slade, P. (2003). 'Gallipoli thanatourism: the meaning of ANZAC'. *Annals of Tourism Research*, *30*(4), 779–94.

Smith, V. (1996). 'War and its tourist attractions', in A. Pizam and Y. Mansfeld (eds), *Tourism, Crime and International Security Issues* (Chichester: Wiley), pp. 247–64.

Stephens, J. (2009). '"The Ghosts of Menin Gate": art, architecture and commemoration'. *Journal of Contemporary History*, *44*(1), 7–26.

Sumatojo, S. (2009). 'Britishness in Trafalgar Square: urban place and the construction of national identity'. *Studies in Ethnicity and Nationalism*, *9*(3), 410–28.

Taps Bugler (2010). 'The evolution of Taps'. Available from: http://tapsbugler.com/247 [23 June 2015].

Toerisme Ieper (2014). *Ypres 2014*. Brochure (Ref. 8900–14-01–2), (Ieper, Belgium: Toerisme Ieper). Available from: www.toerisme-ieper.be/en/brochures.html [11 December 2014].

Tuan, Y. F. (1976). 'Geopiety: a theme in man's attachment to nature and to place', in D. Lowenthal and M. Bowden (eds), *Geographies of the Mind: Essays in Historical Geosophy in honor of John Kirtland Wright* (Oxford: Oxford University Press), pp. 11–39.

Van Alstein, M. (2011). 'The Great War remembered: commemoration and peace in Flanders Fields'. Report (Brussels: Flemish Peace Institute).

Vandaele, D. and Monballyu M. (2008). 'Understanding WW1-related tourism in the Westhoek', in K. Lindroth and M. Voutilainen (eds), *Competition in Tourism: Business and Destination Perspectives: Proceedings of the Travel and Tourism Research Association Europe – 2008 Annual Conference* (Helsinki, Finland : Travel and Tourism Research Association–Europe), pp. 362–71.

Volksbund Deutsche Kriegsgräberfürsorge (2014). 'Abstract'. Available from: www.volks bund.de/en/volksbund.html [10 December 2014].

Westtoer (2013). 'WOI-bezoekers in de Westhoek (2013)'. Powerpoint presentationlocale for local partners (Brussel: Wesstoer).

Winter, J. (2010). 'The performance of the past: memory, history, identity', in K. Tilmans, F. van Vree and J. Winter (eds), *Performing the Past: Memory, History, and Identity in Modern Europe* (Amsterdam: Amsterdam University Press), pp. 11–23.

Winter, J. (1995). *Sites of Memory, Sites of Mourning: the Great War in European Cultural History* (Cambridge: Cambridge University Press).

Ypres Memorial Tattoo (2014). 'Programme for 28 September 2014' (Ieper: Last Post Association and Ypres Surrey Pipes and Drums).

Ziino, B. (2010). 'A lasting gift to his descendants: family memory and the Great War in Australia'. *History and Memory*, *22*(2), 125–46.

Ziino. B. (2007). *A Distant Grief: Australians, War Graves and the Great War* (Crawley, PTH: University of Western Australia Press).

7 The heritage of 'Flanders Fields'

Research, protection, management
and commemoration of World War I
landscapes in Flanders (Belgium)

*Luc Vandael, Hannelore Decoodt, Marc Dewilde,
Piet Geleyns, Koen Himpe, Marnix Pieters
and Hilde Verboven*

Introduction

On the eve of the centenary of World War I (1914–18) the region of Flanders has started preparations for a unique commemoration project in which heritage occupies a key position. Nearly a century after the events took place, tangible and intangible evidence of World War I is still widely present in Flanders, especially in the Westhoek area, the westernmost tip of Flanders adjacent to the North Sea and France (see Figure 7.1). Wartime heritage such as (reconstructed) trenches, bomb and mine craters (Verboven 2014), bunkers and dugouts (Bostyn 1999; Decoodt 2014), and post-war memorials, monuments (Jacobs 1996) and military cemeteries (Geurst 2010; Freytag and Van Driessche 2011) are omnipresent in the Westhoek (Decoodt 2007). In addition, the numerous human remains and the enormous quantities of unexploded ordnance that are being recovered to this day, still testify to the intensity of the battles of World War I (henceforth: WW I) in this region.

From 2002 onwards the region of Flanders, in collaboration with the Province of West Flanders, launched a heritage programme that focused on research, protection and management of WW I heritage. Initially the emphasis was on built and easily identifiable heritage like military constructions, military cemeteries and monuments. Later on, attention shifted towards landscape heritage of WW I and its associated archaeological heritage (Chielens, Dendooven and Decoodt 2006; Verboven 2012).

This chapter will focus on the interesting, but also very complex, debate on the landscape heritage of WW I. It will start with a discussion of the importance of the landscape, followed by a presentation of the strategy that Flanders has developed to deal with this heritage by discussing the research–protection–management cycle related to WW I heritage. Finally, the chapter will conclude with an explanation of the rationale for the UNESCO World Heritage nomination that Flanders is currently preparing together with Wallonia and France, covering a scientifically underpinned selection of WW I sites along the entire Western Front, as the culmination of this long-term heritage strategy.

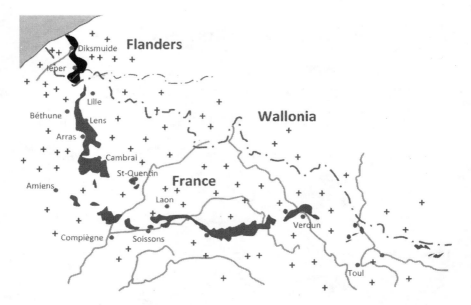

Figure 7.1 Schematic representation of the Western Front in World War I. The shaded areas in France are the so-called 'red zones' where the original landscape was completely destroyed. The front of the Westhoek is at the top of the shaded area, running down from the Flemish coast to the border with France.

Source: (© Flanders Heritage Agency).

The landscape as the last witness

At the end of 1914, after the Battle of the Yser and the First Battle of Ypres, World War I ground to a halt in the Westhoek area (Brown 2001; De Schaepdrijver 2013). In the following four years the deadlock of the trench war would shape the westernmost tip of Flanders into the lunar landscape many have come to identify with World War I (see Figure 7.2).

In fact, the landscape of the Westhoek created the conditions and circumstances in which this trench war was fought. The strategic framework of the war was defined by large-scale geophysical features and conditions. The northern sector of the Westhoek, the so-called Yser front, was dominated by the deliberate flooding of the *polders*, low-lying tracts of flat land (former tidal flats and saltmarshes) reclaimed since medieval times along the Flemish coastline and the Yser river valley. Combat in the southern sector, an area best known as the Ypres Salient, was determined by and revolved around a succession of undulating ridges around the city of Ieper (Ypres) (see Figure 7.3).

From a tactical perspective small landscape elements shaped the battlefield. A ditch became a trench, a farm became a dressing station, a small elevation became an observation post or a row of trees became an artillery position. Once completed these structures were included in the ever-expanding infrastructure of war, even

Figure 7.2 Canadian troops of the 16th Machine Gun Company take up defensive positions outside the village of Passendale, late October or early November 1917, during the closing stages of the Third Battle of Ypres, commonly known as the battle of Passchendaele.

Source: (© Imperial War Museum).

after the original landscape features had disappeared beneath the successive waves of destruction.

Research

After the war, hesitant at first, but quickly gaining speed, daily life took over the devastated landscape and the physical remains of the battlefield slowly disappeared (for an example see Heyde 2014). In many cases, the Western Front of World War I was absorbed in a dynamic cultural landscape created by the complex interplay of natural, cultural, spatial and social processes and developments.

To identify the sites in the Westhoek that today, a century later, still testify to the strong ties between landscape and WW I, a two-tracked research project was launched in 2009 by the Flanders Heritage Agency.

Archaeological research (Dewilde, De Meyer and Saunders 2007; Saunders 2010; Dewilde *et al.* 2014) focused on collecting consistent data concerning the state of conservation of the archaeological features of WW I. Is the conservation geographically differentiated? Which sites present extremely good preservation

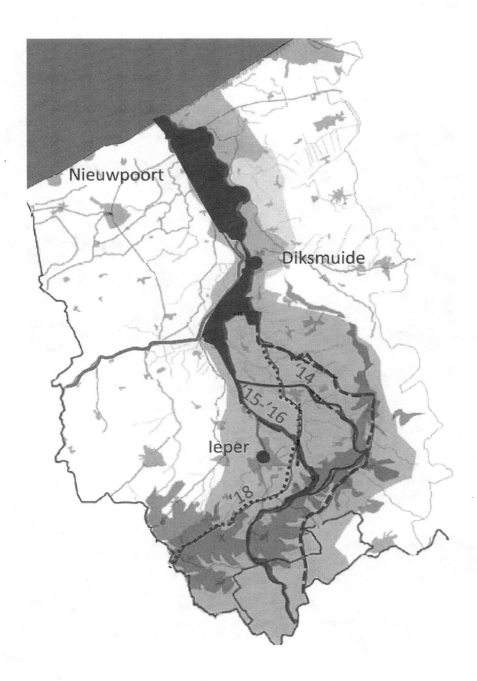

Figure 7.3 Map of the Westhoek with the front lines of World War I highlighted. It clearly shows the static 'No-Man's-Water' of the Yser front in the North and the shifting No-Man's-Land in the southern sector around the town of Ieper.

Source: (© Flanders Heritage Agency).

conditions? Is this archaeological heritage in danger of being destroyed by the current land use? The methodology used to address these questions consisted of trial trenching on a representative selection of test sites. The location of the trial trenches themselves was based on the expertise of local historians, the analysis of WW I trench maps and WW I-period aerial photographs, and on previous archaeological fieldwork (see Figure 7.4). Additional geophysical surveys were performed to corroborate and extend the archaeological results beyond the trial trenches.

Landscape research aimed at identifying the most valuable parts of the landscape in relation to WW I. What is the historical significance of the landscape? In what state of preservation is the WW I war landscape? Is the WW I landscape still present and available for interpretation, by non-specialists or only by specialists? Is there an evident link between the actual and the former landscape? To answer these questions, war-era archival sources such as trench maps (Verboven nd), panoramic pictures, aerial photographs (Stichelbaut 2007; Stichelbaut *et al.* 2009) were digitalised and compared with contemporary data in a geographic information system. The results of this exercise were enhanced through on-site observations (see Figure 7.5).

The results of the archaeological and landscape research combined with the results of earlier studies on built and architectural heritage ultimately led to the identification of 28 'sites of memory'. This term refers to the concept of 'Lieux de Mémoire' as introduced by the French historian Pierre Nora in 1984 (Nora 1984–92). Based on the combined consideration of built heritage, war landscapes and valuable archaeological features, these sites of memory are defined as historically significant sites where the mutual relations between landscape, war and commemoration can still be experienced today.

This two-tracked (archaeology and landscape research) project also resulted in nine important conclusions or recommendations regarding the 28 sites of memory that represent the core of WW I heritage surviving in this part of Flanders (Verboven 2012).

1   It is important to take into consideration the selected 'sites of memory' when establishing new spatial development plans.
2   Large-scale structural features in the landscape such as natural or man-made elevations, forests, drainage infrastructure, etc. should be preserved as far as possible.
3   Special care should be taken to preserve areas still not built on and historically important vistas.
4   Selected parts of the landscape, such as mine and bomb craters and well-preserved trenches, must be protected as landscape relics.
5   Historic grasslands, wooded areas, zones with preserved micro- and/or meso-relief, embankments and zones where the front lines stabilised for long periods are hotspots for archaeological research into WW I.
6   Sites that are characterised by extremely good preservation conditions should be protected archaeologically.
7   Special attention should be given to historic grasslands showing traces of micro-relief.

Figure 7.4 A trial trench in Messines reveals well-preserved remains of trenches and a bunker.

Source: (photo Marc Dewilde, © Flanders Heritage Agency).

Figure 7.5 A seemingly pastoral image of the rural landscape of Heuvelland cannot hide the omnipresence of World War I in the Westhoek: the pond is actually a mine crater.
Source: (photo Kris Vandevorst, © Flanders Heritage Agency).

8   Underground structures such as deep dugouts and mine tunnels must be registered, monitored and thoroughly studied, and preferably kept as non-*aedificandi* zones (zones kept free from construction) since these sites still present risks for subsidence.
9   When touched by new spatial developments, the areas of former military cemeteries should be studied archaeologically as they preserve a valuable archaeological archive even if most of the human remains have been reburied after the war in other cemeteries. Human remains when discovered should be studied archaeologically. Forensics and analysis of the accompanying finds could lead to identification of the victims.

Protection

The intensive survey and research work established an impressive and very diverse list of heritage of WW I. These heritage items were fed into the online database 'Inventaris Onroerend Erfgoed' (De inventaris van het Onroerend Erfgoed nd). The results of the survey and research were used to develop a policy for protecting WW I heritage.

Ever since as early as 1922, WW I heritage has been the subject of protection under different initiatives and heritage laws (Vaesen 2008; Himpe 2013). These protections, while very valuable, did not originate from an all-encompassing and structured policy on WW I heritage. After the results of the different studies became available the approach in Flanders changed substantially.

From 2008 onwards a targeted programme of protections for WW I heritage was launched, based on three themes: military cemeteries, military constructions (mostly bunkers) and memorials. Beside these three major themes several minor themes, such as reconstruction architecture and logistics, and a few unique items were also considered valuable and included for protection. Between 2008 and 2014 this resulted in the protection of almost 300 WW I-related items. Today, for example, all military cemeteries in Flanders, regardless of their nationality, are protected under the heritage law (see Figure 7.6).

Starting from 2011 attention shifted from the protection of single items, such as architectural heritage, towards initiatives focusing on the contextual setting, the landscape, in which this built heritage is situated. Flemish heritage law does provide a possibility to protect sites as 'registered landscapes', but this tool seemed too strict and inflexible to protect the sites of memory identified in the multidisciplinary research. WW I heritage is embedded in a dynamic cultural landscape in which people live, work, build, farm… The protection of sites of memory should not only consider preservation but also aim at durable and sustainable development. To take into account the evolving nature of these sites of memory, Flanders made

Figure 7.6 A British bunker in Heuvelland on the Messines Ridge. One of the many bunkers protected as part of the programme for protecting WW I heritage.

Source: (photo Kris Vandevorst, © Flanders Heritage Agency).

use of a specific spatial planning instrument that allows heritage to enter into a dialogue with other societal sectors, rather than using the instrument of protection via the heritage law that provides a more rigid protection of heritage. This integration of heritage in spatial development plans is the key to protecting large areas without compromising the economic, agricultural, touristic and living qualities of the areas envisaged.

The embedding of heritage into spatial planning instruments is done by a kind of 'heritage landscape plan'. As of January 2015 five 'plan projects' or 'anchor-places' in the Westhoek have been defined specifically based on their landscape heritage values related to WW I, and a sixth project is under preparation. Combined, these six 'anchor places' cover most of the front zone around and near the city of Ieper.

Management

The more and the better sites were understood, valued and protected, the higher the need to develop a management strategy adapted to WW I heritage. This resulted in a programme of specific grants to restore and maintain such heritage. Additional funding to facilitate and improve the public access to WW I sites was provided. Improving access means raising awareness.

An important landscape project in this respect is the Remembrance Park 2014–2018 designed by Geurst & Schulze architects and Lodewijk Baljon landscape architects (Vandael 2012). The aim of this project is to draw up a master plan for an integrated and comprehensive cultural-tourism project covering the former front line in the Westhoek. To strengthen the connection between the individual sites, the Remembrance Park 2014–2018 team has developed overarching principles to facilitate the interpretation and the experience of WW I landscapes and sites. On a more practical level, a lot of proposals have been submitted to improve the quality of the presented sites and landscapes, mainly by removing obstructions or disturbing features and to a lesser extent by adding new elements to the setting (see Figures 7.7 and 7.8).

UNESCO World Heritage Site

The strategy that Flanders has developed for the heritage of World War I culminates in a proposal for a UNESCO World Heritage Site nomination which Flanders is currently preparing, in cooperation with Wallonia and an association of 14 Northern French *départements* (Aisne, Ardennes, Haut-Rhin, Marne, Meuse, Meurthe-et-Moselle, Moselle, Nord, Oise, Pas-de-Calais, Seine-et-Marne, Somme, Territoire de Belfort, Vosges).

This UNESCO World Heritage nomination will not focus on the historical battlefields but rather on the memorial landscapes and sites that have arisen from the conflict. More specifically, the focus will be on the universal values that these landscapes and sites propagate. This is an important nuance as it shifts the focus from war to international remembrance practices and their associated universal

Figure 7.7 The French military cemetery on the Kemmelberg in Heuvelland: current situation.

Source: Photo T. V. Park 2014–2018, © Flanders Heritage Agency.

Figure 7.8 A simulation of the same military cemetery as proposed in the Remembrance Park. By trimming the shrubs and trees behind the cemetery, a direct relation is restored with the landscape where the soldiers buried here fought and died.

Source: Illustration T. V. Park 2014–2018, © Flanders Heritage Agency.

values. We believe that this is a very important concept, in line with the objectives of UNESCO itself.

Exemplary for this memorial landscape are the hundreds of military cemeteries and monuments to the missing, located in a 700km-long linear zone from the North Sea to the French-Swiss border, which still recall the former Western Front (see Figure 7.9).

These military cemeteries and monuments to the missing truly are an exceptional kind of heritage:

- They bear witness to a new tradition in which, for the first time in human history, all killed in action are recognised unanimously and equally in death. In spite of the inhumane slaughter that took place on the battlefields, every victim is buried or remembered individually regardless of nationality, religion, rank or social status. This represents a re-individualisation in death, placed before any other consideration (UNESCO 2014 ; La Valeur Universelle Exceptionelle nd).

Figure 7.9 Landscape, war and memory in one image: Tyne Cot cemetery and memorial to the missing in Zonnebeke is the largest Commonwealth military cemetery in the world. It started as a small battlefield cemetery next to an advanced dressing station set up in a German bunker captured during the Third Battle of Ypres (1917). The design of the cemetery incorporates several bunkers of the German 'Flandern I' defence line constructed on one of the strategically important low ridges around the city of Ieper.

Source: (© Visit Flanders).

- These sites also provide evidence of the creation of a completely new architectural and landscape-architectural typology with exceptional qualities. The aesthetic language is specific to each belligerent, but the particular attention to quality and detail is universal.
- And finally, these cemeteries and monuments are the object of a lasting and living international commemoration that has evolved to an appeal for peace, reconciliation and cooperation. The last post at the Menin Gate memorial to the missing in Ieper is a very well-known example of this aspect.

King George V is recorded to have said, when he visited several WW I sites in France and Belgium:

> We can truly say that the whole circuit of the Earth is girdled with the graves of our dead. In the course of my pilgrimage, I have many times asked myself whether there can be more potent advocates of peace upon Earth through the years to come, than this massed multitude of silent witnesses to the desolation of war.
>
> (11 May 1922, Tyne Cot Cemetery, Zonnebeke)

The partnership mentioned above is convinced that these universal and exceptional values combined do make a very strong case for nominating a selection of the most important and most relevant military cemeteries and monuments to the missing on the former Western Front as UNESCO World Heritage.

Conclusion

From 2002 onwards Flanders has launched an integrated programme targeting WW I heritage. At first this policy focused primarily on built heritage. By studying in more detail the qualities and values attributed to this built heritage it became obvious that the actual landscape with its associated archaeological heritage are equally important and valuable. The government of Flanders therefore started an integrated process of research, protection and management of WW I landscapes. Nomination to become a UNESCO World Heritage Site is meant to be the pinnacle of this long-term heritage strategy.

The partnership (Flanders, Wallonia and 14 French *départements*) is hoping to get the unanimous support of all World Heritage Convention member states for this UNESCO World Heritage nomination and is looking forward to initiatives that would enhance this support.

References

Bostyn, F. (1999). 'Beecham Dugout, Passchendaele 1914–1918'. *Studies 1* (Zonnebeke: Association for Battlefield Archaeology in Flanders).

Brown, M. (2001). *The Imperial War Museum Book of the Western Front* (London: Pan Books).

Chielens, P., Dendooven, K. and Decoodt, H. (2006). *De laatste getuige. Het oorlogslandschap van de Westhoek* (Tielt, Belgium: Lannoo).

Decoodt, H. (2014). 'Belgische en Franse militaire posten aan het Ijzerfront'. *Monumenten, Landschappen en Archeologie, 34*(3), 4–23.

Decoodt, H. (2007). 'De sporen van "den Grooten Oorlog"'. *Monumenten, Landschappen en Archeologie, 26*(1), 4–36.

De inventaris van het Onroerend Erfgoed (nd). Available from: https://inventaris.onroerenderfgoed.be/woi/relict/zoeken. [10 February 2015].

De Schaepdrijver, S. (2013). *De Groote Oorlog. Het koninkrijk België tijdens de eerste wereldoorlog* (Antwerp: Houtekiet/Linkeroever Uitgevers).

Dewilde, M., De Meyer, H. and Saunders, N. J. (2007). 'Archeologie van de "Grooten Oorlog". De Vlaamse situatie'. *Monumenten, Landschappen en Archeologie, 26*(1), 37–54.

Dewilde, M., Stichelbaut, B., Van Hollebeeke, Y., Verboven, H. and Wyffels, F. (2014). 'Bellewaerde en zijn turbulent oorlogsverleden'. *Monumenten, Landschappen en Archeologie, 33*(3), 30–47.

Freytag, A., and Van Driessche, T. (2011). 'Die Deutschen Soldatenfriedhöfe des Ersten Weltkriegs in Flandern'. *Relicta. Archeologie, Monumenten- en Landschapsonderzoek in Vlaanderen, 7*(7), 163–238.

Geurst, J. (2010). *Cemeteries of the Great War by Sir Edwin Lutyens* (Rotterdam: 010 Publishers).

Heyde, S. (2014). 'Het herstel van het bocage-landschap in de zuidelijke Westhoek na de Eerste Wereldoorlog'. *Monumenten, Landschappen en Archeologie, 33*(1), 28–41.

Himpe, K. (2013). 'De zorg voor littekens, een eeuw erfgoedbeleid rond Wereldoorlog I-relicten'. *Ruimte, 20*(5), 12–19.

Jacobs, M. (1996). *Zij die vielen als helden... Inventaris van de oorlogsgedenktekens van de twee wereldoorlogen in West-Vlaanderen* (Brugge, Belgium: Provincie West-Vlaanderen).

La Valeur Universelle Exceptionelle (nd). Available from: www.paysages-et-sites-de-memoire.fr/accueil/notre-activite/comite-prefiguration [10 February 2015].

Nora, P. (ed.) (1984–92). *Les Lieux de Mémoire*, 7 volumes (Paris: Gallimard).

Saunders, N. J. (2010). *Killing Time. Archaeology and the First World War* (Stroud: The History Press).

Stichelbaut, B. (2007). 'Mogelijkheden van historische luchtfotografie voor de slagveldarcheologie van Wereldoorlog 1'. *Monumenten, Landschappen en Archeologie, 26*(1), 55–63.

Stichelbaut, B., Bourgeois, J., Saunders, N. and Chielens, P. (eds) (2009). *Images of Conflict: Military Aerial Photography and Archaeology* (Newcastle-upon-Tyne: Cambridge Scholars Publishing).

UNESCO (2014). 'Sites funéraires et mémoriels de la Première Guerre mondiale (Front Ouest)'. Available from: http://whc.unesco.org/en/tentativelists/5886/ [10 February 2015].

Vaesen, J. (2008). 'Hergebruik of oorlogstoerisme? De omgang met Belgische militaire sites als sporen van de strijd, 1914–1940', in P.-A. Pallier and P. Nefors (eds), *En toen zwegen de kanonnen – Quand les cannons se taisent – When the Guns fall silent*, international colloquium, Algemeen Rijksarchief en Koninklijk Legermuseum, Brussels, pp. 483–518.

Vandael, L. (project coordinator) (2012). 'Masterplan Herinneringspark 2014–18', Brussels.

Verboven, H. (nd). 'De andere kant van het niemandsland. Loopgravenkaarten uit de eerste wereldoorlog revisited'. *Relicta. Archeologie, Monumenten- en Landschapsonderzoek in Vlaanderen*, submitted for publication.

Verboven, H. (2014). 'De Westhoek ondermijnd'. *Monumenten, Landschappen en Archeologie, 33*(1), 6–27.

Verboven, H. (ed.) (2012). 'Syntheserapport over de aanpak, methodiek, resultaten en aanbevelingen van het WO I erfgoed onderzoek', unpublished research report, Onroerend Erfgoed, Brussels.

8 Commemorating dissenting voices and stories

The centenary of the anti-conscription campaign in World War I

Warwick Frost, Jennifer Laing and David Cragg

The Melbourne Trades Hall Council decided on November 14th 1918 to place on record their appreciation of all those soldiers who whilst fighting abroad voted against the introduction of conscription into this country.

(Inscription, Conscription Memorial Mural, Trades Hall Building, Melbourne)

Introduction

On 28 October 1916 – midway through World War I – Australians voted in a referendum to approve military conscription. While the vote was not needed to change the constitution, Prime Minister Billy Hughes saw it as a means to demonstrate widespread support and aid in pushing legislation through both houses of parliament. Following an extensive and bitter campaign regarding the referendum, conscription was narrowly defeated – 1,160,033 votes against, 1,087,557 for. An important moment during World War I, the anniversary of the referendum and the campaigns for and against conscription will *not* be included in the official programme of anniversary events to commemorate the centenary of the War. Such an omission raises critical questions regarding the planning and staging of commemorative events; demonstrating that official anniversaries tend towards a single narrative and are often just as much about forgetting as they are about remembering.

A common difficulty with events commemorating war is the presentation of just a single narrative, often constructed as *official* or absolutely *true*. Such phenomena have been widely recognised in heritage studies, particularly the consequent tendency to ignore or belittle alternative or dissonant interpretations of history. Accordingly, heritage may become contested, with different groups claiming that their version of history is correct and that all other perspectives are wrong (Lowenthal 1998; Tunbridge and Ashworth 1996). For commemorative events, this may be manifested by descendant groups claiming the exclusive right to manage *their* heritage and/or governments attempting to preserve a single narrative by excluding dissenting voices (Frost 2007; Frost and Laing 2013).

The exclusion of the conscription referendum from the Centenary of World War I is a valuable case study for considering issues of heritage dissonance and the selective rewriting of history within the context of official commemorative events. Furthermore, it is important to understand that this is not an isolated instance. What is and what is not included in the official programmes for the Centenary of World War I has given prominence to other dissenting views, particularly the recognition of the ill treatment of conscientious objectors, the Shot at Dawn Memorial in the UK and the anti-war poetry produced by soldiers such as Wilfred Owen and Siegfried Sassoon. Our aim in this chapter is to examine and highlight such dissonance and its exclusion from official commemorative events.

Understanding the special nature of dark commemorative events

The planned World War I commemorative events may be generally categorised as 'dark events', though such terminology needs to be recognised as fluid and open to contestation. The use of the term 'dark' comes from tourism studies (examples include Lennon and Foley 2000; Stone 2006; Stone and Sharpley 2008). Its application to events studies is more recent. In a more general study of commemorative events, Frost and Laing argued for a separate consideration of dark events, particularly noting that many of these commemorative events had limited tourism appeal. They defined dark events as those 'that commemorate or mark the anniversaries of incidents that are distressing, macabre or involve death or suffering' (Frost and Laing, 2013: 31). Many of these dark commemorative events are linked to battles or warfare. In addition to those relating to the centenary of World War I (2014–18), recent years have seen events to commemorate the 70th Anniversary of World War II (2009–15), the 150th Anniversary of the American Civil War (2011–15) and the Bicentenary of the Battle of Waterloo (2015).

That all warfare commemorations are dark is open to discussion. In his study of four UK battlefields, Miles has persuasively argued that 'the visitor experience is multifaceted with an appreciation of the site as a heritage, not specifically dark, tourism site' (2014: 143). He found that the visitors he interviewed had 'a more immediate engagement with the story attached to the site… [and] there were no examples of respondents who were pre-occupied with the more viscerally "darker" aspects of the sites' (Miles 2014: 144). Visitor interest in themes of sacrifice and personal identity – rather than horror and death – has been apparent at previous World War I commemorative events (Frost, Wheeler and Harvey 2008) and has been highly visible in publicity leading up to the centenary.

The emphasis on costumed re-enactment – sometimes resulting in events tending towards the carnivalesque – signifies that some war commemorations can hardly be seen as dark (Frost and Laing 2013; Ryan and Cave 2007; Wallace 2007). The integration of performances into commemorative events raises issues of appropriateness. In 2005, the organisers of the 90th anniversary of Gallipoli received strong criticism for playing pop music videos – including the Bee Gees' *Staying Alive* – on a big screen before the dawn service (Frost *et al.* 2008). The 70th anniversary of the bombing of Darwin included a black-tie dinner and a fashion show. In response to media criticism, the Returned Services League defended the fashion show, stating 'here is a young person with a completely new idea to show what happened in Darwin... she's showing that terrible time in a different light and a way that will attract a younger person' (quoted in Breen Burns 2012: 3). The 70th anniversary of D-Day event featured the history of the War in interpretative dance, including archival film of the discovery of the atrocities at Auschwitz shown on a large screen. In contrast, such an approach was not used at the 70th anniversary of Auschwitz, which was staged less than a year later.

Such examples suggest that the concept of a *spectrum of intensity* (Stone 2006) should be applied to dark commemorative events. At the lighter end of that spectrum are battles like Gettysburg and Bannockburn that took place so far in the past that they might be regarded as having *whitened* over time, with closure largely achieved over what had happened and the reasons why (Lennon and Foley 2000). At the darker end of the scale are acts or episodes connected to war that are so unspeakable that they maintain their dark edge over the years. Examples of these include the Holocaust (Dekel 2013; Macdonald 2012), Hiroshima (Hogan 1996; Saito 2006), Vietnam (Wagner-Pacifici and Schwartz 1991), the Nanjing Massacre (Fengqi 2009) and Northern Ireland (Conway 2009). For commemorative event organisers, understanding where their event sits on this spectrum of intensity is both critical and problematic. Any such judgement is subjective and it will be interesting to see how the centenary of World War I unfolds in this regard.

The uncertainty of commemorative events is a function of their special nature. Major anniversaries are *one-off* events. National Days, for example, are staged annually with the benefit of established organisations and government funding. The public has fixed expectations and there is strong organisational memory as to what will or will not work. In contrast, the organisation of an event like the centenary of World War I is ad hoc, with expertise pulled together in a tight time-frame and limited examples to draw on. This may lead to conservatism and naïveté, manifested in a strong desire to not offend anyone. The 1988 bicentenary of European settlement in Australia has become infamous for following such an approach, offending both radical and conservative stakeholders by trying to strip the event of any meaningful historical interpretation (Frost and Laing 2013). In the USA, the 1995 exhibition commemorating the 50th anniversary of the 'Enola Gay' dropping an atomic bomb on Hiroshima was cancelled by the Smithsonian. This resulted from extensive complaints that the interpretation in the exhibition was too sympathetic to the Japanese and was perceived by some as a *rewriting of history* (Goldberg 1999; Hogan 1996; Lowenthal 1998).

Tunbridge and Ashworth (1996) argue that such dissonance about and contestation over heritage is healthy, recognising that pluralist societies contain multiple perspectives that should be debated. However, there is a tendency for event organisers not to feel this way. A common view is that events should aim to satisfy, to make people happy. In applying this attitude to commemorative events – particularly if they have dark elements – event organisers understand that people will be respectful, reflective and solemn and this leads to ideas that they should not be upset further by controversy. Reinforcing this tendency to conservatism, government funding agencies may emphasise the need for a single national narrative and the exclusion of any dissent.

As detailed in the examples above, the special nature of commemorative events is critical in the shaping of how they are staged and their effectiveness in achieving the strategic goals of organisers and stakeholders. It is particularly important to understand that significant anniversaries may be compromised by their one-off status. We have emphasised naïveté – not in order to disparage, but to highlight that organisers may be limited by a lack of experience in staging similar events and limited knowledge of potential pitfalls. The organisers of the 2001 centenary of Federation, for example, were very conscious of avoiding the criticisms of sanitisation and banality that plagued the 1988 bicentenary. With a gap of only 13 years, the problems of 1988 were still fresh to the organisers, staff and stakeholders. In contrast, the gap between 1988 and 2015 is much greater – essentially generational. A number of our students have commented that they were not born in 1988 and only have vague memories of the centenary of Federation and even of the Sydney Olympics.

Magnifying this lack of experience is the dissonance associated with heritage and heritage events. Complaints of sanitisation are common, as are feelings of bitterness and betrayal from stakeholder groups that feel they are being excluded from the reinterpretation of history that comes with every commemorative event. Organisational naïveté again comes to the fore here, as there is a tendency to try to avoid controversy and stick to a misguided plan of providing a single national narrative. An instructive example of this occurred with the British organisation of the centenary of the start of World War I (4 August 2014). The UK Department of Culture, Media and Sport decided to exclude the poetry of Wilfred Owen and Siegfried Sassoon as 'their work is too critical' and 'would not fit the spirit of the event' (Brooks 2014: 20).

In contrast to the single narrative of official commemorations, dissenters provide alternative perspectives. Two are worth noting. The first is the Shot at Dawn Statue at the National Memorial Arboretum in England. Unveiled in 2000, it graphically represents the 274 servicemen shot for desertion during World War I. It was built as part of a campaign for recognition that many of these men were suffering from severe shell shock and were sentenced after short trials in which they had no legal representation (Black 2004). The second example is the Fallen 9000. Led by artists Jamie Wardley and Andy Moss, hundreds of volunteers stencilled the shapes of dead people on Normandy beaches. This was to commemorate the 9,000 soldiers and civilians who died on D Day and this event was staged on Peace Day, 21 September 2013 (Moss 2013).

The centenary of World War I provides an evocative case study for considering these issues. In this chapter, our aim is to focus on the omission of dissenting views of war, looking in particular at the instance of the centenary of the successful anti-conscription campaign. Our main emphasis is on the Victorian Trades Hall as a major player in the original campaign and in attempts to stage an *alternative* series of events at the same time as the official government-funded programme.

The official centenary programme

As with most major commemorative events, an array of consultative committees were created to ensure consultation and the appropriate distance between the elected parliament and the staging of the anniversary. Under the aegis of the Australian Department of Veterans' Affairs, a National Commission on the Commemoration of the Anzac Centenary was initially formed to scope out the potential range of activities. Later, a separate Anzac Centenary Advisory Board was formed to oversee the staging of the centenary programme. Both bodies were primarily composed of former politicians and military officers.

The National Commission recommended that the main focus be on centenaries of four historical episodes: the first departure of troops in 1914, the Gallipoli landings in 1915, the Battle of Villers-Bretonneux in 1918 and the armistice in 1918. In addition, it recommended that anniversaries of other conflicts – including World War II and the Vietnam War – be included within the official programme. In the appendices to its report, the National Commission identified an extensive list of 'key commemorative dates', which included the centenary of the conscription referendum (National Commission on the Commemoration of the Anzac Centenary 2011).

As the centenary programme has unfolded, the National Commission's suggested approach has been followed, particularly the emphasis on four cornerstone anniversaries and the inclusion of commemorative events regarding other conflicts. What did change, however, was that the list of key commemorative dates was greatly shortened. It now mainly consisted of major battles and did not include the conscription referendum (Anzac Centenary 2014). While this programme does not prevent anybody from organising commemorative events for the conscription referendum, it does provide an official imprimatur that it is not part of the official commemoration.

The Victorian Trades Hall and the commemoration

In 1856, a successful campaign for the 8-hour day led unionists to form a Trades Hall Committee in Melbourne. In 1859, they opened the Trades Hall Building, now recognised as the world's oldest trade union building. When completed, its grand style mirrored that of the nearby Parliament Building and it has been suggested as a prime candidate for UNESCO World Heritage Listing (Ludvigsen 2013).

With the announcement of a conscription referendum, the Trades Hall took a leading role in the opposition campaign. There was a loose coalition of varied groups against conscription but, for the purposes of this study, we are focusing only on the labour movement in Victoria. Leadership of the campaign included John Curtin (who was later Prime Minister during World War II) and Jack Holloway (later Federal Minister for Labour and National Service from 1943 to 1949). Strong opposition to conscription opened a split within the Labor Party, leading to Billy Hughes leaving, forming a new Nationalist Party and remaining Prime Minister until 1923. It is intriguing how often and widely Hughes is being invoked in the marketing of the centenary of World War I, particularly his claim that 'Australia was born on the shores of Gallipoli' (see, for example, the community website Spirits of Gallipoli 2015).

The strong involvement of trade unionists in opposing conscription arose for three reasons. First, during the original enthusiasm for the War in 1914 and 1915, the rate of volunteering amongst unionists was high. This engendered a feeling that volunteering was a personal choice and that military service should not be enforced. Second, by 1916 it was clear that the War was not going well and that casualty rates were extremely high. Gallipoli and the Battle of the Somme were military disasters (the former was a defeat, with forces withdrawing in December 1915). The view that the military commanders and politicians were incompetent began to gain ground. In contrast to the jingoistic enthusiasm of 1914, by 1916 it was clear that the conscripts would have a high mortality rate. Third, within the labour movement, opposition to Hughes was growing, owing particularly to his support of the War at all costs. Religion may also have played a part, with Catholics concerned about the aftermath of the 1916 Easter Rising in Dublin; though it must also be acknowledged that many Protestants were against conscription. And we also need to remember that there had been those who were against the War from the beginning.

The anti-conscription campaign was marked by a series of rallies, drawing crowds of up to 30,000. As campaign HQ, the Trades Hall Building was decked in large banners (see Figure 8.1). For twenty-first century eyes, they present a surprising picture of a media-savvy society. Two themes particularly dominated. The first is the appeal to mothers, especially effective as female suffrage had been in place since 1902. The second is the testimonials from serving volunteers. Such

Figure 8.1 The Trades Hall Building decorated in anti-conscription banners.
Source: (courtesy Victorian Trades Hall).

uniformed military personnel could hardly be seen as disloyal and the message was clearly that volunteers were needed, not conscripts.

Within the Victorian Trades Hall and its associated organisations there has been much debate as to how best to commemorate the centenary of World War I. Planning has focused on the second half of the anniversary, particularly 2016 to 2018. The Victorian Trades Hall's programme will include the following events:

- unveiling a fully restored conscription mural (see Figure 8.2)
- opening a permanent Peace Exhibition, emphasising the 1916–17 Anti-Conscription Campaign
- holding commemorative thanksgiving ceremonies on the anniversaries of both referenda and
- hosting a 'future directions' defence policy conference to bring together peace activists, defence and foreign affairs analysts.

Debating omission

In an opinion piece in Melbourne's *Age* newspaper, politics and history lecturer Dr Julie Kimber voiced some of the frustration at the failure to acknowledge alternative narratives in commemorations to mark the outbreak of World War I:

Figure 8.2 The 1918 Anti-Conscription Mural, Victorian Trades Hall Building, Melbourne. Note that it was unveiled three days after Armistice Day.

Source: (courtesy Victorian Trades Hall).

We will hear, as we have done for years past, how the nation, which had been federated for only 14 years, was 'born' at Gallipoli. But how much of the divisions at home during that war will be acknowledged? It's a story familiar to historians of the period, but one that is largely absent from our public remembrances. Our amnesia risks perpetuating the glorification of war.

She goes on to record her outrage at how this way of thinking put pressure on young men in particular to join up:

That glorification underpinned the kneejerk jingoism that sent men to their deaths. In towns across Australia men were pressured into enlisting by patriotism, yes, but also by local newspapers, recruitment drives, white feathers and bluster. The repercussions of these pressures had devastating effects on families and towns.

(Kimber 2014)

Kimber's mention of white feathers refers to the practice of giving a white feather to any young man of fighting age who was seen around in 'civvies', to denote their cowardice. Its origins are explained by Nicolson (2009: 15): 'In the countryside there was an old rural belief that a white feather in a bird's tail indicated a bird of inferior quality'. Its use was popularised through the novel *The Four Feathers* by A. E. W. Mason (1902), in which, during the late nineteenth century, a young army officer is given four feathers by friends when he leaves the army just as a war starts, but later redeems himself by acts of bravery, allowing him to return the feathers one by one. Nicolson emphasises that these kind of acts were devastatingly effective on their targets and the shame was often too great to bear: 'The humiliation associated with failing to join up was often overwhelming and young men, even those officially unqualified to fight for medical reasons, felt compelled to sign on' (2009: 15).

The crux of Kimber's argument is that the anniversary of the defeat of the vote on conscription is a time to celebrate 'the dissenting voices in our history', not to pretend that they did not (and still do not) exist. For Kimber, '[t]he glory of war sent men to their deaths. Opposition to conscription saved many others from the same fate'. In a personal communication with us, she reveals that this article touched a nerve ('I received many emails, calls and letters'), all positive with one exception, an email which labelled her work 'a puff piece' that lacked 'a more balanced view of the issues'. This email took the line that:

[d]issenting voices can possess the high moral ground only because others are prepared to do the dirty work. It is convenient for these dissenting voices to look the other way without recognising their freedom is come at someone else's cost... Conscription can be seen as a necessary act of desperation to ensure that the freedoms within our community are maintained, solely by putting more resources into the fight. *Unfortunately there is no right or wrong answer in relation to this* [italicised for emphasis by us]. Those who

volunteered did so in the belief that they were doing the right thing, and those who campaigned against military involvement could only do so with the luxury of others being prepared to die to protect their freedom.

(personal communication sent to Julie Kimber)

This email in fact *supports* Kimber's central tenet, as illustrated by the italicised phrase above, that the stories behind the centenary of World War I and the anti-conscription movement in Australia are indeed complex, and that this contestation should be given greater prominence, not swept under the carpet. The fact that this correspondent is so passionate in his defence of conscription and Kimber so equally ardent in her denunciation of it, makes the centenary of anti-conscription an important subject for examination and discussion in 2015. A letter sent to *The Age* after Kimber's article makes the same point (McMillan 2014), observing that there are two sides to this argument, and that Kimber is in error to ignore the 'harsh military and geopolitical realities of 1914 Europe'.

In support of Kimber's article, in a letter sent to and published in *The Age*, Glazebrook (2014) specifically refers to the conscription referendum:

The dissenting voices against military conscription deserve to be commem-orated, not disrespected by deliberately excluding them from our public ceremonies and ignoring their heroic deeds. There can be little doubt that at least another 60,000 young Australians would have been slaughtered if not for the courage and intelligence of those civilians who fought without compromise against an imperialist war and military conscription.

This links in with the importance of 'taking an iconoclastic stance on the Great War and the Anzac myth' (personal communication sent to Julie Kimber), with another correspondent stating '[w]e have to deflect the madness somehow'. The high emotion shown by these correspondents in arguing that World War I is being painted as a purely positive event in history by those promoting the centenary commemoration is palpable in the language they use ('blind loyalty', 'ideological conceit').

Others base their support of Kimber on the perceived waste of public money behind these commemorations, with comments such as '[t]he participation of cash strapped universities in the commemorations (grants, conferences, publications, etc.) provides shocking, gangrene flesh to the abstract skeleton of ideological hegemony' and '[a]lthough we constantly hear about the need for government austerity policies in education and community health, governments nevertheless always find money for promoting the "militarisation of Australian history"' (personal communication sent to Julie Kimber). Zembekis (2014) points out the inequality of the funding of these commemorations, noting '[w]hile hundreds of millions of taxpayers' dollars are to spent laying wreaths and blowing bugles to remember the fallen, little will be spent to remember the dissenting voices whose protestations would have saved millions of lives'.

118   *Warwick Frost, Jennifer Laing and David Cragg*

Conclusion

The beginning of World War I was marked by jingoism and widespread optimism. Starting in late summer, it was forecast to be all over by Christmas. For the European powers, the struggle was to be modelled on the short Franco-Prussian War. The drawn-out attrition and slaughter of the American Civil War was ignored. Once bogged down in trench warfare, strategy focused on a knock-out blow to end the stalemate – a second front like Gallipoli or a big push like the Somme. As the War dragged on and the casualties mounted, this naïve optimism dissipated. Rather than an adventure, this was a war of industrial killing. Confidence in military and political leaders declined. In Russia, the Romanov dynasty was overthrown. Ireland rebelled. All the major powers felt threatened by revolution and dissent.

The centenary commemoration of World War I will follow a similar path. The first twelve months or so – particularly in Australia – have been characterised by enthusiasm and excess. Once past the anniversary of the Gallipoli landing, the trend of the War went downwards and dissent intensified. The challenge for the centenary organisers is in how to appropriately commemorate this different story. Rather than the heroic landing at Gallipoli, the later anniversaries will be of the bungling of the Somme and the opposition to conscription.

As we write in early 2015, changes in mood are apparent. The Australian Chamber Orchestra concert *Reflections on Gallipoli* sparked a review that commented:

> As World War I's commemoration juggernaut ploughs onwards… it can be difficult to see past the bombast… from luxury cruises to key rings, and even a 'lest we forget' cuckoo clock… can it [this production] cut through the usual hubris with a different perspective?
>
> (Evans 2015: 40)

Another example arose with the 2015 television shows *Gallipoli* and *The Story of Us*, which were launched with great fanfare but did not rate as well as might have been expected. According to documentary film-maker Alex West, these programmes 'have not really captured the imagination. I think that's because people are bored with that kind of back-slapping, mateship kind of thing… There's a level where we want more sophistication' (Kalina 2015: 6).

The anniversary of the anti-conscription campaign is an important example of the common problem faced in organising commemorative events. It is very different to the battles, but equally important for understanding the nature and significance of World War I. That it highlights dissent clearly sits uncomfortably with those who aim for the propagation of their single narrative. Nonetheless, commemorative event organisers need to resist the temptation of a single narrative and understand that any commemorative event will be more effective if it recognises and embraces multiple viewpoints.

The centenary of the Anti-Conscription Campaign is one of a series of upcoming anniversaries of difficult and highly contested historical conflicts. Others that will soon be occurring include the 70th Anniversary of the bombing of Hiroshima

(2015), the centenary of the Irish Easter Rising (2016), the centenary of the Russian Revolution (2017) and the 50th anniversaries of the Vietnam Moratoria (2019–20). These are all dark commemorative events that require multiple interpretations, but that no doubt will be marked by attempts to enforce single narratives. Ideally, all of these events will be more meaningful if dissenting voices are incorporated in the official programmes.

Acknowledgements

We would like to thank the Victorian Trades Hall for their assistance and Dr Julie Kimber of Swinburne University, Melbourne for sharing her experiences with us.

References

Anzac Centenary (2014). 'The Program 2014–2018: Significant commemorative dates for the Anzac Centenary National Program'. Available from: www.thefallen9000.info/ [15 January 2015].

Black, J. (2004). 'Thanks for the memory: war memorials, spectatorship and the trajectories of commemoration 1919–2001', in N. J. Saunders (ed.), *Matters of Conflict: Material Culture, Memory and the First World War* (Oxford and New York: Routledge), pp. 134–48.

Breen Burns, J. (2012). 'Darwin bombings inspire a woven lesson in history'. *The Age*, 18 February, 3.

Brooks, R. (2014). 'War poets edited out of memorial'. *Sunday Times*, 29 June, 20.

Conway, B. (2009). 'Rethinking difficult pasts: Bloody Sunday (1972) as a case study'. *Cultural Sociology*, 3(3), 397–413.

Dekel, I. (2013). *Mediation at the Holocaust Memorial in Berlin* (Basingstoke: Palgrave Macmillan).

Evans, K. (2015). 'Gallipoli parable intensified by music'. *The Age*, 14 March, 40.

Fengqi, Q. (2009). 'Let the dead be remembered: interpretation of the Nanjing Massacre Memorial', in W. Logan and K. Reeves (eds), *Places of Pain and Shame: Dealing with 'Difficult' Heritage* (London: Routledge), pp. 17–33.

Frost, W. (2007). 'Refighting the Eureka Stockade: managing a dissonant battlefield', in C. Ryan (ed.), *Battlefield Tourism: History, Place and Interpretation* (Oxford: Elsevier), pp. 187–194.

Frost, W. and Laing, J. (2013). *Commemorative Events: Memory, Identities, Conflict* (London and New York: Routledge).

Frost, W., Wheeler, F. and Harvey, M. (2008). 'Commemorative events: sacrifice, identity and dissonance', in J. Ali-Knight, M. Robertson, A. Fyall and A. Larkins (eds), *International Perspectives on Festivals and Events: Paradigms of Analysis* (London: Elsevier), pp. 161–72.

Glazebrook, J. (2014). 'Blind loyalty to British interests'. *The Age*, 6 September, 32.

Goldberg, S. (1999). 'The Enola Gay affair: what evidence counts when we commemorate historical events?' *Osiris*, *14*, 176–86.

Hogan, M. (1996). 'The Enola Gay controversy: history, memory and the politics of presentation', in M. Hogan (ed.), *Hiroshima in History and Memory* (Cambridge: Cambridge University Press), pp. 200–232.

Kalina, P. (2015). 'Doco-maker debunks myths'. *The Age*, Green Guide, 12 March, 6.

Kimber, J. (2014). 'How jingoistic bluster encouraged our boys to enlist'. *The Age*, 5 September. Available from: www.theage.com.au/comment/world-war-1-how-jingoistic-bluster-encouraged-our-boys-to-enlist-20140904-10c98v.html [15 January 2015].

Lennon, J. J. and Foley, M. (2000). *Dark Tourism: The Attraction of Death and Disaster* (London: Cassel).

Lowenthal, D. (1998). *The Heritage Crusade and the Spoils of History* (Cambridge: Cambridge University Press).

Ludvigsen, P. (2013). 'Workers' assembly halls as a proposition for UNESCO's World Heritage'. *International Journal of Heritage Studies, 19*(5), 408–38.

Macdonald, S. (2012). *Memorylands: Heritage and Identity in Europe Today* (London and New York: Routledge).

McMillan, J. (2014). 'Why we had to fight rampant aggression'. *The Age*, 6 September, 32.

Miles, S. (2014). 'Battlefield sites as dark tourism attractions: an analysis of experience'. *Journal of Heritage Tourism, 9*(2), 134–47.

Moss, A. (2013). 'The Fallen'. Available from: www.thefallen9000.info/ [26 February 2015].

National Commission on the Commemoration of the Anzac Centenary (2011). *How Australia May Commemorate the Anzac Centenary* (Canberra: Government of Australia).

Nicolson, J. (2009). *The Great Silence 1918–1920: Living in the Shadow of the Great War* (London: John Murray).

Ryan, C. and Cave, J. (2007). 'Cambridge Armistice Day celebrations: making a carnival of war and the reality of play', in C. Ryan (ed.), *Battlefield Tourism: History, Place and Identity* (Oxford: Elsevier), pp. 177–86.

Saito, H. (2006). 'Reiterated commemoration: Hiroshima as national trauma'. *Sociological Theory, 24*(4), 353–76.

Spirits of Gallipoli (2015). 'Spirits of Gallipoli: The first Anzacs'. Available from: www.spirits-of-gallipoli.com [8 March 2015].

Stone, P. R. (2006). 'A dark tourism spectrum: towards a typology of death and macabre related tourist sites, attractions and exhibitions'. *Tourism, 54*(2), 145–60.

Stone, P. and Sharpley, R. (2008). 'Consuming dark tourism: a thanatological perspective'. *Annals of Tourism Research, 35*(2), 574–95.

Tunbridge, J.E. and Ashworth, G.J. (1996). *Dissonant Heritage: The Management of the Past as a Resource in Conflict* (Chichester: Wiley).

Wagner-Pacifici, R. and Schwartz, B. (1991). 'The Vietnam Veterans Memorial: commemorating a difficult past'. *American Journal of Sociology, 97*(2), 376–420.

Wallace, T. (2007). 'Went the Day Well: scripts, glamour and performance in war-weekends'. *International Journal of Heritage Studies, 13*(3), 200–223.

Zembekis, L. (2014). 'Military prejudices alive and well'. *The Age*, 6 September, 32.

9 Once more, with feeling

Commemorating Royal Air Force Bomber Command in late modern Britain

Damien Williams

In Richard Flanagan's Booker Prize-winning *The Narrow Road to the Deep North*, the central character is a World War II army surgeon who survives the death camps along the Thai-Burma railway. Later in life, Dorrigo Evans is disturbed by the 'bland new world' around him, especially 'the new age of conformity that was coming in all things, even emotions' (Flanagan 2013: 80).

Like Evans, most readers will be familiar with the way that testimony has set the tone for the public expression of emotion and authenticity in recent years. It is seen and heard in myriad public performances: on talk shows, in memoir, in commissions of inquiry and in the tears shed by public figures while they reckon with their infidelities or reflect on the pain of others. With that shift there has come a growing awareness of the concept of 'trauma' and an expectation that citizens will witness testimony and validate it by listening. In the Australian context, contemporary stories of white suffering (including those of prisoners-of-war) came to the fore in the late twentieth century as the settler nation began to reckon with public testimony by refugees, Aboriginal and Torres Strait Islander people and other marginalised groups (Twomey 2013; Butler 2009). Having witnessed so much emotion from people on the margins, the settler majority began to take pleasure in stories of its own hardships and trauma.

In the example looked at here – in the planning and dedication of a memorial to RAF Bomber Command in Green Park, London – it is evident that, in late modern Britain, a similar pleasure is taken in witnessing stories of white suffering and sacrifice in war. In important respects, this stems from the official recognition of subaltern groups that rendered military service in defence of the empire. These groups included people of colour and animals, in addition to individual branches of the armed forces not previously recognised with their own memorials.

Moreover, for some descendants of Bomber Command crews, the 2012 unveiling brought a sense of pleasure in seeing their parent or relative given prominent recognition in the centre of the metropolis. Legal secretary Sandy Cannings, whose father flew with the elite Pathfinder force, attended the day with her father. On her blog, she recounts their arrival at Green Park:

> I looked around the crowd and had a massive lump in my throat at how many veterans had managed to attend this very special day. Dad was one of the

youngest to join Bomber Command and at 88 he is still very fit and active, unlike some of the other older veterans who were in wheelchairs but proudly displaying their medals and I'm sure wouldn't have missed the day for anything… each and every one of them with their own story to tell. You could see how proud they were etched in all their faces. All had lost comrades from Bomber Command so this day was to proudly remember them.

(Cannings 2012)

In claiming that 'each and every one of them' had a story to tell Cannings has unwittingly gone some way to identifying how testimony has played a role in shifting the official reception of Bomber Command since the end of the war. During the campaign for this memorial, its planning and especially its unveiling, testimony about the emotional cost of war to airmen and their families allowed for feelings of pride to be elevated, which Cannings sees in the faces of old men. Their war service had long been overshadowed by questions over Bomber Command's efficacy and its deadly harvest of civilian lives. Heritage scholars talk of 'dark events' being *whitened*, or sanitised, over time, which in this case has a double meaning (Frost and Laing 2013, pp40–2). The commemoration of Bomber Command in 2012 smoothed over its tactical and strategic shortcomings while restoring to prominence a largely white fighting force. Added to this was the serendipity in how the campaign for a new Bomber Command memorial aligned personal stories of wartime triumph over adversity with wider national narratives of the need for shared suffering in the face of crisis.

Along with significant changes in testimonial culture in the early twenty-first century, contemporary politics contributed greatly to giving stories from World War II a new prominence. At the time the Bomber Command campaign began, Britain was still mired in the aftermath of an illegal invasion of Iraq and an ill-fated war in Afghanistan. In the case of Iraq, subsequent inquiries had established that the Blair government had indeed exaggerated claims that Saddam Hussein's regime had possessed weapons of mass destruction. From 2008, political attention centred on 'the crisis' that followed the collapse of Lehman Brothers and the state bail-out of financial institutions such as the Royal Bank of Scotland. The austerity measures that followed would further diminish the public sphere and play into the hands of protest parties such as UKIP, which advocates the nation's withdrawal from the European Union and tougher restrictions on immigration. As trust in elected politicians and democratic institutions fell, it became easier to make claims that the British public – and, indeed, Europe – owed a debt to the military for safeguarding its freedoms.

Against that political, economic and cultural backdrop, my principal aim in this chapter is to illustrate the pleasure taken in honouring RAF Bomber Command in late modern Britain. Elsewhere I have gone into the longer history of how this branch of the armed forces has been commemorated in the United Kingdom (Scates *et al.* 2013). 'Remembering' Bomber Command in 2012 was predicated on forgetting existing memorials to the force, and downplaying others that commemorate all of Britain's war dead (such as the Cenotaph) or the RAF as a whole. The individuals and groups whose views won the day in Green Park were those that made the most successful appeals to emotion, utilising the mass media in telling 'forgotten' stories of Bomber Command. While the campaign for a new memorial was stridently contested, it was all the more powerful for the way supporters drew on stories of suffering during and after the war, and the pleasure with which such stories were received.

While World War II has long been a crucial marker across the British political spectrum, publicly testifying to the trauma of the conflict is a more recent innovation. For the left and for liberals in the Whig tradition, the 1939–45 war represented the planned mobilisation of the nation's talents in the defeat of fascism, a 'people's war', that culminated in the election of the Attlee government in 1945. For the right, Churchill's example as wartime leader saw the adjective 'Churchillian' become a byword for tenacity, pluck and political courage. Crucially, too, the war became the high water mark of empire, the last moment that India, Pakistan, Burma, Ceylon and other colonies were held (if somewhat shakily) under the crown. After fighting a war in the name of democracy and freedom, the empire would never be the same again. Neither would Britain: decolonisation brought people from every part of the new Commonwealth to the imperial centre. With them came cultural practices and religious beliefs that contributed to what scholars describe as 'post-Christian' Britain.

Amidst such great social change, the remarkable thing about the most recent efforts to commemorate Bomber Command was the degree to which they reached back in time to a Britain still largely untouched by those developments. At the unveiling, officiating clergy from the established church and kirk were at centre stage to dedicate a memorial in the name of Jesus Christ that unambiguously presented all in Bomber Command as heroes. In doing so, the memorial and its advocates studiously ignored the historical debates that have presented differing interpretations of Bomber Command's tactics, efficacy and place in the wider Allied war effort. Furthermore, the cause that boosters claimed these airmen to be fighting for was most often reduced to 'freedom', a word that had taken on a radically different meaning since the end of the Cold War. In this case, the 'new age of conformity' that so mystifies the fictional Dorrigo Evans was clearly on display in London in 2012: the memorial and its dedication service left precious little room for ambiguity about the men and women of Bomber Command, or their leaders. Elevated on a stone plinth, super-sized in bronze and housed in an 85 metre-long pantheon stretching 8 metres into the sky, it was difficult to see the men of Bomber Command's aircrew as anything less than heroes. Indeed, as former Bee Gee and chief memorial advocate Robin Gibb told the BBC in 2010, they were 'heroes that literally saved the world, [who] in essence, brought peace to Germany and freedom to Germany and Europe itself' (BBC 2010).

As overblown as such claims were, the price in lives that Bomber Command paid in proportion to the size of its force was very high. As proponents of the new memorial were keen to remind people, 55,573 men from Britain and the empire died in the service of the RAF while flying bombers over Europe. Only U-boat crews in the Atlantic suffered a higher death rate; Bomber Command's men went

Figure 9.1 The Bomber Command Memorial as seen from Piccadilly.
Source: (D. Williams).

into combat facing odds similar to those of Tommies on the Somme in the summer of 1916. Despite those losses, members of Bomber Command were not awarded a clasp to their Aircrew Europe medals, in contrast to 'the Few' who flew in Fighter Command during the Battle of Britain.

In the immediate aftermath of the war, such claims to proportionality held little weight when assessed against the millions of murdered Jews and the even greater numbers of Chinese and Soviets who died during the conflict. For its part, Bomber Command had contributed to hundreds of thousands of civilian deaths in firebombing German cities such as Essen, Berlin, Düsseldorf and Dresden, particularly in the second half of the war. Its earlier attempts at daylight 'precision' raids had ended in farce, with high losses and few targets hit. From 1942 it was transformed into a night force that rained high explosive and incendiary bombs on German industry and urban areas. Those tactics were endorsed in the Combined Bomber Offensive agreement that the Allies made at Casablanca in January 1943. Subsequent directives reflected the new reality, such as Bomber Command Operation Order No. 173 of 27 May 1943, which simply read 'destroy Hamburg' (Armitage 1999: 141). By war's end, the order was almost carried out to completion. Seventy-five per cent of Hamburg's built-up area had been razed and more people were killed than in the raids on Dresden in February 1945.

As Ian Buruma has shown in his history of 1945, the scale of wartime loss across the world contributed to a strong feeling of wanting to return as quickly as possible

Figure 9.2 Admiring Philip Jackson's sculptures in the atrium
Source: (D. Williams).

to something resembling everyday life (Buruma 2013). In such a climate, singling out Britain's aerial bombing force for special praise ran counter to the larger political project of rebuilding Western Europe and, later, to a human rights discourse that placed great emphasis on protecting non-combatants during times of conflict (Keegan 1976: 27–8). By the early twenty-first century, however, the postwar consensus around a planned economy and Britain's place in a united Europe had given way to a cult of the market in which the public sphere was hacked away and so-called 'Euroscepticism' came to the fore. Popular feelings of being threatened and isolated in this new economic climate further chipped away at trust in politicians and government, which had been severely eroded following revelations that Tony Blair's administration had fabricated evidence that Saddam Hussein's regime had possessed weapons of mass destruction. While many Britons had come to see the folly of Blair's decision to join the US-led invasion of Iraq in 2003, support for the armed forces remained high, even while the British Government's war aims in the Middle East were unclear. Never was there a better time for the ageing veterans of Bomber Command to be held up by their supporters as unsung heroes, deserving of special recognition.

My focus in the following two sections of this chapter is on the ways in which the past and present coalesced in the unveiling of the Bomber Command Memorial in 2012. I look first at the immediate pressures that were applied to Green Park as it was reinterpreted as a war landscape. The second section gives an account of the dedication ceremony itself, focusing on the range of public performances, the actors involved and the audiences they addressed.

Pressures on Green Park

The campaign for a new 'national' memorial to Bomber Command followed a serendipitous luncheon hosted by the Heritage Foundation in October 2007. The foundation is a philanthropic organisation of British performers and celebrities whose members had included the sports broadcaster Kenneth Wolstenholme, best known for his commentary on the 1966 World Cup. Significantly for this story, Wolstenholme had served with Bomber Command during the war. After the Heritage Foundation had led a successful campaign to honour him with a blue plaque on his house, members of the Bomber Command Association (formed in 1985) were invited as regular guests to its luncheons (Scates *et al.* 2013: 218).

In the preceding seven years, a rash of World War II memorials had been unveiled in London: to the Royal Tank Regiment (2000), the Memorial Gates monument to colonial servicemen and women (2002), to animals in war (2004) and to the Battle of Britain (2005), which carries the crest of RAF Fighter Command. The animals in war monument and the Memorial Gates were the most visible signs of the new recognition given to subaltern groups in Britain's armed

Figure 9.3 The Memorial Gates on Constitution Hill, designed by Liam O'Connor.
Source: (D. Williams).

forces. The inscription for the animals reads 'they had no choice' (the same could be said for conscripts) while the Memorial Gates lists the countries of Africa, the Caribbean and the subcontinent from which troops came to serve the British crown. In their own ways, both memorials would become significant in the campaign for, and design of, a new monument to Bomber Command.

During the course of the Heritage Foundation lunch in 2007, its chairman mentioned to one of the Bomber Command men his admiration of the animals in war memorial. His interlocutor's response was pointed: 'Yeah, and where the bloody hell's ours?' (Scates *et al.* 2013: 217–8). The Bomber Command Association found a willing ally in their campaign for a new memorial when Robin Gibb became annual president of the Heritage Foundation in 2008. Gibb, best known as a member of the Bee Gees, was also a keen amateur history enthusiast. He was highly sympathetic to the Association's claims that it was suffering from monumental deficit in the nation's capital. Gibb's visibility and celebrity status was a boon for the Bomber Command Association. With the help of other members of the Heritage Foundation, the *Sunday Telegraph* took up the cause in March 2008, publishing feature articles that gave the Foundation's details for a memorial appeal (9 March 2008). The *Telegraph*'s enthusiasm followed the successful campaign run by the *Daily Mail* for a Battle of Britain memorial, unveiled by the Prince of Wales and the Duchess of Cornwall in 2005.

Figure 9.4 Holding on to St Paul's at the Battle of Britain Memorial on the Embankment.
Source: (D. Williams).

Figure 9.5 The Fighter Command crest on the Battle of Britain Memorial.
Source: (D. Williams).

The *Telegraph*'s reports of wartime daring, valour and suffering, in addition to pathos-filled accounts from the children of Bomber Command veterans, proved effective in helping to raise £1.5 million in the first two years of the memorial appeal. The largest single donation (£1 million) was made by businessman and Tory peer Michael Ashcroft, an avid collector of Victoria Crosses and author of a series of books including *Victoria Cross Heroes* (2007)*, Special Forces Heroes* (2008) and *George Cross Heroes* (2010), among other work on politics. In time, two other major benefactors enabled the project to proceed to fruition. The first was John Caudwell, who made his fortune selling mobile phones and was the nephew of a Bomber Command serviceman (*Daily Express*, 25 April 2011: 12). Second was Richard Desmond, businessman, television porn broadcaster and publisher of the *Daily Express, OK!* magazine and, until 2004, British *Penthouse*. He matched donations made by *Express* readers pound-for-pound and, according to his newspaper, donated 'a further £500,000 from his own pocket' (*Daily Express*, 25 April 2011: 12). By April 2011, £5.6 million had been raised.

With its £6 million target nearly reached, the Bomber Command Association turned its attention to the question of where to locate its desired memorial. Under planning rules passed by Westminster City Council, proponents of new memorials had to demonstrate a link between their design and the site on which it was to be built. In the case of the Royal Tank Regiment memorial at Whitehall, this had been

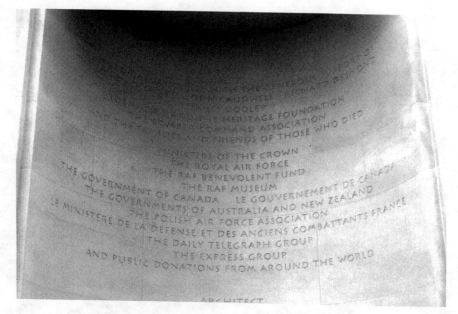

Figure 9.6 Donors recognised in a Bomber Command Memorial alcove.
Source: (D. Williams).

established by its proximity to the offices of the Ministry of Defence. The Battle of Britain monument at the Embankment was next to the Royal Air Force memorial on the Thames, dedicated in 1923 to the memory of British airmen killed in World War I. Significantly, the following inscription was added to the RAF monument in 1946: 'in remembrance of the men and women of the air forces of every part of the British Commonwealth and Empire who gave their lives 1939–1945'. For the 2005 Battle of Britain Memorial, establishing a link with that site was straightforward enough, primarily as the skies above the city had been the scene of aerial battles between British fighters and German bombers.

For the Bomber Command Association, however, establishing a connection with a London location was not as straightforward. During the war, British recruits had been inducted near Lord's cricket ground and billeted close to London Zoo. But the Association deemed this area unsuitable. Instead it cast its eye across the road from the RAF Club towards the western tip of Green Park, on Piccadilly. This was a prominent location on a major thoroughfare (and 2012 Olympic route), close to the Memorial Gates monument to Commonwealth troops. As critics of the design would later point out, there was no direct link between Bomber Command and the park.

Green Park has been part of the network of Royal Parks since at least the sixteenth century and was enclosed by Charles II in 1668. According to legend, his wife discovered that the king had been picking flowers during his morning walks in the park to give not to her, but to another woman. Furious, the queen ordered that

Figure 9.7 World War II service recognised on the RAF Memorial at the Embankment.
Source: (D. Williams).

all of its flower beds be ripped up. Since that time, there have been no formal flower arrangements or manicured lawns in Green Park. Part of its distinctive character stems from the way its 19 hectares 'are presented in an informal rural landscape of pasture, meadows and trees' (Royal Parks 2008: 2). Monuments began to encroach on Green Park when the City of Westminster granted permission for the Canada Memorial in 1994 (City of Westminster 2010: 18). In 2000, the council approved the design of the Memorial Gates and it followed this, in 2009, with permission for a cycling docking station at the park's western end (City of Westminster 2010: 18). These changes to the park's landscape became crucial considerations for the council when the Bomber Command Association submitted its designs.

Impressed by the Memorial Gates, in 2010 the Bomber Command Association engaged the architect of that project to create plans for a memorial to their 'boys'. Compared to other World War II monuments in the English capital, Liam O'Connor's design for Bomber Command was of a scale never previously seen in London. Its 85 metre-long colonnade of Portland stone drew on Decimus Burton's screen (1824–5) near Hyde Park, albeit in the Doric, rather than Ionic, order. The proposal was also 37 metres longer than Burton's screen, and twice as deep (City of Westminster 2010: 22). An open pavilion in the middle of the design housed a bronze sculpture by Philip Jackson, depicting seven airmen returned from an operation, mounted on top of a stone plinth. O'Connor's design would necessitate the removal of four mature silver lime trees (to be replaced by 25 new trees), as well as the railing and hedge growing along the perimeter of the site.

Once the plans were made public, Westminster Council began to take consultations, eventually receiving 92 submissions from various individuals and organisations interested in the matter (City of Westminster 2010, pp25–7). Of the 36 letters that raised objections, the strongest voices raised in protest were from conservation and residents' associations such as the Thorney Island Society, the London Society, the Knightsbridge Association, the Westminster Society and the London Parks and Gardens Trust (City of Westminster 2010, pp11–14). Most were sympathetic to the principle of commemorating Bomber Command, but opposed the scale and form of O'Connor's design. The Thorney Island Society was 'at one in regard to remembering the sacrifices made by those who died for the defence of the nation and the freedom of others; but find the concept which requires the destruction of parkland to be completely at odds with the ethos of those who died'. Surely, such a memorial could be 'expressed more modestly with gravitas and sensitivity'? (City of Westminster 2010: 12) For the London Society, the design was 'too dominant and assertive and will radically change the character of this part of the park... compounded by an inscription such as that from Churchill: "The fighters are our salvation but the bombers are our means of victory" which makes it seem more a triumphal arch than a monument to the dead' (City of Westminster 2010: 13). The London Parks and Gardens Trust drew attention to the City of Westminster Council's policy of approving no new memorials in the Hyde Park area, and the Royal Parks moratorium on future monuments. These were 'eminently sensible policies ... based on the premise that it is the green space of parks that should be pre-eminent and that all other considerations should be secondary to the aim of ensuring the public's continued enjoyment and appreciation of the park's quasi natural and quasi rural qualities' (City of Westminster 2010: 13–14).

On architectural and commemorative grounds, the plans came in for even more strident criticism. As the London Parks and Gardens Trust was keen to remind Westminster's councillors, 'there are many servicemen and women to remember and commemorate, and it is the role of the Cenotaph in Whitehall to be the focus for such remembrance'. The Trust saw bigger problems with O'Connor's use of the stripped Doric order: it did 'not bring to mind the buildings of Decimus Burton or Sir Edwin Lutyens so much as the rather chilly Greek revival style promoted by Schinkel and von Klenze in Berlin and Munich... [i]f the references are accidental they are unfortunate, and if deliberate the irony is misplaced' (City of Westminster 2010: 14).

Planning officers at Westminster had similar concerns about the scale of the proposal. They supported the principle of a memorial to Bomber Command in Green Park, but were of the opinion that the proposal 'whilst of considerable architectural and artistic merit, causes substantial harm to the special character of the designated heritage asset of the park, principally as a result of its physical dominance in this parkland setting' (City of Westminster 2010: 5). The proponents had not made a case, in their view, for why the policy for new development in this part of the city ought to be overturned on the basis of exceptional circumstances. Planners were of the view that 'a more modest proposal comprising the principal element of the bronze statue with a suitable scaled supporting plinth only is likely to be considered more favourably' (City of Westminster 2010: 5). In their more detailed considerations of why the proposal was not suitable, planning officers at Westminster gave one final reminder to the council's planning committee: 'officers are mindful that Bomber Command is already remembered in Westminster at the RAF Church of St Clement Danes and the memorial to Air Marshal Harris. They are mindful also that there are no particular links between Bomber Command and The Green Park whereas there are such links with the Embankment, St John's Wood and Regent's Park'.

The committee chairman, Councillor Alastair Moss, took the opposite view. Green Park was nowhere near as saturated with memorials as was, for instance, Hyde Park Corner. Moreover, the Canadians had set a precedent for locating monuments in Green Park when a memorial to their war dead was unveiled near Buckingham Palace in 1994. A member of the Conservative Party and an army reservist, Moss was made chair of the planning committee hearing that considered the Green Park proposal only 24 hours beforehand, filling in for another councillor

Figure 9.8 An open Book of Remembrance, in which are recorded the names of over 155,000 Air Force dead in St Clement Danes, the Central Church of the Royal Air Force.

Source: (D. Williams).

who was ill. Moss walked to the church of St Clement Danes to inspect the Harris statue after reading the Westminster officials' view that Bomber Command was already commemorated there. Beneath Harris's statue, an inscription reads: 'In memory of a great commander and of the brave crews of Bomber Command, more than 55,000 of whom lost their lives in the cause of freedom. The nation owes them all a great debt'. When interviewed, Moss disagreed that the statue constituted a proper memorial to those thousands of men from Britain and the Commonwealth who had died in the skies over Europe: 'It's not. You look at the memorial of Lord Harris: that is a memorial to *him*. If you put a 5-year-old child or a 50-year-old

Figure 9.9 A Bomber Command crest illuminated in St Clement Danes.
Source: (D. Williams).

Figure 9.10 Sir Arthur Harris watching over the forecourt of St Clement Danes.
Source: (D. Williams).

man in front of it and say "Well, what's that about?" they'll say it's about Harris' (Cr Alistair Moss, personal communication, 2 July 2012).

The Harris statue was the last impediment to creating a new site for Bomber Command commemoration in Green Park. In a general election year and with UK forces still on deployment in Afghanistan, the leaders of the Conservative, Labour and the Liberal Democratic Parties all gave their support to the Bomber Command Association's proposal. Moss's committee approved the application without significant modification.

During the consultation period planning and architecture critic Tom Ball, a committee member of the Thorney Island Society, became one of the best-known opponents of the design. After the design was approved by council he published a scathing letter in the press:

> The Bomber Command memorial proposed for Green Park is a very serious misuse of the park, of the powers of democracy, and of the media. The myth that there is no memorial to Bomber Command in central London has duped many into being supporters. Those who died are individually remembered in the books of remembrance in the RAF's memorial church, St Clement Dane's, where there are also statues to Harris and Dowding, and there is a memorial in Lincoln Cathedral, near several airfields. ...
>
> The failure to protect Green Park, which has existed as 'countryside in the city' for centuries, amounts to a major injustice. Westminster set aside its policies, which said no more memorials in the Hyde Park area; the royal parks waived their policy of a moratorium on any more memorials; and the mayor, Boris Johnson, would not comment, although the park is metropolitan open land. There are alternative sites, but there is no alternative to the precious space, which, once lost, cannot be replaced.
>
> (Ball 2010)

The extent to which the views of organisations such as the Thorney Island Society diverged from the Bomber Command Association (and its supporters) made for sensational reporting of the issue in the press. In the main, the well-informed views of Ball and others were 'balanced' with the opinions of ageing Bomber Command ex-servicemen, whose outrage at any criticism of the memorial was almost guaranteed (*Camden New Journal*, 7 May 2010). Furthermore, newspapers such as the *Daily Telegraph*, which had been advocating the memorial, had been letting veterans get away with making blatantly incorrect statements since the beginning of the campaign. In the *Telegraph* article by Alec Lom that marked the beginning of the Heritage Foundation's appeal, Bomber Command Association president Sir Michael Beetham stated that Bomber Command had 'nothing' when it came to memorials (9 March 2008). Such reporting, however, was consistent with the lionising of veterans that reached giddy heights in the unveiling and dedication ceremony itself, to which I shall now turn.

Figure 9.11 RAF side chapel in Lincoln Cathedral.
Source: (D. Williams).

'What they did for us was simply quite extraordinary': unveiling the memorial to Bomber Command.

Thursday 28 June 2012 was a bright, sunny day in London: a perfect day for a celebration held during Armed Forces Week. The Bomber Command Association could scarcely have hoped for better conditions to welcome the Queen, members of the Royal Family, VIPs and guests to Green Park for the memorial's dedication and unveiling. Given the warm weather, scores of Air Force officer cadets and members of the RAF Benevolent Fund (which was to take on responsibility for the memorial's upkeep) were on hand to give out bottles of water. Hydration, however, came too late for some who fainted in the heat.

Two major spaces were fenced off from the rest of Green Park for guests attending the ceremony. An area just to the south of the memorial, with a view of proceedings, was allocated to the Royal Family, visiting dignitaries, senior officers, Bomber Command veterans and a scattering of British celebrities that included actors Stephen Fry and Vicki Michelle (Michelle had succeeded Robin Gibb as president of the Heritage Foundation after his death). Further to the east was a larger 'Salute Area' that seated about 3,000 people, mostly ex-servicemen and women, their families and friends who had been allocated tickets in a ballot. Being unable to see the ceremony from there, people in those seats watched and listened to a broadcast projected onto large screens, compered by television host and RAF Benevolent Fund patron Carol Vorderman.

Figure 9.12 Bomber Command memorial window, Lincoln Cathedral.
Source: (D. Williams).

Figure 9.13 RAF officer cadets feeling the heat in Green Park, while civilians head for the Spitfire Bar (far left).
Source: (D. Williams).

Vorderman kept those in the Salute Area entertained by interviewing ageing Bomber Command men on their war service while the crowd waited for the Queen to arrive. Vorderman had little difficulty in holding her interlocutors' attention while doing her best to channel a wartime pin-up model. Next to her, they were young men again (repeatedly, the crowd was told that the average age of aircrew had been just 22).

In between those dialogues, music by Vaughan Williams, Elgar and Grainger was played by the Central Band of the RAF and the Band of the RAF Regiment. For the benefit of people not so familiar with Bomber Command's history, a three-part documentary on the force was shown to the crowd. Occasionally the film's producers flicked the switch to vaudeville: in one scene, the narrator mimicked the voice of a German general who was surprised at the news of an attack by Bomber Command. The voice exclaimed (in English, with a thick German accent) 'Vhat is dis?!' Most people, however, paid little attention, preferring instead to take in the carnival atmosphere, talking to those around them and fortifying themselves at the Spitfire Bar.

At noon, a trumpet fanfare and a colour party signalled the arrival of the Queen, dressed in purple, accompanied by the male members of her family in RAF uniform. The able-bodied stood to sing 'God Save the Queen' before the chairman of the Bomber Command Association, Air Commodore Malcolm White, gave his

Figure 9.14 Young men again: Carol Vorderman interviewing veterans in the Salute Area.
Source: (D. Williams).

Figure 9.15 'Vhat is dis?' Hitler and henchmen appear in the Salute Area.
Source: (D. Williams).

welcome address. He was the first of several speakers. Not one of them was an elected representative of the people. 'What they did for us', White told the assembled crowd, 'was simply quite extraordinary'. The Queen and the Duke of Edinburgh made their way over to Jackson's statue, which was shrouded by a large sheet of fabric. After a couple of royal tugs on a long rope, the sheet fell away, exposing the huge bronze aircrew that dwarfed the monarch and her husband. Applause from people gathered on both sides of Piccadilly filled the atrium. The wall behind the royal party was inscribed with a dedication to the 55,573 war dead who had flown with Bomber Command. On the opposite wall, Churchill is quoted from 1942: it was with the 'bombers alone' that victory would come. It was evidence of this kind that the Bomber Command Association liked to cite as *post hoc* justification for its memorial – the wartime prime minister's later reticence about the bombing campaign notwithstanding. Those seated in the bleachers directly opposite would not easily have been able to read a third inscription, subtly located just below the aluminium canopy: 'This memorial also commemorates the people of all nations who lost their lives in the bombing campaigns of 1939–1945'.

Jackson's statue now unveiled, the RAF's chaplain-in-chief followed with prayers for peace and fellowship before he led the audience in reciting the Lord's Prayer. Hymns and readings from Isaiah followed and then the Chief of the Air Staff, Air Chief Marshal Sir Stephen Dalton, addressed the audience. His speech emphasised that the aircrew in Bomber Command had been volunteers, that they

Figure 9.16 Flocking to watch the royals arrive.
Source: (D. Williams).

had suffered greatly, had engaged in individual acts of great bravery and had relieved the starving Dutch towards the end of the war during Operation Manna. On the greater part of Bomber Command's work – bombing cities – Dalton referred only to 'their dedication to doing their duty'.

The idea of freedom being paid for through blood sacrifice was a constant one during the ceremony. When the chaplain-in-chief dedicated the memorial in the name of the Trinity, he prayed that it would 'remind us … of the freedom and liberty that was bought for us through the bravery and skill of the aircrew'. Part-way through his dedication, he was interrupted by an Avro Lancaster from the Battle of Britain Memorial Flight. Somewhat fittingly, given Bomber Command's patchy record as a precision bombing force, its payload of red poppies missed the target over Green Park, appearing like a spray of blood against the blue sky. The Ode to the Fallen, the Last Post, a minute's silence and Reveille followed, to which those present listened with a solemnity learned from the liturgies of remembrance developed after World War I.

Of the speakers on the day, the clergy were the most effusive in their praise. But in reports of the event, nothing quite matched the hyperbole of the *Telegraph*'s online correspondent who observed: '[The] Ingenuity of veterans knows no bounds, [as] many have now crafted their complimentary copies of the RAF news into paper hats. Brollies brought in anticipation of rain are now parasols' (Holehouse 2012).

Given the *Telegraph*'s active role in pushing for the memorial, such coverage was perhaps unsurprising. But it was not markedly different from that broadcast and printed by other outlets. The media had time to plan around the spectacle of the event and its promise of moving testimony. When asked why he thought the Bomber Command commemorations had attracted such a large crowd, BBC deployment editor James Buchanan reiterated the value of veterans' stories:

> It's taken years to get this point and here we are and suddenly everybody's waking up to what happened and what they all did and as the publicity has grown people have begun to realise that if you speak to any one of these guys, they've got incredible stories to tell, amazing stories to tell.

Buchanan expanded on the stories that resonated with the BBC audience:

> I was just talking earlier to a veteran from Canada … who was shot down, captured by the Gestapo, sent to a concentration camp, was about to be shot and then the German air force heard about where he was and rescued him shortly before he was due to be executed. These are great stories and most of the men here can tell you astonishing stories about what they did and it was just normal for them. It has a real resonance among today's generation and I think with the [Queen's] jubilee this year we've been looking back and this event has kind of captivated people.
>
> (James Buchanan, personal communication, 28 June 2012)

In the events surrounding the planning and unveiling of the Bomber Command Memorial we can see how the late modern appetite for 'amazing', 'great' and 'astonishing' stories of suffering aligns with a contemporary politics of distrust in elected representatives and the lauding of moneyed interests. Combined, this allowed the organisers to take those surviving airmen, and us, back to a retro version of 1942, just without the rationing, the fear and the uncertainty over which side would prevail. Vorderman's channelling of a pin-up girl, the Spitfire Bar, the comical digs at the Nazi commanders, the young men and women in RAF uniform; they all could have been from 'some sunny day' that Vera Lynn sang about during the dark days of the war. Only the Iraq and Afghanistan campaign medals that many of those younger officers, airmen and women wore on their chests served to remind us that this was a very 2012 moment. For those people in attendance who had flown in 1942, and then survived the other long years of the war, evidently catharsis brought its own consolation. As one Bomber Command man told the BBC after the service:

> I lost my brother, I lost close relatives, school mates, friends that I made in the service and to see them all going down, disappearing, never having known the joy of having a life [pauses]. I used to get choked. But they've done such a lovely job here. I feel different. That's all I can say on there. I do feel different. I think it's marvellous.

(BBC 2012)

References

Armitage, M. (1999). *The Royal Air Force* (London: Cassell).
Ball, T. (2010). 'Letter to the editor'. *The Guardian*, 17 July. Available from: www.theguardian.com/uk/2010/jul/17/there-are-peace-memorials-too [13 November 2014].
BBC (2010). *Breakfast*, 14 May. Available from: http://youtu.be/WfCJaaGCdHk [27 October 2014].
BBC (2012). 'HM The Queen unveils Bomber Command Memorial' (video file). Available from: http://youtu.be/jVnanoHzE3U [26 October 2014].
Buruma, I. (2013). *Year Zero: A History of 1945* (London: Atlantic Books).
Butler, K. J. (2009). 'Their culture has survived: witnessing to (dis)possession in Bra Boys' (2007). *Journal of Australian Studies, 33*(4), 391–404.
Cannings, S. (2012). *Sandy's Blog*, 2 July. Available from: www.sandycanblog.blogspot.com.au/2012/07/bomber-command-memorial-dedication.html [29 October 2014].
City of Westminster (2010). Temporary Planning Applications Sub-Committee, 'Report of Strategic Director Built Environment', 13 May. Available from: http://transact.westminster.gov.uk/CSU/Planning Applications Committees/2008 onwards/2010/17 – 13 May/ITEM 01 – The Green Park, Piccadilly, W1.PDF [18 August 2012].
Flanagan, R. (2013). *The Narrow Road to the Deep North* (Sydney: Vintage).
Frost, W. and Laing, J. (2013). *Commemorative Events: Memory, Identity, Conflict* (London: Routledge).
Holehouse, M. (2012). 'Bomber Command memorial service: as it happened'. *Daily Telegraph*, 28 June. Available from: www.telegraph.co.uk/history/raf-bomber-command/9361572/Bomber-Command-memorial-service-as-it-happened.html [28 October 2014].

Keegan, J. (1976). *The Face of Battle* (London: Jonathan Cape).

The Royal Parks (2008). 'St James's Park and The Green Park Management Plan (2008–2018)'. Available from: www.royalparks.org.uk/__data/assets/pdf_file/0008/41768/st-james-and-green-park-management-plan.pdf [12 November 2014].

Scates, B., McCosker, A., Reeves, K., Wheatley, R. and Williams, D. (2013). *Anzac Journeys: Returning to the Battlefields of World War II* (Melbourne: Cambridge University Press).

Twomey, C. (2013). 'Prisoners of war of the Japanese: war and memory in Australia'. *Memory Studies, 6*(3), 321–30.

10 The ghosts of Changi

Captivity and pilgrimage in Singapore

Kevin Blackburn

On the morning of every 15 February, to mark the anniversary of the surrender of Singapore to the Japanese in 1942, Australian veterans and their families gather around the Cenotaph at Martin Place in the centre of Sydney. An army band marches playing the stirring strains of 'Waltzing Matilda'. A dwindling band of veterans from the battalions turn up with their banners and wreaths. The guest of honour is always the Governor of New South Wales, and members of the armed services are represented by senior serving officers. This ceremony has been occurring since 1946, soon after the veterans returned to Australia. At the ceremony in 2006, Rowley Richards, a former President of the veterans' association of the 8th Division, said of the event 'It's a responsibility we owe our mates that are not here and who did not come back'. He added that, for many of the veterans, the date was of equal importance to Anzac Day, while for some it was of greater significance to them. Richards was quick to add 'but it doesn't denigrate in any way Anzac Day. I mean they're two that complement one another' (*ABC Online,* cited in Jung 2010).

On the same day at the same time, in Singapore, ever-decreasing numbers of the ageing wartime generation who lived through the Japanese Occupation gather around the Civilian War Memorial in the heart of the civic district to remember their common experience of suffering during the war. This ceremony has been held since 1967 when the monument was first unveiled by Lee Kuan Yew, Singapore's Prime Minister (1959–90), only two years following Singapore's independence. The memorial was erected after Singapore had exhumed the bodies of thousands of civilians massacred by the Japanese in the days following the fall of Singapore in 1942. The monument consists of four pillars that represent the collective wartime suffering of the four main racial groups of Singapore, the Chinese, Malays, Indians and Eurasians. The pillars are joined at the base and extend 67.4metres into the sky. Under the memorial are 600 urns filled with the remains of 20,000 Singapore Chinese massacred by the Japanese after the British surrender. They are known as the *sook ching*, meaning 'to purge'. At the 2007 service Madam Tan Siew Gek, a grandmother in her 70s, mentioned in Chinese 'I left the house without telling my family. I felt I must come to pay my respects to those I knew who died'. Present at the ceremony have also been war veterans from Australia and Britain and their families who later make their way to Changi and the war memorial to the

Figure 10.1 The Kranji War Cemetery with the Singapore Memorial (known locally as the Kranji War Memorial) in the background.
Source: The Author.

Commonwealth military dead at Kranji. Australian veterans travelling to Singapore to mark 15 February have attended the ceremony since the unveiling of the monument in 1967.

The battle for Singapore

The history of the fall of Singapore, its captivity and the Japanese Occupation is a compelling one. Japan's attack on Malaya and Singapore began at the same time as Japanese planes were bombing Pearl Harbor, on the morning of 7 December 1941 Hawaiian time. In the early hours of the morning of 8 December 1941 Malayan time, Japanese bombs rained down on the Singapore civilian population, while 600 kilometres to the north at Kota Bharu Australian aircrew in Hudson bombers were dropping their own bombs on Japanese seaborne invasion landing parties. Out of the 5,000-strong Japanese Kota Bharu invasion force, 320 Japanese soldiers lost their lives before they took the town.

In Singapore, thousands of civilians died in Japanese air raids. While the first air raid was on the day of the outbreak of war, the second did not occur until the night of 29 December 1941. Then on 31 December 1941 there were two air raids. From 2 January 1942 Singapore was bombed almost every day. Tragic events occurred: the Japanese bombers mistook the rickshaws parked at Clifford Pier in Singapore for anti-aircraft guns, killing the rickshaw pullers and their passengers.

THE MALAYAN CAMPAIGN
8 DECEMBER 1941–31 JANUARY 1942

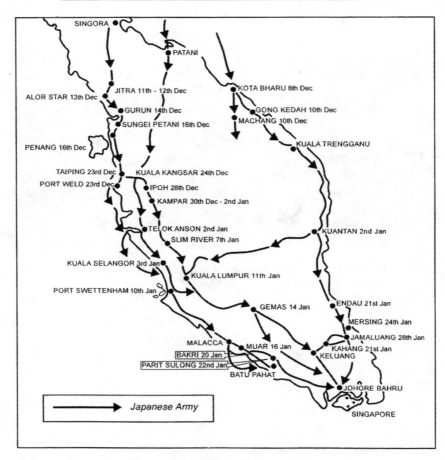

Figure 10.2 Map of the Malayan Campaign, 8 December 1941–31 January 1942.
Source: The Author.

Landing unopposed on the beaches of Southern Thailand, the Japanese main force quickly crossed over the border with Malaya. British commanders had long suspected the Japanese would attack Singapore this way and had prepared Operation Matador to send troops into Thailand to prevent the Japanese landing on the Thai beaches. But they dithered and never implemented the plan for fear of violating Thailand's sovereignty. After this initial failure, British and Indian troops were caught on the back foot with hastily prepared defences as they lost a succession of battles down the west side of Malaya, first at Jitra on 12 December, then at Gurun on 15 December.

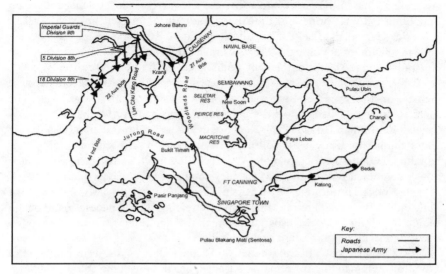

THE ATTACK ON SINGAPORE
8 FEBRUARY - 9 FEBRUARY 1942

Figure 10.3 Map of the attack on Singapore, 8–9 February 1942.
Source: The Author.

From New Year's Eve into the first few days of 1942 the only real prospect of significantly delaying the Japanese was fighting by British and Indian troops at Kampar, a naturally defensive position on a mountainside that overlooked Japanese approaches. However, there was little air support because the British government had sent the best planes to the Middle East and Russia. When war broke out in Malaya there were a paltry 158 planes out of the 336 that the British high command estimated it needed to defend Malaya and Singapore, most of them obsolete or inferior to Japanese planes. With little air support, the British and Indians at Kampar were eventually outflanked by boat landings behind them, and forced to withdraw. On 7 January 1942, at Slim River further down the western side of Malaya, another disastrous battle occurred when the Japanese used tanks to smash through the British and Indian positions. The British government had refused to supply the defence of Singapore with tanks, believing that they could not be used in the terrain.

During the first month of the fighting retreat down the Malay Peninsula the Australian Army had yet to be in combat. This soon changed when its commander, Maj Gen Gordon Bennett of the Australian 8th Division was given the job of defending the Malay state of Johore. An ambush on 14 January 1942 at Gemencheh Bridge on the inland trunk road resulted in its being blown up after several hundred Japanese had crossed over. B Company of the 2/30th Battalion machine-gunned the Japanese who had crossed the bridge, but when a promised artillery barrage failed to follow up this success the Australians were forced to hastily retreat since more than a battalion of Japanese soldiers had already crossed the bridge. For the Australians this initial success in their first encounter with the Japanese meant upholding national pride and the Anzac tradition of martial prowess. Lt Col Frederick Gallagher 'Black Jack' Galleghan of the 2/30th said before the ambush: 'The reputation of not only the AIF [Australian Imperial Force] in Malaya, but of Australia, is in the hands of this unit' (Galleghan, cited in Wigmore 1957).

At the same time as the Australians were having their initial success around Gemas, disaster was befalling them on their western flank at the coast. The Japanese Imperial Guards had crossed the Muar River and overwhelmed the poorly trained 45th Indian Brigade. The New South Wales 2/19th Battalion was sent to shore things up. They were followed by the 2/29th 'Boys from Melbourne' battalion. Despite the Victorian 4th Anti-Tank Regiment having success stopping a tank column at Bakri behind Muar, they soon had to retreat as a large force of Japanese began infiltrating behind them. The 2/19th, 2/29th and soldiers of the 45th Indian Brigade were prevented from retreating by a Japanese roadblock at the Parit Sulong Bridge. Desperate to break through, they resorted to bayonet-charging machine-gun positions on the bridge.

On 22 January 1942, Lt Col Charles Anderson, of the 2/19th Australian Infantry Battalion, commanding the remaining troops, began to lead the able-bodied men around the Japanese road blocks and through the swamps back to Australian lines. The wounded had to be left to surrender, but were later massacred by the Japanese at the bridge. Left behind were 110 Australian and 35 Indian wounded. Out of these, only three Australians survived the Japanese massacre. Anderson won a Victoria Cross for the amazing feat in breaking out of the encirclement, with only 550 Indians and 400 Australians making it back to their own lines (Percival 1948). He needed 690 reinforcements to raise the strength to his battalion to around 900 men, since only 219 men were left (Australian War Memorial 52 8/3/19/9).

The collapse of the western flank of Johore's defences forced a general retreat back to Singapore, where preparations were made for the final defence of the island once the last troops had crossed over the Causeway and it was blown up on 31 January 1942. When the Japanese marshalled their forces and attacked Singapore on the night of 8–9 February 1942 they passed through widely dispersed Australian battalions along the western coast of Singapore. Another attack was launched between the Kranji River and the Causeway on the night of 9–10 February 1942. Lt Gen Arthur Ernest Percival, the General Officer Commanding, Malaya Command, had believed the Japanese attack would come in the east, so had kept the fresh British 18th Division there.

The Australian battalions, including the badly mauled 2/19th and 2/29th, crumbled under the full onslaught of three Japanese divisions. From the west, Japanese troops came down Lim Chu Kang Road then onto Jurong Road. From the north, they barreled down Woodlands Road. Within a matter of days they were on the outskirts of Singapore town and surrender was inevitable. On 15 February 1942, Lt Gen Percival met his Japanese counterpart Lt Gen Tomoyuki Yamashita at Japanese military headquarters in the Ford Factory around the Bukit Timah area of Singapore. He surrendered unconditionally to Yamashita 130,000 Allied soldiers who became prisoners. The majority of the prisoners, more than 55,000, were Indians who were separated from the Australian and British soldiers and taken to various camps on Singapore island.[1]

Captivity in Changi

On 17 February, the Japanese sent 50,000 British and Australian prisoners into the Changi area, the former barracks of the soldiers guarding the big guns of Singapore. Out of the 50,000 in Changi, 14,972 were Australians, while the rest were mainly British (Wigmore 1957). The statistics for battle casualties as compared to losses in captivity are startling. A total of 138,000 Allied soldiers took part in the Malayan campaign. More than 8,000 were killed. In the Malayan campaign, out of 18,490 Australian soldiers, 1,789 were killed, while 1,306 were wounded. Of the 14,972 Australians taken prisoner at the fall of Singapore, 4,766 would die in captivity under the Japanese between 1942 and 1945. Overall, almost one in three Australians would die as PoWs compared to about 10 per cent who were killed in battle.[2]

Very few, however, would die in Changi. Conditions at Changi were much better than at other camps, such as those on the Burma–Thailand Railway and in Borneo. As Australian ex-PoW Fred Stringer recalled to Hank Nelson and Tim Bowden on ABC Radio in 1984, Changi seemed 'like Heaven' when compared to many of the places to which the PoWs were later sent to labour for the Japanese (Nelson 1985). Of the 87,000 PoWs who went through Changi en route to other places, 809 died (*Straits Times*, 7 September 1945). They were buried in Changi's own cemetery. The breakdown of the PoWs buried in the Changi cemetery is 549 British, 165 Australians, 94 Dutch and 1 other (Lewis Bryan 1946: 66). Thus, Changi had a death rate lower than 1 per cent, compared to the Burma–Thailand Railway's 20.4 per cent (12,619 died out of the 61,811 PoWs on the railway). Of the 2,434 prisoners in the Borneo camp of Sandakan only 6 survived its deprivations and death marches, and they were the ones who managed to escape (Beattie 2007: 41; Silver 2000).

Perhaps because Changi is the best-known Japanese PoW camp it has been assumed in the popular imagination that it was a 'hell-hole'. This image is generally not held by many of its ex-PoWs who were transferred from Changi to camps along the Burma–Thailand Railway, or who came through Changi from Indonesian PoW camps on their way to the Railway. Former PoW Stan Arneil of the 2/30th Battalion has noted the discrepancy between the public image of Changi and the perceptions of many ex-PoWs who had spent time in other Japanese PoW camps. Arneil wrote that 'the portrayal of the "dreaded Changi" camp brings a smile to the faces of many former prisoners of war who longed for Changi as almost a heaven on earth compared to some of the dreadful places to which they were taken' (Arneil 1982).

Changi, especially in its early days, was unlike other Japanese PoW camps. The camp was virtually semi-autonomous, and run day-to-day, not by the Japanese, but by the prisoners' own military commanders. Ex-PoWs have often commented that in Changi, because their own military administration was responsible for the camp, they did not come into regular contact with Japanese guards (Havers 2003: 56–8, 60, 114–17; Havers 2000: 17–36). Kenneth Harrison, of the Victorian 4th Anti-Tank Regiment, recalled that, in 1942 at Changi, 'one could go months without seeing a Japanese' (Harrison 1966). Hugh Clarke, of the Queensland 2/10th Field Regiment, explained why: 'One virtue of Changi was that the Japanese guards remained outside the camp, the administration being left to our own officers' (Clarke and Burgess 1992: 112). Roy Whitecross, from the 8th Division headquarters, elaborated:

> Generally speaking, we were left to ourselves. In the main camp area Japanese soldiers were rarely seen. Day to Day administration of the camp was at the time almost entirely in the hands of our senior officers. The camp headquarters were certainly in daily contact with the Japanese... Orders and instructions were received by headquarters from the Japanese, passed on to the troops through our established routine of brigade headquarters, unit headquarters, and finally to the rank and file of the division.
>
> (Whitecross 1951)

This relative autonomy meant that the prisoners had time on their hands in the early days of captivity during 1942. To fill in this time they arranged many activities. They held frequent concert parties, played a lot of sport, had a library and even conducted educational courses on topics from mechanics to ancient history. This educational centre was colloquially referred to as 'Changi University'. Food and medical conditions were also better than those at many other camps. Loet Velmans, a Dutch PoW, described the life of the Changi camp after arriving in late 1942 from the Java camps:

> The barracks were a cosmopolitan mini-metropolis. Bandung had been a provincial backwater compared to Singapore. The PoWs who were already there had developed an amazing menu of activities to keep us occupied – from international soccer matches, chess and bridge tournaments, art shows, comedy theatre, and classical and jazz concerts to lectures in mathematics, drawing, philosophy, English literature, history of art, ancient and modern history, French, Chinese, and many other subjects.
>
> (Velmans 2011: 93)

The area the PoWs occupied for most of their imprisonment consisted of the former Changi British military barracks, which had been part of the British defence of Singapore. However, as George Aspinall of the 2/30th Battalion observed, in the popular imagination the PoWs were always in Changi Prison, which was a civilian prison built in 1936 (Bowden 1984: 134). Only in May 1944 were between 7,000 and 8,000 PoWs moved to Changi Prison proper. The prison had been built for 600 inmates. The Japanese wanted to use the barracks to accommodate their own air force personnel who operated the military airfield that the PoWs had built. The PoWs were kept both inside and outside the walls of Changi Prison proper, surrounded by barbed wire and fences on the outside. The prison had been used since 1942 to house about 3,400 male and female civilian internees, who in May 1944 were moved to the Sime Road camp.

The PoWs in Changi often went 'under the wire' to trade with the Chinese in order to get extra food. Aspinall remembered:

> Just about every second PoW was a scrounger by fair means or foul. We regarded the Japanese as fair game. If we could pinch something from them, we would. The native population had much the same idea, and a lot of the material we scrounged would be sold to the Chinese for food – the Japanese money wasn't worth anything. Petrol was a good commodity. A couple of gallons of petrol was worth about a dozen coconuts or a hand of bananas. We developed quite a complex trading system with the Asian community and it was very successful. Our prime needs were food, medicines or drugs if possible, and they needed materials of any description to help in their local businesses. We had a very good relationship with the local people.
>
> (Bowden 1984: 135)

George Williamson of the 2/18th Battalion recalled 'I tell you, what the Chows had was absolutely fantastic. Leave K-Mart for dead' (Elliot and Silver 2006: 96).

At home: imagining captivity of loved ones

Many of the relatives of the PoWs waited for long periods to hear whether their loved ones had been killed in the last days of battle or been taken prisoner. They imagined all kinds of fates that might have happened to them in places that many had heard of but few had seen.

Flt Lt Oscar Diamond had piloted one of the Royal Australian Air Force (RAAF) Hudsons that had bombed the Japanese landing at Kota Bharu. His squadron moved to Singapore and then to Java, where he was taken prisoner. He went through Changi on the way to labour for the Japanese in the mines of Manchuria. It was not until 22 November 1943 that the RAAF sent Diamond's mother, Rosetta, a telegram confirming that her son was a PoW. They had received a letter from him addressed to her.

As early as March 1942, Rosetta had some indication that her son was a PoW. On his way home to Rockhampton, Oscar's comrade Cpl Walter Kenneth Hams dropped by Rosetta's house in Brisbane and told her that he had last seen Oscar with a group of airmen who were cut off and had no means of escape, just before the surrender of Java on 8 March 1942. Oscar's mates kept her informed and she was able to prod the RAAF authorities to provide more details on her son. In November 1943, Rosetta had written to the RAAF when she had heard that her son had made a broadcast in July 1942 over Japanese radio: 'I ask you to be so kind to give details if possible of this Broadcast made from Batavia regarding this officer. I might mention I am his mother, and both his father and I are most anxious to know anything you may have to tell us' (Diamond 1942). Only then in November 1943 did the RAAF confirm the fate of her son.

When another broadcast to his mother and father was made over Japanese radio on 1 October 1944, the authorities cautioned Rosetta not to fully believe it despite Oscar mentioning his girlfriend Norma whom he would later marry when he returned to Brisbane: 'I am well and keeping fit. I spend my time reading and doing light exercise. You are always in my thoughts. Hope we may be together again. Remember me to Norma. Love, your son, Oscar' (Diamond 1942).

Oscar's 'light exercise' was of course heavy labour in the mines, but apart from that, the message was genuinely from him. Oscar did return in September 1945, flown back from Mukden after having slaved in the mines of Manchuria. Along with his family and girlfriend's warm embraces he also received the Distinguished Flying Cross for his bravery at Kota Bharu and later in Sumatra and Java.

The wait of other mothers did not end as happily as Rosetta's did. Amelia Grace Hall, of Prahran in Melbourne, was the mother of Jack Russell Hall, who was aged 25 when he was killed with many members of his unit, the 2/29th Battalion, in the Battle of Muar on 20 January 1942. Her other son, Raymond Lindsey Hall, died in Changi on 30 March 1945. For 12 years she prayed 'Let me live until I see my sons' graves in Singapore'. In 1957 she was selected to be one of the 17 members of the Australian official delegation to be present at the opening of Kranji War Cemetery in Singapore, where her two sons were buried. Upon flying into Singapore aboard a government-paid Qantas flight, she said 'It's wonderful how one's dreams can come true' (*Straits Times*, 28 February 1957).

Early pilgrimages to the sites of captivity and the battlefields

In early post-war period, air travel to Singapore was expensive. The first veteran to fly there and visit Changi was 'Black Jack' Galleghan. Now a brigadier, he arrived by flying boat on 9 January 1948 and was met by three former 2/30th Battalion members who were now part of Singapore's colonial administration. They presented him with a 'bouquet' of one egg, soya and a tin of bully beef. The card on the bouquet read 'Memo: Black Jack – your ration sir'. His ex-PoW comrades then took him on a tour of Changi Prison (*Straits Times*, 9 and 10 January 1948; *Malaya Tribune*, 10 January 1948).

After the war, many former PoWs worked in the colonial administration of Singapore. They began in the 1950s to turn the Changi area into a commemorative site for themselves and the small number of returning veterans and their families. In August 1957, the chapel in Changi Prison, which had been created in 1953, was rededicated to the ex-PoWs who were arriving in increasing numbers. Major W. L. P. Sochon, the Commissioner of Prisons, remarked that 'many visiting relatives asked to see Changi but there had been no lasting memorial there for them to visit'. He added that during the war '[t]here was no chapel in the jail so we have converted an isolation ward in the hospital block into a chapel which is to be dedicated as a memorial to those who lost their lives here' (*Straits Times*, 14 August 1957).

Among the organisations that contributed to the new chapel were the Returned Servicemen's League of Australia, the Young Wives' Association of the RAF,

Changi, the Chaplain General of the Forces stationed in Singapore, the Rotary Club, the PoW Association of Melbourne and the Dutch and United States Consulates in Singapore. In attendance at the dedication was William A. C. Goode, the colonial administration's chief secretary, who became Governor of Singapore at the end of 1957.

In the same year that the Changi Prison Chapel became a memorial for the PoWs and civilian internees who had died at Changi, the Kranji War Cemetery was officially opened and its memorial to those with no known grave unveiled. All the 809 PoWs buried at the Changi PoW cemeteries were exhumed and moved to Kranji in order to make way for expansion of the airfield that the PoWs had had to build under the Japanese. It became an RAF airfield for the returning and eventually Changi International Airport after the British gave up the base in the 1970s. The first large group of Australians visiting Changi to refer to themselves as being on 'an Australian pilgrimage' came to Singapore to witness the official unveiling at Kranji War Cemetery on 2 March 1957 of the memorial to 24,000 members of the Commonwealth armed forces who had lost their lives in the war against Japan in Southeast Asia. Among the names were 1,647 Australians. Of the 3,955 graves at Kranji, 1,121 contain Australians (Department of Defence nd).

Gordon Bennett led the Australians on this 1957 pilgrimage. He toured by car, with his wife and *aide-de-camp* Captain L. Logan, to the Malayan battlefields around Gemas and Muar where many Australians had fought and died. Bennett then revisited the Western and Northern battlefields of Singapore. The official group he was leading included members of the Australian armed forces, war widows and Australian ex-PoWs, such as the surgeon Albert Coates (*Sunday Times* (Singapore), 3 March 1957: 11; *Straits Times*, 4 March 1957).

Battlefield tours of Malaya (after 1963 known as Malaysia) and Singapore became an important element of return visits and pilgrimages by Australian veterans and their families during the 1960s. In February 1962, Reginald William James Newton, a former officer in the 2/19th Battalion, visited both Malaya and Singapore with six other ex-PoWs for three weeks. They travelled by train from Singapore to Kuala Lumpur, where they had been locked up in Pudu Gaol after being taken prisoner at the Battle of Muar. At the Parit Sulong massacre site they embedded a plaque in the bridge in memory of their comrades who had been killed there. In Singapore they unveiled another battalion plaque at the Changi Prison chapel. Newton commented that the places he and the other veterans had visited 'all bring back memories of the war and of friends, some of whom were unlucky and did not survive' (*Straits Times*, 7 February 1962).

There were changes in the commemorative sites because of the increasing number of veterans visiting Changi on pilgrimage during the 1960s as the age of mass air travel emerged. In 1963 the Changi Prison Chapel was completely refurbished. The significance of the Chapel was recognised by the Returned & Services League of Australia (RSL), which donated 20 pews, a carpet and wall fittings to renovate the chapel in memory of the PoWs and civilian internees who had died at Changi. These were presented on behalf of the RSL by the Australian High Commission in Singapore. As a result of this refurbishment Changi Prison

Chapel was re-dedicated on 5 May 1963 by Bishop Hobart Amstutz of the Methodist Church in Singapore (Singapore Tourism Promotion Board records nd, ref PD/PRJ/45/87, vols 2 and 8). Bishop Amstutz had himself been a civilian internee in Changi Prison during the Japanese Occupation, and had conducted religious services there.

By the early 1970s, with the introduction of the jumbo jet, the cost of air travel decreased and large numbers of Australian and British veterans and their families began making the pilgrimage to Singapore. In October 1972, a group of British relatives of PoWs arrived in Singapore on the 'Memory Lane' tour of Singapore and the Burma–Thailand Railway. Journalist Nancy Bramji evocatively described meeting them at the airport:

> They walked out of the arrival hall of the Singapore airport and looked around rather cautiously, unlike other groups of tourists. Then tears filled their eyes…'We're here! We made it!' some of them whispered to their relatives and colleagues among the group of 40, including 22 former prisoners-of-war who were held here during the Japanese Occupation.

The growth of battlefield tourism in Singapore

In the 1970s and 1980s there was a growing consciousness among Singapore government officials of the value of battlefield tourism as an activity that could be promoted to assist Singapore's economic development. These tourists might want to spend their money seeing new battlefield attractions. The decision to embark upon promoting such tourism in Singapore was initiated by Prime Minister Lee Kuan Yew. In November 1970, Lee sent a memorandum to Runme Shaw, Chairman of the Singapore Tourist Promotion Board, instructing him to turn Singapore's World War II sites into tourist attractions:

> I have visited Gettysburg when I was on my way to Washington. Herewith some pamphlets. It occurred to me that whilst we do not have our own Gettysburg, there were some battles fought as the Japanese crossed the Causeway into Singapore…

(Lee 1970)

Lee's memo prompted the Singapore tourism officials to add to the commemorative sites that the colonial administration had created. In 1974, a waxwork was created of the surrender of the Japanese to Lord Mountbatten and the returning British army on 12 September 1945. It was followed in 1981 by another waxwork of the surrender of the British to the Japanese in 1942. Lee maintained an interest in battlefield tourism, setting up in 1983 a high-level After the Battle Committee to assess which sites could be promoted to tourists (After the battle file nd, ref. TPB/J-2/81). When in 1986 Changi Prison Chapel was closed to visitors after hostages were taken in a prison in neighbouring Malaysia, the officials of the

Singapore Tourism Promotion Board replaced it with a replica of a PoW chapel and a museum standing next to the Changi Prison.

Singapore tourism officials meticulously planned the new Changi chapel and an accompanying museum to target Australian and British tourists' eye for rustic simplicity and desire for close historical authenticity when gazing at relics of the PoW past. The problem of what the chapel was to look like was resolved when one of the consultants on the project, Robertson Collins, glanced through a book from the library of Changi Prison's chaplain, the Reverend Henry Khoo. The book, *Churches of Captivity in Malaya*, from 1946, showed in watercolours, sketches and photographs more than 16 chapels that had been used by the PoWs around Changi and Singapore. Collins selected as the chapel that the Singapore Tourist Promotion Board would recreate a simple outdoor chapel pictured against the wall of Changi Prison, St Paul's. The chapel was an open-air structure made from rough wooden planks erected with a simple, high, 'A'-framed roof, covered in attap palm leaves and tropical flowers from creeping vines (Collins 2003: 47; Lee 2004, pp177–8; for original image see Lewis Bryan 1946: 65).

Pamelia Lee, the director of the project, wanted the chapel to be in the shadow of Changi Prison for atmosphere. She picked a site for the chapel where the tourists could see Changi Prison's 'gurkha guards on duty at their turret towers' in the near background. She reasoned '[i]f I could not preserve the real thing, I wanted to make sure that tourists at least had a real glimpse of prison activity' (Lee, personal communication, 23 September 1997; Lee 2004: 177). Collins suggested that Lee make it a 'real church' that was consecrated and had a minister and a congregation. This suggestion was implemented, and the Changi Chapel was formally conse-crated on 15 February 1988 by the Reverend Khoo. He was also able to form a regular congregation from prison workers and residents in the Changi area who held formal services at the Changi Chapel every Sunday.

A similar understated style was adopted by Pamelia Lee for the museum that was to go with the chapel. According to Collins, she 'felt [the museum] should not be air-conditioned; the windows should be open at all times. Initially she ordered wicker chairs so people could sit and relax in the area'. Collins noted that the 'museum was never "slick" or professionally polished' (Collins 2003, pp49–50; see also Blackburn 2000). Roney Tan, the Singapore Tourist Promotion Board Regional Director in Sydney, offered his observations on how these ideas would be received. In his memo he wrote that that the 'proposed open-air Chapel' is '"quaint" and will certainly be a hit among Australian war veterans and their families'. Tan expressed his opinion about developing more sites for battlefield tourism: 'I see a lot of potential in this project. We should plan big and integrate all the WWII historical sites/monuments that we currently have' (Tan 1987, ref. PD/PRJ/45/87 vol. 1).

Singapore tourism authorities publicly appealed for mementos from the ex-PoWs for the museum. Thus, they cleverly advertised the new attraction to the site's key visitors. They were keenly aware that endorsement by the veterans and their families would give the new Changi Prison Chapel and Museum an aura of authenticity and credibility. Previously, Singapore prisons personnel had ignored requests by PoWs and their families to deposit their mementos in the Changi Chapel inside the prison

(Quek 1987, ref. PD/PRJ/45/87, vol. 1). The new marketing strategy worked, as the response was very positive. Desmond Bettany, a former British PoW who headed the Ex-Prisoners of War of Australia Association, responded to a letter asking for mementos from Quek Shi Lai, the Director of Prisons, with his ringing endorsement and a desire to visit: 'Good luck with the project. I know I speak with the support of all ex-PoWs when I say we are very pleased to learn of this effort to record a dark period of our lives for prosperity' (Bettany 1987, ref. PD/PRJ/45/87, vol. 1). H. K. Mawby, also of the Ex-Prisoners of War of Australia Association, replied to Pamelia Lee: 'I have tried to promote the project as much as possible via the public, relatives, working with the Ex Service organisations I belong to in Australia and the UK' (Mawby 1988, ref. PD/PRJ/45/88, vol. 6).

For the museum's main exhibits, the tourism authorities mainly settled on watercolours by W. R. M. Haxworth, who had been a civilian internee, and the photographic collection of George Aspinall. Both of these collections had to be formally acquired. The Haxworth watercolours came from the National Archives of Singapore and the Aspinall photographs were contained in a book collection. Despite the very public call for PoW mementos few were used in the end. Singapore tourism officials were pleased with acquiring these two collections. In their brochures, the Haxworth watercolours were described as being meant to 'illustrate with good humour the high morale among the PoWs despite overcrowding, poor hygiene and lack of food in the prison' while the 'shadowy and evocative series of photographs taken secretly by an Australian soldier, Mr George Aspinall, graphically depict the day-to-day experiences of PoWs'. Haxworth had died, but Aspinall visited the Changi Chapel and Museum, twice giving his endorsement to the new re-creation.

The Changi Prison Chapel and Museum was crafted to engage British and Australian visitors emotionally. On 17 February 1997, Adam Berwick, who described himself as the 'grandson of Clyde Berwick, Australia', placed the following card on the Changi Chapel's notice board:

> To my grandfather who survived but told no-one of the horrors he faced here. Yet he did tell his young grandson stories of the mateship and comradeship that allowed those fortunate ones to endure.

The planned demolition and expansion of Changi Prison in the first decade of the twenty-first century brought an opportunity to recast the Changi Chapel and Museum as it moved to a new location two kilometres down the road. What was planned was a more complete history of the war experience that integrated the PoW story and the story of the local population during the Japanese occupation. Singapore Tourist Promotion Board studies on visitors to Changi and other battlefield tourism sites revealed that increasingly large numbers of schoolchildren on class field trips were being bussed to and from these historic locations (Lee 2000a). The notice board in the Changi Chapel often featured notes posted by Singapore school students.

In 1997, with the launch of National Education in the Singapore school system, the fall of Singapore and the Japanese occupation were used to highlight the government message: 'we ourselves must defend Singapore' (Wong 2001, pp225–7). From 1998 15th February, the date of the fall of Singapore, became marked as Total Defence Day. The defeat of the British at the hands of the Japanese and the subsequent suffering of the local population became crucial in highlighting what might happen if Singapore did not have compulsory military service for males once they reached 18 years of age.

During 2000, in preparation for the opening of the new Changi Chapel and Museum, the Singapore Tourism Board began to create storyboards that blended the local population's experience of the Japanese occupation with the PoW story. The panels had names such as 'The Experience Lingers', 'Darkest Days', 'Living in Fear' and 'Suffering under Japanese Hands'. A gallery of the new Changi Chapel and Museum also reproduced the Changi Murals which, although preserved, after 2001 and the threat of terrorism were effectively closed to the public because they were in a high-security military base.

In August 2000, Singapore tourism officials came up with a new proposal for the museum. Their idea was to use two fictional characters, Nicholas, a young PoW, and Lin Mei, a Chinese girl, to narrate their stories. The use of a fictional young girl was intended to engage the school students with the story of the local population. She was to tell of the suffering of the local population from a child's perspective. The Australian PoW was also to be young in order both to interest foreign tourists and to appeal to local schoolchildren. According to this proposal, each panel was to have one fictional narrative from the perspective of the PoW and another from the point of view of the young child living through the occupation (Ser Yong & Associates 2000). This proposed division of the war history of Singapore into two different narratives illustrated the perception that the suffering of the local population during the Japanese occupation was intermixed with the story of the PoWs. In turn a commonality of shared experience is apparent throughout the interpretation in various galleries at Changi Chapel and Museum.

The use of fictional characters for the new Changi Chapel and Museum was dropped in late November 2000, in favour of utilising the power of direct quotes from real people who had lived through the occupation to give the same perspectives of the local population and the PoWs. At a meeting of tourism officials and historians convened on 22 November 2000, Lily Tan, the head of the National Archives of Singapore and Oral History Centre, made the case that oral history quotes would give the visitors the impression that the past was speaking to them and that narration should be kept to a minimum. She advised: 'Don't say something directly; let the quotes do it for you. That has worked for our exhibitions' (Lee 2000b). This mimicked exhibits in the Australian War Memorial where recorded interviews with PoWs were played.

Anzac journeys and British pilgrimages today

In the decade following the opening of the new Changi Chapel and Museum on 15 February 2001 Australian and British visitors on their pilgrimages warmed to this blend of stories and its simplicities. Prominent was the Changi Chapel notice board that Robertson Collins devised so that there would be a spiralling of emotional depth as each writer reacted to another's emotional outpourings. Next to the notice board was placed a wooden sign on which was carved: 'Whosoever thou art that entereth this Church leave it not without prayer to God for thyself and those that minister here'. On the other side of the notice board was paper on which to write the messages. The messages are snapshots of the emotional reactions of visitors, from those who regard themselves as pilgrims to schoolchildren caught up in the spiralling of emotional reactions to the site.

From the first year of its operation, the two most striking letters pinned on the chapel notice board from British and Australian visitors were kept on display by the management of the Changi Chapel and Museum to illustrate the power of the site. A British family wrote the following on 13 September 2001:

In memory of dear Uncle Jack Wayling, whose remains are somewhere here in Singapore, from Susan Wayling your niece. How I would love to have known you and to have brought you home to your Mum and Dad. They could not believe you were never coming back, but now with the passing of the years, God has reunited you all. I am your bother Robin's daughter and I am here just for 3 days with your son, Richard whom you never saw. We have tried to be close to you here, at Kranji, Mount Pleasant Road and Alexandra Hospital and we are glad we have stood on the same land.

Loved always by

Your wife, Kathleen

Your daughter Jillan

Next to the British response was a letter by an Australian visitor dated 6 November 2001:

In loving memory of my dear Uncle Ernie McBurney who lost his life in Changi. My godfather, Uncle Ron McBurney who survived this horror has finally after 53 years started to talk of life in Changi to his family members. Let's pray there will never be another war and thanks to the men who lived and died during World War II. We have a peaceful and safe place to live in today. Lest we forget.

Kay Barclay

(Australia)

A survey of 214 random respondents, conducted from 15 to 24 September 2001 at the Changi Chapel and Museum, revealed that 30 per cent of visitors were there to commemorate the PoW experience, while a further 13 per cent described themselves as being on a pilgrimage. Australians and British tourists formed the majority of visitors, at 35 per cent and 36 per cent respectively. Singaporeans constituted 19 per cent of the visitors. Among them, 10 per cent were Singapore pupils on a school trip. The British and Australian visitors, when asked about their activities at the site, revealed that 6 per cent wrote a card, 5 per cent lit a candle, and 10 per cent said a prayer. Most visitors, 42 per cent, opted not to do anything. However, when asked whether the site had emotionally touched or affected them 40 per cent used words indicating that it had, with the most frequently occurring words being 'sad', 'emotional' and 'moving' (BAG 433 2001).

The Australian emotional connection with the Changi site remained strong. In 2004 when it was made publicly known that Changi Prison would be demolished and replaced by a new prison, Australian ex-PoWs and their families lobbied the Australian government, which in turn put pressure on the Singapore government, to preserve the front wall of the prison with the iconic gate (Beaumont 2009).

Following the 2004 demolition of the Prison, the families and loved ones of the PoWs have continued to use the notice board at the Changi Chapel for their outpouring of emotion. On 15 February 2006, the 64th anniversary of the fall of Singapore, Helen Bradford wrote of her father who had been in the Queensland 2/10th Field Regiment:

> In loving memory of my dear father Kevin Adcock who passed through Changi on his way to Burma and lived through the worst years of his life knowing of my mother's love. He returned home to die in 1958.

Next to this message was posted a remembrance note from a young Australian visitor, Xavier Clemens, reacting to Helen Bradford's message and other evocative remarks from relatives also on an anniversary pilgrimage:

> As ever, I am in simple awe of those that survive places like these. Sacrifices were made that, as a younger Australian, I will never truly be able to comprehend for my ignorance. I thank those who were incarcerated.

For many relatives, it appears that the recent death of their PoW relative prompted their visit. A message from a young Collette Day posted in early 2008 is just one of several indicating their reasons for their journey:

> In memory of Ernie Day who was a prisoner of war and survived. He passed away last year and allowed me to travel and learn more of his past.
>
> Rest in Peace Granddad
>
> Love Collette Day

It is not only at the Changi Chapel and Museum that there are evocations of the spirits of the deceased and conversations with the dead left by relatives. At the Kranji War Cemetery, opening the books that contain the lists of the fallen often reveals little messages from relatives. Even old photos of their loved ones are put between the pages of these volumes in order to leave something behind. In 2010, Glenys Tangey placed in these volumes a photograph of her uncle and two of his army mates sculling beer from VB bottles. Glenys embedded a red poppy in the photograph. She then wrote:

> James Joseph Tangey. VX 33332 Born 19.12.23 Died 11.2.42 AIF 4A/Tank Regiment. Royal Australian Artillery.
>
> Although I never knew you I know you were a character and loved to have fun. You probably thought war would be such an adventure.
>
> I wonder what your last moment of life were like *[sic]*. I hope you didn't suffer.
>
> I am visiting Kranji in honor of your mother Moya father Herbert and brother Kevin.
>
> May you and your mates Rest in Peace.
>
> Glenys Tangey x
>
> 23.10.10.

In the same volume, during December 2010 a British visitor also placed photographs and the story of her relative who had been lost at sea and had no known grave. His name appears on the Kranji War Memorial of the fallen who have no known grave. She wrote:

> There's a little town in England.
>
> Wigan is its name. It's where this lad was born and bred. Dick Ollson was his name. For years we tried to find you. Alas it was in vain. We didn't know your resting place until a letter can, your friend from your Battalion Charles Frisby was the name. For all the loving memories and the ones we have never made, we send you Hugs and kisses until we meet again.
>
> From your loving family
>
> in Wigan
>
> xxxxx Lancashire xxxxx

The battlefields of Malaysia, while less frequently visited, also bring out emotions similar to those expressed at Kranji and Changi. In the first week of September 2007 seven veterans and two widows were part of a trip sponsored by the Australian Department of Veterans Affairs to unveil a new memorial to the Australians massacred by the Japanese at the Parit Sulong Bridge. As well as taking in Changi and the war sites of Singapore they toured the places in Malaysia where the Australians had fought, and also Pudu Gaol in Kuala Lumpur. Jim Kerr, a veteran from the Battle of Muar, commented: 'Well, it's going to be very moving to go back. I have never been back to where the actual battle took place. I have never been back to Parit Sulong where the massacre took place'. Jack Varley, another veteran, when asked how he felt, commented: 'Quite emotional; my first time back here for 60 years'. Rowley Richards, who was also involved in the Battle of Muar, was asked what younger generations of Australians should know about the battle and massacre: 'There is no doubt that they need to know more about it but the important thing is that they are far more interested' (News report, *Australian Network*, 4 September 2007).

Significantly, the large Parit Sulong memorial was prominently inscribed in Malay, the national language of Malaysia, as well as English in recognition of the local people who had helped generations of visiting Australians identify the location of the massacre site.

At the Changi Chapel and Museum there is also this acknowledgement that there is a wider history to be commemorated. Inside the chapel is a box with the words:

> This box contains sand from Changi Beach.
>
> On this and many other beaches around Singapore many civilians and PoWs were sacrificed.
>
> This once blood soiled beach is today filled with laughter and peace. We pray that those who were sacrificed have found their peace too.

Thus, Australian pilgrimages to Singapore, particularly Changi, Thailand and the battlefields of Malaysia, are consciously part of remembering a larger history that includes PoWs of other nationalities and members of the local population who also suffered under the Japanese occupation. In a sense the history of the Australian PoWs and the pilgrimages associated with it are best understood as a strand of a larger narrative of war experience associated with the Asian theatre of war during World War II. It is hard not to be aware that many different people are on pilgrimages and that journeys there are not just 'Anzac Journeys' that focus only on the Australian experience and ignore the commemorative activities of other groups and the experiences of Malaysians and Singaporeans.

References

Arneil, S. (1982). *One Man's War* (Melbourne: Macmillan).

Beattie, R. (2007). *The Thai–Burma Railway: The True Story of the Bridge on the River Kwai* (Kanchanaburi, Thailand: TBRC).

Beaumont, J. (2009). 'Contested trans-national heritage: the demolition of Changi Prison, Singapore'. *International Journal of Heritage Studies*, *14*(4), 298–316.

Beaumont, J. (2001). *The Australian Centenary History of Defence: Vol. VI, Australian Defence: Sources and Statistics* (Melbourne: Oxford University Press).

Blackburn, K. (2000). 'Commodifying and commemorating the prisoner of war experience in Southeast Asia: the creation of Changi Prison Museum'. *Journal of the Australian War Memorial*, *33*. Available from: www.awm.gov.au/journal/ [19 June 2015].

Bowden, T. (1984). *Changi Photographer: George Aspinall's Record of Captivity* (Sydney: Allen & Unwin).

Clarke, H. V. and Burgess, C. (1992). *Barbed Wire and Bamboo: Australian POWs in Europe, North Africa, Singapore, Thailand and Japan* (Sydney: Allen and Unwin).

Collins, R. (2003). *A Disorderly Excursion: ASEAN Profiles* (Singapore: Pepper Publications).

Elliot, D. and Silver, L. (2006). *A History of 2/18th Infantry Battalion AIF*, rev. edn (Sydney: 2/18th Infantry Battalion (AIF) Association).

Hack, K. and Blackburn, K. (2004). *Did Singapore Have to Fall? Churchill and the Impregnable Fortress* (London: Routledge).

Harrison, K. (1966). *The Brave Japanese* (Adelaide: Rigby).

Havers, R. P. W. (2003). *Reassessing the Japanese Prisoner of War Experience: The Changi POW Camp, Singapore, 1942–5* (London: RoutledgeCurzon).

Havers, R. P. W. (2000). 'The Changi POW Camp and the Burma–Thailand Railway', in P. Towle, M. Kosuge and Y. Kibata (eds), *Japanese Prisoners of War* (London: Hambledon Press), pp. 17–36.

Hirsch, M. (2008). 'The generation of postmemory'. *Poetics Today, 29*(1), 103–28.

Jung, Y. K. (2010). 'Voices of the fallen: Singaporean and Australian memories of the fall of Singapore', PhD thesis (Wollongong, NSW: University of Wollongong).

Lee, P. (2004). *Singapore, Tourism & Me* (Singapore: Pamelia Lee Private Ltd).

Lee, P. (2000a). 'Singapore Tourism Board Meeting of Changi Chapel and Museum', convened by P. Lee, notes taken by K. Blackburn, 1 August.

Lee, P. (2000b). 'Singapore Tourism Board Meeting of Changi Chapel and Museum', convened by P. Lee, notes taken by K. Blackburn, 22 November.

Lewis Bryan, J. N. (1946). *The Churches of the Captivity in Malaya* (London: Society for Promoting Christian Knowledge).

McKernan, M. (2001). *This War Never Ends: The Pain of Separation and Return* (St Lucia, QLD: University of Queensland Press).

Nelson, H. (1985). *Prisoners of War: Australians under Nippon* (Sydney: ABC Books).

Percival, A. (1948). 'Operations of Malaya Command from 8 December 1941 to 15 February 1942', in *Second Supplement to the London Gazette of 20 February 1948*, No. 38215, 26 February, pp. 1245–346.

Ser Yong & Associates (2000). 'Drafts from 15 September 2000', held by K. Blackburn.

Silver, L. R. (2000). *Sandakan: A Conspiracy of Silence*, rev. edn (Sydney: Sally Milner Publishing).

Velmans, L. (2011). *Long Way Back to the River Kwai: A Harrowing True Story of Survival in World War II* (New York: Arcade).

Wigmore, L. (1957). *The Japanese Thrust* (Canberra: Australian War Memorial).

Whitecross, R. H. (1951). *Slaves of the Son of Heaven* (Sydney: Dymock's Book Arcade).

Wong, D. (2001). 'Memory supression and memory production: the Japanese occupation of Singapore', in T. Fujitani, G. M. White and L. Yoneyama (eds), *Perilous Memories: The Asia–Pacific War(s)* (Durham, NC: Duke University Press), pp. 218–38.

Survey

BAG 433 (2001). Survey conducted in September 2001 by 15 student interviewers under Brian Shaw for BAG 433 Geography of Tourism at the National Institute of Education, called BAG 433 'A Research Study on Changi Prison Museum'.

Archival material

The After the Battle file (nd). Serial number 23, file reference number TBP/J-2/81, microfilm AJ005, in the Singapore Tourist Promotion Board records (National Archives of Singapore).

Bettany (1987). Bettany, D. to S. L. Quek, Director of Prisons, 7 September 1987, in 'The Battle for Singapore', Changi Prison Chapel and Museum, serial number 57, file reference number PD/PRJ/45/87, vol. 1, in the Singapore Tourist Promotion Board records (National Archives of Singapore).

Changi East Coast Tour, in 'The Battle for Singapore', Changi Prison Chapel and Museum, serial number 58, file reference number PD/PRJ/45/87, vol. 8, in the Singapore Tourism Promotion Board records (National Archives of Singapore).

Changi Prison Chapel, in 'The Battle for Singapore', Changi Prison Chapel and Museum, serial number 58, file reference number PD/PRJ/45/87, vol. 2 in the Singapore Tourism Promotion Board records (National Archives of Singapore).

Department of Defence (nd). Unveiling of Kranji War Memorial – Singapore. A663, O100/1/428 (National Archives of Australia).

Diamond, O. N. – (Flight Lieutenant); Service Number – 270544; File type – Casualty – Repatriation; Place – Java, Netherlands East Indies; Date – March 1942 A705, 166/9/445 (National Archives of Australia).

Lee, K. Y. (1970). Memorandum from Prime Minister to Chairman, Tourist Promotion Board, 26 November 1970, in 'Selective Historical Sites into Tourist Attractions', TPB/F/72 (A) vol. 1, in the Singapore Tourism Promotion Board records (National Archives of Singapore).

Mawby (1988). Mawby, H. K. to P. Lee, 8 August 1988, in 'The Battle for Singapore', Changi Prison Chapel and Museum, serial number 66, file reference number PD/PRJ/45/88, vol.6 in the Singapore Tourist Promotion Board records (National Archives of Singapore).

Quek (1987). Quek, S. L. to D. Bettany, 31 July 1987, in 'The Battle for Singapore', Changi Prison Chapel and Museum, serial number 57, file reference number PD/PRJ/45/87, vol. 1, in the Singapore Tourist Promotion Board records (National Archives of Singapore).

Tan, R. (1987). Re: Changi Development, 20.8.87, in 'The Battle for Singapore', Changi Prison Chapel and Museum, serial number 57, file reference number PD/PRJ/45/87, vol. 1 in the Singapore Tourist Promotion Board records (National Archives of Singapore).

War Diary of 2/19th Infantry Battalion, AWM 52 8/3/19/9 (Australian War Memorial, Canberra).

Notes

1   For an up-to-date, concise analysis of the Malayan campaign see Hack and Blackburn (2004).
2   See Beaumont (2001), p. 345; Wigmore (1957), p. 382 and p. 511; and Nelson (1985), p. 4.

11 Reading Darwin as a landscape of war

Laura James

Through a detailed look at the war memorials and performances of remembrance that occur in Darwin's Bicentennial Park, this chapter hopes to show how landscapes can be developed to reflect a particular historical narrative and promote a specific agenda. In recent years, perhaps as a result of the Anzac centenary, there has been a significant growth in war commemoration practices within Australia. While today we see Australians of all ages and races and every gender participate enthusiastically in a range of commemorative events, this has not always been the case, with interest in war remembrance rising and falling at different times in Australia's history. Through an examination of how landscapes can help shape our remembering of war, and how they are utilised at different times to unite communities and express political agendas, this chapter will analyse why war remembrance in Darwin has become so discernible today.

The best -known example of war commemoration in Australia is of course Anzac Day, when millions of Australians (and New Zealanders) gather together across the suburbs, small towns and large cities to remember those who have fought and died in international wars. Days like Anzac Day often recall those well-told stories of campaigns and battles fought in Europe or Asia, rarely remembering that war too was once fought on Australian soil. However, as these previously forgotten conflicts, battles and sites of war on Australian soil are rediscovered within the landscape, the desire to commemorate the experiences of Australians who fought and died at these locations has also grown. Darwin, the remote tropical city in Northern Australia, has in recent years become one such place to undergo a boom in war tourism. The city itself has experienced warfare and destruction in a way that is unmatched by any other Australian city. It is this unique past, along with Darwin's present status as one of Australia's largest military centres, that has led the city to be seen by many as a significant landscape of war.

Today, when people think of Darwin, the capital city of the Northern Territory, they picture a tropical oasis, a modern metropolis, the home of crocodiles, monsoonal weather and the beer can regatta. In the minds of many Australians, and more than a few Territorians, Darwin has always been, and remains unique in the country. With a population of 120,000, Darwin's cultural background is shaped by over 50 nationalities, with 32.5 per cent of the population born overseas, and another 9.2 per cent identifying as Indigenous Australians (Australian Bureau of

Statistics 2011). It is this difference, along with Darwin's remote positioning within Australia, that has led to the city's distinctive subsistence. Darwin has long been known as 'Australia's gateway to Asia', and is nearer to the Indonesian capital, Jakarta, than to Canberra. This geographic isolation from the Australian government and from the southern states is reflected in the psyche of its population and is evident in how many of them have come to see themselves as Territorians first and Australians second.

Along with the equally transformative experience brought about by the devastation caused by Cyclone Tracy, the unique experience of warfare in the Northern Territory can be seen to have helped frame the city's identity. Although other parts of the nation have encountered conflict – be that during Australia's colonisation, or similar World War II bombing raids by the Japanese – it is Darwin that stands apart. This difference may also be attributable to the continuing presence of the Australian Defence Force in the city today. Darwin certainly remains a town with a strong military heartbeat. Just over 7 per cent of Darwin's population are employed in defence, and this is not counting the tens of thousands of other Australian and international service personnel who pass through the city annually (Australian Bureau of Statistics 2011). However, until recently the city's military history was little known outside the Northern Territory. Before the 70th Anniversary of the Darwin Bombings in 2012, and the extensive media coverage of the day, many Australians remained unaware that Darwin had been bombed during World War II, let alone a total of 64 times. Where once the bombing of Darwin was considered 'a day Australia would rather forget', today it is something that many Australians pause to remember.

As Debbie Lisle has remarked, 'war and tourism are strange bedfellows', and in Darwin, it is precisely this notion that the community has begun to negotiate with in recent years (Lisle 2000). Where once the majority of tourists came to visit Darwin for its rich indigenous heritage, today there are a number of tourist attractions designed for those interested in discovering the experience of Australia at war. Through the medium of war heritage sites Darwin has succeeded in packaging a version of the bombing of Darwin for the tourist to consume, and in doing so has developed a profitable war heritage industry. Today, the war tourist has the opportunity to actively participate in a number of specially designed experiences in a way that simply did not exist a decade ago. These include a smartphone app that acts as a guide to significant war heritage sites, a number of museums and exhibition spaces for the tourist to connect with the story and visit to discover the military history of the town, as well as guided tours, souvenirs and a plethora of books. However it is the landscape itself that speaks the most of Darwin's war experience and allows the tourist to engage with the past. The bombing of Darwin both physically and culturally changed the landscape of the city forever. The warfare waged in this area instilled a new meaning into the surroundings, reflecting the change of identity of the community itself. The redevelopment of part of the city's landscape to reflect its war heritage is at once both a masterstroke for the city's tourism industry, and a way for the Australian government to present Darwin as historically significant to Australia's defence policies.

In order to truly understand the impact the bombing of Darwin has had on both the community and the landscape, it is necessary to first explain how the Japanese attack came to take place. On 3 September 1939, Australia as a nation entered World War II vowing to stand behind Britain as they sought to 'check the march of force' launched by German leader Adolf Hitler in his ambition to seize substantial areas of Europe (*Sydney Morning Herald* 1939). As thousands of Australian service personnel enlisted and departed once more to fight in far-flung battlefields, they remained largely unaware that war closer to home threatened. However, by 1941, the increasingly aggressive actions of Imperial Japan (which had successfully attacked Manchuria and China in 1931 and 1937 respectively) had become a real source of concern to Australians, who felt somewhat isolated in the Pacific region and in danger of a Japanese invasion. The Australian government cautiously chose to position thousands of Allied troops in Darwin to reinforce the city against a Japanese attack in early 1941, and by mid-December of the same year the majority of Darwin's civilian population had been evacuated and the town left for the military to defend. On 7 December this threat became even more apparent, when Japan attacked the United States Naval base at Pearl Harbor in Hawaii, as well as numerous other locations in the Philippines, Guam, Malaya, Thailand and China as a response to US economic sanctions. Australia immediately declared war on Japan, along with Britain and the United States, with Prime Minister John Curtin rationalising that Australia's 'vital interests are imperilled and … the rights of free people in the whole Pacific are assailed' (*Sydney Morning Herald* 1941).

After a series of victories it took Japan just over nine weeks to march from Malaya to Singapore, the place believed by Australians to be the last bastion between the enemy and the Australian mainland. When Singapore fell on 15 February, the threat that war might reach the Australian mainland became a terrible possibility. These fears were almost at once confirmed when four days later the city of Darwin was bombed by the Imperial Japanese Naval Air Force. Despite preparation, when the attack eventually came, confusion and disbelief reigned as the Allied defenders realised just how unprepared Australia was to resist an enemy airstrike on Darwin.

In the two raids conducted by the Japanese on 19 February, approximately 246 people died, including 25 civilians (Lowe, 1942). Although a warning about 'an unusually large air formation bearing down on us from the northwest' was received at 9:35am from Father John McGrath, stationed at a Catholic mission on nearby Melville Island, it was ignored as it was believed to be returning US Kittyhawks from Timor. Not until 9:58am, as the attack started, was an air-raid warning finally sounded. Because of this unpreparedness, much of the town was destroyed, as first 188 attack aircraft and later 54 land-based bombers, assaulted the area, defended only by the returning Kittyhawks, 45 unprepared Allied ships stationed in the harbour and 2 anti-aircraft batteries.

The Japanese attack was led by Mitsuo Fuchida who had commanded the raid on Pearl Harbor ten weeks before; he later referred to the Japanese bombing of Darwin as 'hardly worthy of us, if ever a sledgehammer was used to crack an egg, it was then' (White and Frew 2013). However, for the people of Darwin the bombing raids are remembered as a complete disaster that destroyed their city, and demonstrated the disorder of the military's preparedness and the complete inability of the administration to respond to an enemy attack.

After 64 wartime raids, a displaced community (many of whom were never to return) and the old city structures ravaged by warfare and the defending soldiers, post-war Darwin was left an altered place, forever changed by its experience of war. Even after decades of rebuilding and despite the best efforts of its struggling population, Darwin remained blighted. Tragically, any semblance of normality and resurrection gained was once more destroyed by Cyclone Tracy in 1974, forcing the community to begin again from nothing. Only the altered landscape of Darwin remains as a memorial to the city's tragic past.

Landscapes are complex, multiple and always transient spaces that are shaped by a constant interaction with the community. Their meanings have been embedded to reflect aspects of time, belief practices and past events. They are reflections of what a community wants to be remembered in a specific location, and can always be read in more than one way. Although Darwin and its surrounds are dotted with sites of war, the space that this chapter will specifically focus on is that of Bicentennial Park, located behind the city's centre and overlooking Darwin's harbour. A reading of this space, analysing its military connections, will aim to demonstrate not only how a landscape can become imprinted with meaning, but how the physical scars left by the wartime bombing raids are used by the Australian government to suit its own purposes.

Today, Bicentennial Park, or as it is known locally, the Esplanade Gardens, is a calm and tranquil space or, as one Darwin resident was to remark, 'a wonderful refuge of peace in the city of Darwin, a reflective gem' (TW 2011). Stretching for over a kilometre, the space is dotted at regular intervals with a number of monuments, memorials and other heritage features denoting Darwin's military past. The landscape has been created specifically to reflect on this aspect of Darwin's history, and says something about how the community values its past and present as a military town today.

This site has undergone a process of what can be termed deliberate memorialisation, or the deliberate act of commemorating an experience through the erection of commemorative structures with the intention of communicating a story. From the early 1990s (perhaps as a result of the interest shown after the 50th anniversary commemorations of the bombing of Darwin), the Northern Territory Government, with the help of a team of professional architects, designed the space with the intention of marrying the Northern Territory's experience of warfare and conflict with this unique former battlefield. It was at this time that a number of books and television series on the bombing of Darwin began to appear and the wartime history of the city slowly became more widely known, causing attendance figures at commemorative events to rise steadily. Eventually it was decided that Bicentennial Park was a perfect location to create a war memorial precinct not only catering to the demand for extra space to accommodate growing crowd numbers, but also to tell the story of Darwin at war. Finally completed in 2007 for the 65th anniversary

Figure 11.1 The Northern Territory War Memorial in Bicentennial Park, Darwin.
Source: Laura James.

of the bombing, the landscape now attracts thousands of individuals annually to war remembrance services, as well as countless thousands of others who are able to visit the memorial space and engage with the story throughout the year (*Defence News*, 21 February 2013).

The central focus of the garden landscape is the cenotaph, set within a large cleared space known as 'The Oval', and designed as a place of remembrance and reflection. The Oval was once the location of the 14th Heavy anti-aircraft battery who defended Darwin from the Japanese airstrike and has become a focal site of memory in the commemoration of the bombing raids ever since. As historian Susan Mary Grant discovered when researching the Civil War landscapes of America, 'the military landscapes of the battlefield become the civilian landscapes of memory' (Grant, 2006). The cenotaph, originally located elsewhere, was moved to this site in 1998, during the construction of the war memorial precinct. Architects, drawing on the history of the landscape, saw the Oval as 'ideally placed' in which to memorialise the city's war experience and therefore decided to unite the two elements (Voss 2011).

The cenotaph structure itself is layered with meaning, and can be seen as a visual expression of the Northern Territory's military history. The structure is composed of a large, grey marble column, set upon a granite plinth and flanked by two sweeping wings that list the Northern Territory's involvement in international wars. Although originally constructed for the dead of World War I, over time, just like many other war memorials across Australia, new plaques were added to the existing structure to commemorate the service and sacrifice of men in subsequent conflicts, setting up a line of succession, an inherited debt. Instead of conveying one story, the monument now exists to communicate many, each plaque a different chapter of a larger narrative.

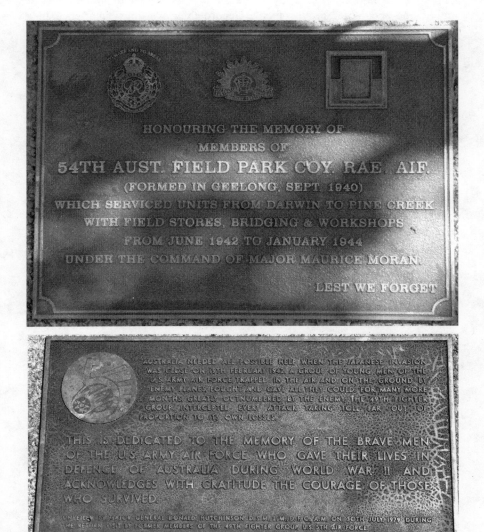

Figure 11.2 The lookout over Darwin Harbour: 2 of the 73 plaques bordering it. The first commemorates the service of the of 54th Australian Field Park Company, Royal Australian Engineers in the Northern Territory during World War II, and the second remembers the sacrifice of the men from the United States Army Air Force who died in the defence of Australia during World War II.

Source: Laura James.

Lying behind the cenotaph is a small lookout over Darwin Harbour. Framed in a semicircle, the lookout is bordered by 73 plaques, which stand as memorials to a wide variety of military organisations and associations that claim a connection with Darwin's military past. These plaques represent the need that a number of individuals and larger groups feel to record their wartime experience in a meaningful way and bind themselves permanently to the landscape. Where the cenotaph lists those from the Northern Territory who have fought and died in wars, the plaques enable other groups to commemorate their own, and otherwise forgotten experiences within this place.

At the far end of Bicentennial Park is a space known as Doctors Gully. The waterfront site, once covered by thriving costal plants is today crowded by a large wartime jetty and two large oil-storage tanks erected in 1943 as part of a World War II maintenance base for Catalina flying boats. The Catalinas are important in the story of Darwin at war, as they not only assisted in defending the town through mine-laying, and observation missions, but also took part in rescue operations over the Timor Sea. A thriving wartime hub, the space was abandoned by the RAAF following the end of the conflict and taken over by a government caretaker, only briefly being visited by salvage teams at a later date who began pulling the wrecks of ships and equipment out of Darwin Harbour (Lewis 1999). Former Governor-General of Australia Paul Hasluck once remarked that Doctors Gully remained 'a junkyard' for many years into Darwin's post-war life, and even today it is possible to see war remains dumped in the harbour during this period (Hasluck, 1992). Lumps of twisted metal, parts of old US Army jeeps and rusted machinery litter the space, which in recent years has been used as a popular fish feeding spot for tourists. The oil-storage tanks too have now been repurposed and become an indoor rock-climbing gym for the Darwin community. It is the physical transformation of landscapes by the activity and destruction of war that enables the war tourist today to engage with their surroundings and reimage the past from their own perspective, even once those lanscapes have been repurposed (like the oil-storage tanks) as something else.

While these memorial features of the landscape help create Bicentennial Park as a meaningful space for the Australian war tourist, it is not only Australians who find importance within this space. During the bombing raids on Darwin, a number of American, Canadian, Dutch and British service personnel were also stationed within this region. Like their Australian allies, scores of these foreign defenders came to feel a special connection to the Darwin landscape, with many returning and reconnecting with the space in subsequent years (*Sydney Morning Herald* 2012). For these individuals, Darwin came to represent an important part of their military lives. Aside from their own personal experiences of war within this space, many of these ex-servicemen lost and buried friends here while others contributed to the post-war reconstruction of Darwin through such initiatives as rebuilding St Mary's Star of the Sea Cathedral in the centre of town (St Mary's Star of the Sea Darwin War Memorial Cathedral 1972). Just as Darwin had made its mark upon them, these foreign servicemen sought to make their mark on the Darwin landscape in return.

American memorialisation of their wartime experience in Darwin is particularly noticeable within Bicentennial Park. As of 2012, 5 out of the 73 commemorative plaques that border the cenotaph lookout have been commissioned by US individuals and military organisations that served in the Northern Territory during the Pacific War. These plaques assist in tying the US experience of the conflict into the military history of the landscape in an obvious and lasting way. The American experience of war in Darwin is further commemorated by its own monument, the USS *Peary* memorial, located in the middle of Bicentennial Park. Constructed using a salvaged deck gun and positioned facing out into Darwin Harbour to indicate the location of the sunken ruin, the *Peary* memorial is expressly dedicated to the American servicemen who died as a result of the first Japanese airstrike on Darwin, and remains one of the most visited heritage sites within the precinct. Surrounding the deck gun are memorial tablets that narrate survivors' recollections of the sinking of the *Peary*, and provide detailed accounts of the role of the US forces in the defence of Darwin. Ninety-one crew of the *Peary* died during the raid, all of whom are named within the space, permanently tying these men to the landscape of their deaths. As historian Kirk Savage has noted, '[t]he most cherished axiom of the memorial landscape is its permanence, its eternity' (Savage, 2009). For the families and friends of these men, a physical memorial to them on the other side of the world speaks of a continued promise to remember these men at the site of their deaths for generations to come.

As a tourism/heritage site, the significance of the USS *Peary* Memorial continues to grow each year as more and more individuals become familiar with the story and find importance in the sacrifice of the American sailors who died in Australia. The *Peary* memorial is often part of American pilgrimage tours to Pacific wartime locations, and annually on the Bombing of Darwin Day, serving US Naval personnel in conjunction with the Australian-American Association conduct a commemorative service that culminates with the US Navy laying a wreath over the *Peary* in the harbour.

As well as former US Naval and Army personnel and their families, many of those who come to visit the *Peary* are current members of the US Navy passing through Darwin. Each year, many of these American men and women, dressed in full dress whites, participate in Darwin's Anzac Day ceremonies and the city's Anzac Day parade. In 2011, three US naval officers remarked how excited they were to be included in the day, and how honoured they were to represent the American Naval men who had died here during the Pacific War (interviews conducted by the author, 2011).

While primarily standing to remember the dead, the commemoration of the American experience of war in Darwin through monuments and memorials can also be seen to relate to the current political relationship between Australia and the United States. Formed out of the strategic defence alliance that Australia continues to maintain with the USA known as the ANZUS treaty, the memorialisation of US experience of war in Darwin can be seen to have a twofold purpose. With the growth of China, and to a lesser extent India, as new superpowers within the Asia-Pacific region, the alliance between Australia and the United States continues to be of vital importance. While the governments of both countries have stated their desire for the 'rise of a peaceful and prosperous China' both have also expressed the need for a strong US presence in the region in order to achieve this (Obama 2011). As well as the physical presence of American troops within the Asia-Pacific region, continued remembrance and memorialisation of past conflict involving the United States, such as what is displayed in Darwin, can also be seen to assist in demonstrating America's historical hegemony of the region since World War II. Through the media of war memorials and monuments, America's sustained involvement in Asia-Pacific conflicts can be read, especially now the United States' gaze is firmly back on the Pacific region.

Out of a relationship with the USA, Australia receives not just a sense of security and protection but the use of modern weaponry, training courses and intelligence resources. However, now, just as when the ANZUS treaty was signed between America, Australia and New Zealand in 1952, the United States both wants, and benefits from, an alliance with Australia. Where else in the Pacific region could the United States find a stable, secure ally with intersecting interest in the Pacific, and one which has strong economic ties to a potentially circumspect superpower? With Australia as a firm ally, the United States gains not only influence in the Pacific, but also a secure base for US forces to train and benefit from Australian Defence Force programmes and facilities.

The decision made by the Australian government to permanently host 2,500 US marines at Darwin's Robertson Barracks on a rotational basis has been a heated topic of conversation amongst the community. In other parts of the world in which the United States have military bases, US troops remain unpopular and are often blamed for increasing crime and vice rates, as well as civilian deaths (Tennant-Wood 2011). While the Darwin community was not without its reservations, a recent study by the Lowy Institute found that more than 50 per cent of Australians believed the United States were very important to the nation's security (Lowy Institute for International Policy 2014) and more than 70 per cent of the population were in favour of American military bases within Australia (Lowy Institute for International Policy 2012). The stationing of a permanent US Marines base within one of Australia's largest defence force bases is one way to reaffirm the permanent nature of the alliance that exists between Australia and the United Sates, but it is not the only way.

The need to demonstrate this alliance as the continuation of a historical relationship in a tangible way has been easily achieved through the medium of war heritage sites in Darwin. The USS *Peary* monument in Bicentennial Park not only firmly places the US military in the history of Darwin, but assists in justifying to the community why they are there now. When visiting Darwin in November 2011, President Barack Obama spoke of the 'unbreakable alliance' that existed between the two nations, drawing on the shared military history of Australia and the United States, asserting '[t]he bonds between us run deep. In each other's story we see so much of ourselves' (Obama 2011). By reaffirming this shared history through US war memorials and plaques on Australian soil, the Governments of Australia and the United States are overtly legitimising the presence of US troops in Australia, and sending a message to potential aggressors that the presence of democratic power, established out of the Allied victory in the Pacific War, will continue to focus on peace in the region into the twenty-first century.

By the military too, much is being done to persuade the community of the valuable presence of the United States. The US Navy have also added something to the Darwin war experience, recently hosting an open day on a visiting US Naval vessel to encourage the community and visiting war tourists to engage with their allied friends. By allowing the public to venture on to a US Navy ship and experience what life is like for American service personnel, the Australian-United States relationship is further strengthened through friendship and thus legitimised. Executive Officer, Cdr T. J. Zerr of the USS *Kidd*, when questioned on the relationship, supported statements made by Australian and US politicians and asserted that '[a]side from the significant strategic aspects of our relationship, there is also an important personal and cultural connection that Americans and Australians share; this mutual respect and admiration was evidenced in *Kidd*'s passageways as our crew had the chance to interact with nearly 600 civilian Darwin residents' (Schaffer 2014). Interactions between the military and civilian populations further assist the work achieved by the deliberate memorialisation of the Darwin landscape and ensure that the city's militarisation is welcomed and supported.

Heath McDonald has suggested that heritage 'plays a critical role in linking the past with the future, specifically by acting as a medium for storytelling and intergenerational communication' (McDonald 2011). The story of the bombing of Darwin and the role of the United States in the defence of Australia during the Pacific War is something that remains relevant in the twenty-first century. The memorials and monuments recognising the role of the United States in Australia have been purposefully positioned within Bicentennial Park, to facilitate the need for this particular aspect of Australia's past history to be remembered today. In no meaningful way are the British, Canadian or Dutch service personnel who fought and died in Darwin remembered. But then again, none of these countries are critical to Australia's defence interests in the future.

Likewise, despite pressure from members of the community, the Japanese are also without a memorial in Darwin, demonstrating once again Australia's inability to present an ambivalent war narrative. However, it is possible that this too may soon change. In 2011, the Japanese Consul-General to Australia Dr Masahiro Kohara attended the bombing of Darwin commemorations. It was the first time in nearly seventy years of remembrance services that an official Japanese Government representative had participated. A local Japanese woman who now resides in Darwin, Sachi Hirayama, also took part in this service, laying a wreath in remembrance of the Japanese who died during the Pacific War. After making a request to the Darwin City Council, Sachi, who was initially worried at the risk of offending Australian veterans, spoke about her decision to participate, stating 'Japanese soldiers are not remembered in my country… so if I can commemorate at least the one who died in Darwin, I think the souls of the soldiers will be pleased' (Coggan 2011). Historian and director of the Darwin Military Museum Dr Tom Lewis likewise believes that it is time for the Japanese to be remembered in

Darwin. Dr Lewis, who has been commended for including the perspective of Japanese soldiers within the Military Museum's exhibitions, asserted publicly in 2011 that 'these are all warriors and they were doing their job. In the end, they died, our people did too. It's nearly 70 years and I think even old soldiers put this behind them' (Coggan 2011). The changing dynamic of the memorial landscape is again possibly reflecting the Australian government's political ambitions.

While the landscape today can be seen to project Darwin as Australia's front line, the same space could just as easily be read as an important Indigenous heritage site, if this is what the larger community and those in power wanted to be remembered here. Recently, the local (indigenous) Larrakia community unsuccessfully attempted to reclaim the space using native title legislation. Lameroo beach in Bicentennial Park has existed as a site with significant cultural meaning to the indigenous people of the area for thousands of years; today this is superseded by the desire of the government to present a narrative of war heritage within this space, pushing all other interpretations aside. In all landscapes there can always be an alternative reading, an alternative history. The transformation of the Bicentennial Park into memorial space that denotes the Australian (and indeed international) experience of warfare in Darwin is just one interpretation of a site of great cultural significance.

References

Australian Bureau of Statistics (2011). '2011 Census Quick Stats Greater Darwin'. Available from: www.censusdata.abs.gov.au/census_services/getproduct/census/2011/quickstat/7GDAR?opendocument&navpos=220 [4 May 2014].

Coggan, M. (2011). 'Push to remember Japanese war dead in Darwin'. *ABC*, 2 March.

Grant, S. M. (2006). 'Landscapes of memory: Susan-Mary Grant argues that the cult of the fallen soldier has its origins at Gettysburg and other battlefield monuments of the American Civil War'. *History Today, 56*(3), 18.

Hasluck, P. (1992). 'Pioneers of post war recovery', Sixth Eric Johnson Lecture, delivered at the State Library of the Northern Territory, 7 November 1991 (Darwin: State Library of the Northern Territory).

James, L. (2011a). 'Anzac Day interviews', 25 April 2011 (unpublished).

James, L. (2011b). 'Interview with Hans Voss on the Darwin Cenotaph, 2011' (unpublished).

Lewis (1999). *A War at Home: A Comprehensive Guide to the first Japanese Attacks on Darwin* (Darwin: Tall Stories).

Lisle, D. (2000). 'Consuming danger: reimagining the war/tourism divide'. *Alternatives, 25*(1), 91.

Lowe, Mr Justice F. (1942). 'Darwin Air Raid Report'. Report commissioned by the Australian Government, NAA MP1185/8, 1806/2/31.

Lowy Institute for International Policy (2012). 'Lowy Poll 2012 – Strong support for US marines in Australia'. Available from: http://m.lowyinstitute.org/news-and-media/hot-topic/lowy-poll-2012-strong-support-us-marines-australia [12 September 2012].

Lowy Institute for International Policy (2014). 'The US alliance'. Available from: www.lowyinstitute.org/lowyinstitutepollinteractive/the-us-alliance/ [29 June 2015].

McDonald, H. (2011). 'Understanding the antecedents to public interest and engagement with heritage'. *European Journal of Marketing, 45*(5), 789.

Obama, B. (2011). 'Remarks by President Obama to the Australian Parliament'. Available from: https://www.whitehouse.gov/the-press-office/2011/11/17/remarks-president-obama-australian-parliament [29 June 2015].

Savage, K. (2009). *Monument Wars* (Berkeley: University of California Press).

Schaffer, B. (2014). USS *Kidd* visits Darwin. Available from: www.navy.mil/submit/display.asp?story_id=79197 [29 September 2014].

St Mary's Star of the Sea Darwin War Memorial Cathedral (1972). *St Mary's Star of the Sea Darwin War Memorial Cathedral* (Darwin: St Mary's Diocese Church).

Sydney Morning Herald (2012).

Sydney Morning Herald (1941). 9 December.

Sydney Morning Herald (1939). 4 September.

Thompson, M. (2011). 'Is a US Marines base in Darwin really a good idea?' Available from: http://theconversation.com/is-a-us-marine-base-in-darwin-really-a-good-idea-4260 [22 June 2015].

White, L. and Frew, E. (2013). *Dark Tourism and Place Identity* (Abingdon, Oxon: Routledge).

12 Examining Vanuatu's World War II memorial places and events

Keir Reeves and Joseph Cheer

The John Frum ceremony is an enduring annual event on 15 February that commemorates the legacy of the American presence during World War II (also known as the Pacific War) on Tanna Island situated in the southern region of the Vanuatu archipelago. It has attracted the interest of tourism researchers, anthropologists, film makers and notable authors including Paul Theroux and David Attenborough. This chapter examines the World War II ceremonial event by John Frum movement villages near the north-eastern side of Tanna's Mount Yasur volcano. In it we contextualise this event as part of travel to the broader area that comprises the World War II-era warscape with associated memories and landscapes including Million Dollar Point and the SS *Coolidge* in Espiritu Santo. This discussion enables greater examination and understanding of the present-day significance of war heritage and commemoration to the ni-Vanuatu community as well as tourists and official visitors associated with former combatant countries. In doing this we emphasise that John Frum commemoration in Tanna, far from being an idiosyncratic commemorative event, is instead a logical continuation of cultural expression stemming from the arrival of the Allied forces in the 1940s.

The following presents the purport of John Frum's message. After a natural catastrophe, Tanna Island would unite with the surrounding islands to form a powerful kingdom. The volcanic hill would collapse and fill the valleys. The land would become flat and fruitful. Men would retain their youth and no illness would harm them. Hard labour would no longer be necessary. John Frum would appear in human form and give his followers everything their hearts desired. The Europeans would leave and freedom would reign. Frum would provide new money and distribute it to all according to their needs. The one condition is that the peoples should take up the old customs again and drive the Europeans away (Steinbauer 1979: 86). They hoped a white ship would arrive with cargo and the Europeans would acknowledge the islanders' dignity as human beings (Steinbauer 1979: 93). The introduction of new morals and customs meant the loss of a traditionally integrated life. The resultant feeling of inferiority had to be balanced by a defensive reaction. Thus antagonism arose against Europeans who had to defend themselves as a consequence (Steinbauer 1979: 104).

World War II memory and heritage in the Pacific remains a contentious issue in the early twenty-first century. This is particularly the case in regard to the question of what is remembered and what is forgotten in Vanuatu (formerly known as the New Hebrides). While in Vanuatu conducting fieldwork over the past decade, the legacy of the broader historical sweep of World War II became apparent. The significance of this realisation was one that was totally removed from research questions of sustainable livelihoods, preserving historical landscapes and heritage tourism that our recent research had been concentrating upon. Instead, it was simply that the memory of World War II still resonates throughout the ni-Vanuatu community regarding the impact of the experience, the actual layout of towns and villages that was, in many cases, determined by military-constructed airstrips, subsequent settlement patterns and also in the oral history of the region. The most enduring and visible is the John Frum Day ceremony driven by villagers from the John Frum movement. There is also a solemn weekly flag-raising ceremony (irregular at times) that, although not as spectacular and wide-scale as John Frum Day, commemorates the arrival of John Frum (or John from America) during World War II (see Figure 12.1).

It is not the purpose of this chapter to extensively or historically analyse the war in the Pacific from a ni-Vanuatu perspective. Nonetheless some historical context is required to understand the commemorative events that continue unbroken well into the twenty-first century. What is important to note is that the Allied bases on Efate and Espiritu Santo, a northern island in Vanuatu, were central to the launch of Allied offensives. They also played an important logistical part in the Allied victory in the Pacific over the Empire of Japan, particularly in the build-up and during the key Battle of Guadalcanal in the Solomon Islands during the second half of 1942 until February 1943. Sometimes this is not readily acknowledged, partly because vicious fighting was taking place in Papua New Guinea and the Solomon Islands and accordingly the New Hebrides (Vanuatu) were conveniently out of sight.

Cargo cults and John Frum

Cargo cults originate well before World War II, back as far as the early 1900s. Peter Worsley agrees that the chronology is correct – cargo predictions predated the arrival of the American military (Worsley 1968). Yet what is clear is that when the American military arrived during World War II, cargo cult predictions were literally realized.

Writing in the early 1980s Pacific studies expert Lamont Lindstrom observed that:

> US military uniforms and insignia... are prized possessions. A few men were lucky enough to secretly retain the numbered dog tags issued to them during tours of labor for the US military. Others still recall the songs they learned from American servicemen and are pleased to sing creditable rendering of 'God Bless America' and 'The Marine's Hymn'.

Figure 12.1 John Frum Day poster, 15 February 2014.
Source: Image © Sebastian Bador, 2014.

Lindstrom's close reading of the events explained that:

> [e]very 15 February, a military drill team marches with bamboo rifles and the logo USA painted in red across the marcher's chests and backs. The team is commanded by a sergeant, 'with stripes', who calls out still recognizable commands (which are, however, unintelligible to the Tannese) such as 'to the right!'

This ceremony still continues and little has changed in terms of it as a commemorative event. Much of the commemoration ceremony is driven by a patriarchal cohort led by longstanding leader Chief Isaac Wan (see Figure 12.2). US Army military regalia are evident in Chief Isaac's personal presentation during John Frum Day celebrations, including uniforms and insignia.

Figure 12.2 Chief Isaac Wan (seated).
Source: Image © Sebastian Bador, 2014.

The military persona adopted is clearly a direct acknowledgement of the American presence during World War II and performed as a mark of respect to John Frum and his imminent return. Chief Isaac is understood to be in regular contact with John Frum and is one of few members of the movement to have direct interaction with him.

The reverence for John Frum and for America is wholly evident during the John Frum Day parade in which meticulous attention is placed on recreating the atmosphere and ceremony emblematic of the US Army's presence during World War II. During the parade, 'soldiers' from the John Frum group are on show with attention placed on recreating the appearance of US Army personnel from the military band, to locally fashioned berets and ammunition belts, and rifles shaped from bamboo (see Figures 12.3 and 12.4). The parade is surrounded by an audience made up of Tannese from elsewhere on the island as well as significant numbers of international and domestic tourists. What is most noticeable is the presence of the American flag in and around the parade area, highlighting that the cargo cult phenomenon is inextricably linked to the largesse of foreign forces; in this case the US Army.

In the case of the John Frum movement, much revolves around a new dawn in which islanders will find a prosperity and emancipation that colonisation and

Figure 12.3 John Frum Group parade band.
Source: Image © Sebastian Bador, 2014.

Figure 12.4 John Frum Group soldiers.
Source: Image © Sebastian Bador, 2014.

Christianity had removed, and tradition or *kastom* would once again reign supreme. This is characterised by Steinbauer (1979: 86) with the statement:

> John Frum who would appear in human form, would give his followers everything their hearts desired. The Europeans would leave and freedom would reign. Frum would provide new money and distribute it to all according to their needs. The one condition is that the peoples should take up the old customs again and drive the Europeans away.

Much interest in the John Frum Movement is framed around its fame as an archetypal case of a cargo cult (Cochrane 1970; Lindstrom 1993; Rice 1974). The phenomenon of cargo cults is captivating outside its actual context because of the seeming implausibility of many of their underlying tenets rooted in mythology, cosmology, religion and traditional narratives. To argue that cargo cults can be simply defined and neatly characterised belies the fact that their formation is complex and subject to the vicissitudes of 'indigenous concepts of leadership, and notions regarding the nature of power and status' (Cochrane 1970: xxix). In arguing that cargo cults are 'not a series of dissociated social phenomena' (ibid.), Cochrane acknowledges the multifariousness in the way cargo cults evolve and take shape. That cargo cults became a curiosity for researchers is therefore unsurprising and reaffirmed in Lindstrom's (1993: 3) probing: 'Who can help being absorbed by stories of Pacific Islanders earnestly scanning the horizons for fleets of great white cargo ships bringing them chocolate, radios and motorcycles?'

That cargo cults are inherently tied to material goods is a plausible theoretical and practical position given that much store is placed in the prospect of future largesse and empowerment in exchange for a lifetime of veneration. Such attitudes arise when the 'gap between wants and the means of their satisfaction' is very wide (Firth 1955: 141). Thus the intersection between traditional and developing country contexts harbours the ferment of the cargo cult phenomenon.

Movements such as John Frum have also been described as millennarian and very often centre on islander responses to colonial and missionary impositions on traditional ways of life and the ruptures and dislocations that followed. Further, such movements are predicated on future events including the arrival of a charismatic leader and the conferral of material largesse to correct deficits wrought by past losses and disjunctures. In the eyes of Lamont Lindstrom (1993: xiii) there is little that distinguishes a millennarian movement from a cargo cult, and the term cargo cult 'exposes a heritage of powerful motifs and themes', the vast majority of which are rooted in islander history and actively enacted in a variety of ways in the present.

External and non-indigenous commentary and analysis of cargo cults has characteristically projected sceptical and overly simplified rationale that ignores what can be both logical and plausible explanations, as well as improbable and fantastical imaginings. More importantly, cargo cults appear to be the demonstration of belief systems stemming from historical antecedents and mythological storylines, and no different to Christianity or any other religious leaning. Indeed, how much more plausible is Jesus Christ than John Frum?

As was pointed out to Marsh (1968) in his conversation with a John Frum Movement member, Christians had been waiting for Jesus Christ far longer than he had for John Frum. Indeed, arguably Christian visualisations of Jesus Christ and the associated array of symbolisms, prophecies and beliefs are not dissimilar to John Frum Movement ideologies, animisms and acceptances.

The question concerning who or what is John Frum necessarily provokes a range of discourses, all of which outline a plurality in conceptualisation; some arguably more fanciful than others. The extent to which John Frum is the physical manifestation of a man, or a multi-faceted, intangible phenomenon, or both, is irrelevant; 'whether or not he is physically present, he is very much a spiritual and psychic reality' (Rice 1974: 242). This reaffirms the 'problems of explanation' (Jarvie 1963: 1) and that the fascinating and compelling nature of cargo cults makes them 'believable and emotionally compelling' (Lindstrom 1993: 210).

Indeed, cargo cults and millennarian movements are intrinsically part of the myth making and cosmologies that frame islander lives. As Roslyn Poignant (1967) points out, 'myths continue to give force and meaning to the lives of the people'. In many other ways they reflect the social, economic and political changes the people are undergoing. This is what makes historical events such as World War II a powerful marker for the creation and adaptation of cosmological, religious and mythological narratives. Although fighting did not occur on Tanna, the presence of American military might and the flood of material goods were fertile grounds for the reaffirmation of movements that suggest the ushering in of profoundly monumental change.

To truly understand the ways of cargo cults is to accept indigenous reaffirmation of cosmologies and customary narratives that abut uncomfortably in non-indigenous contexts. How such narratives are conceptualised and understood is vexed given that a plurality of rationale is inevitably the case. Furthermore, the work of cargo cults is also intrinsically tied up in emancipation and the attraction of material goods as a *quid pro quo* for veneration of the idea or the charismatic identities that act as custodians for it. As Steinbauer (1979: 93) points out, John Frum would give his followers 'everything their hearts desired'.

However as Rice (1974) argues, much of the discourse on John Frum has been dominated by non-indigenous actors, especially academic anthropologists who have striven to rationalise and give meaning to the Movement. Doubtless the particularities and quirks of such a phenomenon render it ripe for examination and argument. Inglis's (1957: 261) assertions that isolating 'the external conditions which are the common and peculiar antecedents' and that a 'general historical explanation cannot be given' (ibid. 263) suggests that the best articulations perhaps come from Movement members themselves. However, local articulations are rare and, in their absence, the prominent discourse is preoccupied with deconstructing cargo cults, lending reason and simplified generalisations as to why they endure. 'John Frum came to help us get back our traditional customs, our *kava* drinking, our dancing, because the missionaries and colonial government were deliberately destroying our culture' (Chief Isaac Wan in Raffaele 2006).

The appearance of intangible war heritage in the John Frum Movement case has for the most part been seen externally as a curiosity embedded in dual conceptualisations. The first is the view that this was precipitated by the unprecedented appearance of American soldiers and military hardware during World War II, the likes of which Tannese had never seen. Second, the Movement is considered a typical response to external interventions, especially Christianity and colonisation, that interrupted and undermined long-held cosmological and religious attitudes. Colonisation and Christianity have undoubtedly shaped contemporary Vanuatu and, alongside World War II, this triumvirate has shaped contemporary local narratives and wider political, sociocultural and economic discourse.

Most starkly, the Pacific War unsettled the expatriate community in Melanesia. It interrupted for several years its internal dissensions and competition to control islanders and secure access to their labour, lands and hearts (Lindstrom 1993: 17). In an attempt to trace the incidence of cargo cults in Melanesia, Lindstrom (1993) suggests that World War II is characteristic of the types of catalytic influence that are required to bring about its inception. Such conditions provide a gateway for islanders to pursue ways of life and beliefs that are counterposed against that which has been imposed upon them.

Linking tourism and tradition (or *kastom*), especially traditional culture and customarily owned land, and understanding the attendant cultural change playing out, was a wider concern in the research related to this chapter (Cheer, Reeves and Laing 2013). This highlights what is an overtly awkward and potentially volatile coupling. Tradition or *kastom* underlines the way of life in Vanuatu, particularly in the outer island and remote rural villages (Keesing 1993; Tabani 2009). It arbitrates over disputes, confers ownership to property, allocates resources and provides ni-Vanuatus with a way of being that is an inheritance from ancestors.

However, the sanctity of *kastom* is increasingly undermined as communities embrace an increasingly monetised existence, led to a large extent by tourism expansion. In embracing such an existence, *kastom* or tradition is acknowledged as a commodity conveying invaluable comparative advantage that only they are best positioned to develop. Unsurprisingly, it is the tourism enterprise and the tourist that are most amenable to consuming traditional culture and the enactment of the colonial and missionised past (Cheer and Reeves 2013).

Cargo cults: Tom Navy

Like John Frum, the Tom Navy cult emphasised the significance of American paraphernalia and ephemera associated with World War II that was given to the local tribesmen as talismanic mementos of the war. Both cults have also come to be emblematic of the second coming of the Americans that, in all likelihood, will never transpire. For Tom Navy devotees the departure of the Americans following the end of the conflict reified John Frum devotees' faith in American salvation as an American return was framed as the second coming of Christ.

This idea of a second coming is not unlike the Prince Philip Movement on Tanna (named in honour of, and venerating, His Royal Highness Prince Philip as a divine being and brother of John Frum). This Tannese viewpoint is understandable in a culture where the external is always revered and tied into Melanesian mythology about a greater, more powerful, being coming to the islands. Prince Philip was known as *husban blong kwin* (husband belonging to Queen) and Prince Charles was known as *nambawan san blong kwin* (number one son belonging to Queen). Because of the propensity of the Tannese to look towards the horizon for a providential sign of a mythological homecoming the Pacific War made visits such as Tom Navy and John Frum appealing.

Despite these cults appearing fantastic or absurd to some, it is worth further considering the intangible heritage from a Tannese perspective. During the late 1930s and early 1940s when the troops started to arrive in ships and supply planes, the artillery, permanent barracks and the soldiers themselves would have been akin to a second coming of the missionaries in impact. Only this time the message was to save the Pacific from the Japanese. Perhaps one way to understand the impact of the arrival of the Allied forces, predominantly Americans, upon ni-Vanuatu society during this period is statistically. The base at Efate and the airstrip on Espiritu Santo processed approximately half a million soldiers at a time when the entire native population of Vanuatu was 60,000 (Lindstrom 1981: 104). So, when considered from this perspective, the cosmological views of the John Frum and Tom Navy groups are totally understandable and do not seem as irrational as initial perceptions may lead one to conclude. Likewise the names of the cults, sometimes seemingly ridiculed on television programmes such as the US version of *Meet the Natives*, are not preposterous when understood in context. To paraphrase anthropologist Kirk Huffman's observation: his name was Tom and he was in the navy, hence Tom Navy.

A few important points about Tannese cults and the Pacific War need to be made. The Tannese were not willing participants in this process although they later lent their support (effectively the Allies dropped out of the sky or arrived on ships). The second thing is that we cannot claim a uniformity of the experience across the country or within Tannese society. Indeed, certain villages have embraced John Frum and are known as John Frum settlements with commemorative events that attract large followings of locals, observers and tourists, while neighbouring villages may lead *kastom* life or indeed modern lives. A pattern is hard to discern, if present, because of linguistic and cultural diversity and also because the experience of the Pacific War was complex and diverse. The question arises whether the war had a lasting effect on the people of Tanna. Clearly the answer is yes, evidenced by the continuation of John Frum Day.

In the past five years America has re-engaged with the Pacific Island nations and increasingly it regards the region as an important theatre of regional security. So the Tannese desire for recognition of their historical role in the Pacific War and of their ongoing cultural practices associated with the war is again topical and has recently gained new relevance. During a delegation visit to America Chief Mangau, a Tom Navy chief, was awarded a World War II Victory Medal by Maj Gen Tony Cucolo, then commander of the 3rd Infantry Division, in recognition of his father's contribution to the war effort opposing the Japanese, and following an audience with the former United States Secretary of State and retired army general Colin Powell. Today there is a clear sense that the United States and Australia no longer dominate islander regional agendas and accordingly there has been a diminution of interest in war heritage throughout Melanesia and Polynesia to such an extent that war commemoration is less relevant than it once was throughout the region. This has meant that the bulk of the war debris from the Allied effort is not curated and is still strewn across the landscape where it is turned into souvenirs or utilised as required. The question that arises for islanders is why should they conserve and curate this war *matériel*?

Some of the most important remnant war *matériel* is the extensive maritime heritage found near Luganville in Espiritu Santo. The wreck of the SS *Coolidge* is a renowned scuba diving site noted for the degree of difficulty and the fact that you can dive the entire length of the ship. Also located near Espiritu Santo is Million Dollar Point. Here an anecdotal story asserts that, upon their departure from the Vanuatu, the US Forces offered military surplus that had been stockpiled for sale to the returning British and French colonial powers as per the post-war settlement. A price could not be agreed with the former colonial administrators so as part of Operation Roll-Up, the American military, operating from Buttons base, dumped literally billions of dollars-worth of the war *materiel* that remained off Million Dollar Point.

Second, while the cult ceremonies, alongside maritime heritage such as SS *Coolidge* and Million Dollar Point, may be the obvious visual reminders of the war, the most potent political one ultimately is the intangible, heritage folkway, tradition associated with the war such as John Frum ceremonies or the Tom Navy story. They are the most enduring throughout the communities we have observed and spent time with. In a sense this is similar to discussions about Blackbirding (the practice of indenturing labour and forced removal of Pacific Islanders to work on the Queensland and Fijian sugar cane plantations), whereby the population of Vanuatu is still at pre-European contact levels and the desire for redress is apparent throughout much, although not all, of the community and at the highest levels, including the *Mulvatumauri* – Council of Chiefs. The issue here is that colonialist and neo-colonialist dialogues take the level of remembrance amongst ni-Vanuatu for granted or monetise it for commercial purposes (recently an Australian entrepreneur released John Frum's Cargo Cult Rum after he 'stumbled upon a tall-but-allegedly-true tale that draws on folklore, war, and even a second coming of sorts' as retold by his father). In doing this the extent and nature of how Pacific Islanders remember the war or other difficult heritage is often underestimated.

Conclusion

Underlying our discussion of the key commemorative event of John Frum Day and other associated World War II heritage is the contention that subaltern voices, particularly Melanesian ones, and specifically for the purposes of this chapter those of ni-Vanuatu, are often not heard, ignored and in some cases subdued in many of the discourses about their respective role in the Pacific War and the support that they provided in assisting the Allied war effort throughout the region.

Ultimately there is ambivalence amongst islanders who largely feel that, unless war heritage has a livelihood imperative, it is unlikely that there is the capacity or desire to preserve it, irrespective of the high level of significance attributed to World War II heritage by former combatant countries such as America, Japan, Australia and New Zealand. This narrative of providence in the John Frum and Tom Navy stories and their associated events explains their enduring appeal whilst the other war-related heritage (such as Million Dollar Point) has less significance; it is an excellent scuba-diving site and for many it continues to serve a cautionary tale of waste in an impoverished country. Hviding and Rio (2011: 325) argue that 'throughout the Pacific, local cultural heritage has been a central element in political innovation in and beyond the local'; the commemorative events of World War II are emblematic of this where islanders will remember and re-enact the war legacy as they see it.

At the time of writing the final draft of this chapter Vanuatu, and Tanna especially, is reeling from the cataclysmic impacts of Cyclone Pam on 13 March 2015; an unprecedented Category 5 cyclone that has caused widespread damage. In Tanna, not only have housing structures been demolished, but food gardens on which most subsistence is based have been severely depleted. In the weeks to follow, the rebuilding process has seen Australian and New Zealand military and civilian assistance arrive on Tanna. Helicopters and barges disgorging food, building supplies and vehicles have been prolific. In many ways this is analogous with the arrival of United States Army personnel during World War II. How this will be interpreted and enacted in years to come is a curious question in light of this discussion concerning the John Frum Movement.

References

Cochrane, G. (1970). *Big Men and Cargo Cults* (Oxford: Clarendon Press).

Firth, R. (1955). 'The theory of "cargo" cults: a note on Tikopia'. *Man, 55*, 130–2.

Hviding, E., and Rio, K. (eds) (2011). *Made in Oceania: Social Movements, Cultural Heritage and the State in the Pacific* (Wantage, Oxon: Sean Kingston Publishing).

Inglis, J. (1957). 'Cargo cults: the problem of explanation'. *Oceania, 26*(4), 249–63.

Jarvie, I. C. (1963). 'Theories of cargo cults: a critical analysis'. *Oceania, 34*(1), 1–31.

Keesing, R. (1993). *Kastom* re-examined. *Anthropological Forum, 6*(4), 588–96.

Lindstrom, L. (1993). *Cargo Cult: Strange Stories of Desire from Melanesia and Beyond* (Honolulu: University of Hawaii Press).

Lindstrom, L. (1981). 'Cult and culture: American dreams in Vanuatu'. *Pacific Studies 4*(2), 101–23.

Marsh, D. (1968). 'The surprising gospel of John Frum'. *Pacific Islands Monthly, 32*(10), 87.

Poignant, R. (1967). *Oceanic Mythology: The Myths of Polynesia, Micronesia, Melanesia, Australia* (London: Hamlyn).

Raffaele, P. (2006). 'In John they trust'. *Smithsonian Magazine,* February. Available from: www.smithsonianmag.com/people-places/in-john-they-trust-109294882/?no-ist [23 June 2005].

Cheer, J. M., Reeves, K. J. and Laing, J. H. (2013). 'Tourism and traditional culture: land diving in Vanuatu'. *Annals of Tourism Research, 43*, 435–455.

Cheer, J. M. and Reeves, K. J. (2015). 'Colonial heritage and tourism: ethnic landscape perspectives'. *Journal of Heritage Tourism*, pp. 1–16.

Rice, E. (1974). *John Frum he come* (New York: Doubleday & Company).

Steinbauer, F. (1979). *Melanesian Cargo Cults: New Salvation Movements in the South Pacific* (Brisbane: University of Queensland Press).

Tabani, M. (2009). 'Dreams of unity, traditions of division: John Frum, *kastom* and inter-manipulation strategies as cultural heritage on Tanna (Vanuatu)'. *Paideuma 55*, 27–43.

US Navy (1948). 'Operation Roll-Up: the history of surplus property disposal in the Pacific Ocean', prepared for the United States Government Department of the Navy (Washington, DC: Naval Historical Archives), pp. 1–32.

Worsley, P. (1968). *The Trumpet Shall Sound: A Study of 'Cargo Cults' in Melanesia* (second edn) (New York: Schocken Books).

13 The community museum and the heritage of conflict in the Kelabit Highlands, Sarawak, Malaysian Borneo

Jonathan Sweet, Toyah Horman and Jennifer Rowe

The Kelabit Highlands in the heart of Borneo are the traditional lands of the indigenous Kelabit people. In 1944, 'Z Special Force' member Major Tom Harrisson (anthropologist, archaeologist and a member of Mass Observation) parachuted into the Plain of Bah, where, from the village of Bario, he organised and led the Kelabit people in a campaign against the Japanese. The isolated tropical highlands of Borneo had become part of the theatre of modern warfare.

The memories of the events of World War II and later on the experiences of The Confrontation with Indonesia in the 1960s are still with the Kelabit people, vividly manifested in intergenerational stories shared between members of the community. As the elders with knowledge of life prior to and during these conflicts pass on, there is a strong desire to document the history of the Kelabit and to review the management of cultural landscapes associated with the memories and experiences of these conflicts in the Kelabit Highlands. The community sees the sustainable management of the landscape as essential to the preservation and representation of heritage values; values that are integral to Kelabit identity. They are also concerned to create a tangible facility through which to express their cultural heritage values. This chapter will contextualise and discuss initiatives that are being undertaken to document and prioritise the heritage of the Kelabit people, with particular reference to the legacies of these wars. It will consider how the decisions being made by the community are being shaped by the influences of the past, the perceived need to ensure the preservation of a distinct culture and the potential economic benefits of cultural tourism. This account is based on source material drawn from archival research and from fieldwork, during which the authors have worked directly with members of the Kelabit community in the process of developing a community museum and cultural centre.

When the heritage values of the World War II experiences of the people of Sarawak were discussed at the 'Workshop on War and Memory in Malaysia and Singapore', in 1995, the emphasis was primarily on the experiences of the Malay, Chinese and Indian residents of the capital Kuching. The experiences of indigenous people received little attention, despite their engagement with wartime events. Furthermore, it is evident from more recent research that the experience of the

Kelabit during The Confrontation in the 1960s has added another layer of significance to the cultural landscape of the Kelabit Highlands.[1]

This chapter addresses this by discussing the efforts of the Kelabit people of North Central Borneo to incorporate heritage values into a community development model that includes conservation and educational goals, and has been informed by the ideals of sustainable cultural tourism. This is seen as a way of building a meaningful and engaging means of managing a complex and contested landscape. Within this broader objective, this chapter highlights the intersections that have emerged between heritage values and the memories and legacies of remote, jungle-based warfare. The methodology is guided by the understanding that heritage construction is a process informed by the social, cultural and political contexts in which it is occurring. In this chapter, we argue that, since World War II, heritage awareness has been shaped in the community through the participatory process of dialogue and exchange between the Kelabit people and their friends and allies. As Gegner and Zino have asserted recently, 'the heritage of war... is not natural but contingent, and dependent on the work of those agents, who bring it into being and sustain it' (Gegner and Zino 2012: 2).

In Malaysia, the representation and memorialisation of experiences of war is evident in museums, and Ahmad (2015) has discussed some interpretations of the Japanese occupation. However, in the main the experiences of the Kelabit appear to be absent from this representation. The Kelabit people are a Christian minority in the multifarious Malaysian political system in which they are represented by the Rurum Kelabit Sarawak (RKS). In recent years this community organisation has sought to address the representation of their culture. They have facilitated collaborations with resource-rich partners in Sarawak and beyond who share development and conservation interests. These partners have included the University of Malaysia (Sarawak), with which the RKS has worked to utilise communications technology for educational purposes (in particular the e-Bario project); the Sarawak Museum, which has supported efforts to research and document movable cultural heritage; and the McDonald Institute for Archaeological Research, University of Cambridge, which has surveyed and documented highland cultural sites under the leadership of Professor Graeme Barker. Barker's interest in understanding the landscape as a 'cultural and historical artifact' (Barker cited in Coates 2007: 34) has very real ramifications for land rights claims and for cultural tourism in the Kelabit Highlands, and dovetails with the work of Dr Ramay Bulan (2003), who has argued for an analysis that takes account of intangible heritage traditions, to recognise in law the long-standing Kelabit connections to the land. Heritage-focused research and associated projects have therefore been supported by the RKS as a key way of fostering the development of the town of Bario and its surrounding villages. The Kelabit Highlands Community Museum Development Project, for which Deakin University, has provided assistance, is part of this loose constellation of heritage programmes. Evaluation has suggested that the success of these kinds of heritage management programme may be contingent on the degree to which they are incorporated into social networks and help to sustain relationships within the community. This community involvement underpins the conceptualisation of the museum and cultural centre, which is intended to have a key role in the commemoration of the community's experiences of war.

World War II heritage values

This research adds a new dimension to the discourse addressing the management of the heritage of war by considering the agency of a fragile community that is attempting to address the fragmentation and submersion of their culture and to construct a robust representation of identity. A key aspect of this is drawn from the heritage significance accorded to the alliance between the Kelabit people and the allied forces operating in North Borneo during World War II, and the legacies of this fellowship in the following decades. In 1959, Tom Harrisson wrote of this fellowship in the memoir *World Within. A Borneo Story,* and the biographical accounts of others have continued to reinforce the significance of this relationship in post-war generations.

In his memoir, Harrisson recounted wartime experiences in the Highlands as a leader of the Z Force commandos (Operation SEMUT). He documented essential wartime operations such as the initial establishment of relationships between the members of Z Force and the Kelabit through the use of commodity exchange (predominately parachutes); activities, such as the innovative communal construction of a bamboo airstrip; and the strategic support of local traditions, such as the taking of enemy heads. Reflecting on his experiences, Harrisson acknowledged his profound personal debt to the Kelabit people who, he wrote, 'have looked after me, in war and peace, for years' (Harrisson 1959: xii).

In his writing prior to the war Harrisson (1933) had promoted the scientific and cultural richness of Borneo, having undertaken an exploratory collecting expedition there in 1932. Indeed, he was privileged to get close to the remote Kelabit at that time because during the government of the Brooke dynasty (1841–1940) this small tribe had largely 'remained beyond effective contact' (Pringle 1970: 320). Their situation was distinct from that of the largest indigenous group, the Iban, whose lands were more accessible from Kuching. Some Iban were employed in the pre-war Brooke administration, and in some cases they continued to work in the Japanese occupation government. Kelabit attitudes to the sovereignty of their forest homelands also distinguished them from the coastal Malays, whose attitudes to the occupation (it has been argued) 'were mostly ambivalent' (Talib 2000, pp.135–6), and for whom the return to colonial rule after the war may have been tolerated as a prelude to national independence. From the mid-1940s, the experiences of the war and the impact of modernity were thus distinct for the Kelabit because, critically, the alliance they formed with allies during the war was clearly focused on vanquishing the Japanese occupiers.

The Confrontation and transformation of identity

A second phase of significant community transformation as a result of the experience of conflict was experienced by the Kelabit in the 1960s, and was a major factor in influencing a change in the cohesiveness of community identity. In

1963 Sarawak, formerly a British Crown Colony protectorate, was incorporated into the newly formed Federation of Malaysia. Indonesia laid territorial claims to parts of Sarawak, and the incursion of its forces into border areas and attacks against local tribal Dayak and other indigenous peoples constituted an undeclared war known as The Confrontation (*Konfrontasi*), which lasted until 1966. These events had a significant impact on the Kelabit owing to the tribe's proximity to the Sarawak–Kalimantan border.

The location of the main Kelabit settlement of Bario in the Plain of Bah was again recognised as being of strategic importance amidst the challenging terrain, and Commonwealth forces utilised Kelabit Border Scouts in intelligence-gathering activities, because of their local knowledge and extended family networks. Bario became the operational centre for British SAS forces tasked with defending other Kelabit longhouses deeper in the interior. Small-scale air raids were launched by Indonesian forces and many Kelabit in the area were too dispersed to be properly defended, prompting the SAS to relocate a number of longhouse communities away from the border area and resettle them on the Bario plains where they were well protected from the enemy. This move had the effect of concentrating the Kelabit population into a more centralised community group and created an uninhabited frontier region to the east. Amster describes this as 'a pivotal event that shaped local attitudes towards the border' (Amster 2009: 317), and resulted in conditions that have been examined by Kelabit sociologist Poline Bala (2002). Bala has highlighted that local awareness of political allegiances and boundaries was minimal until The Confrontation, when land was granted to those Kelabit who had been relocated. Involvement in this new political environment and the imposition of constraints by the nation-state therefore signified a 'key

Figure 13.1 Kelabit longhouses that housed Commonwealth forces during The Confrontation. In the foreground the remains of defensive bunkers are a reminder of
the incursion of the Indonesian military.

Source: Jennifer Rowe.

transformation' in social relations and cultural legitimacy whereby 'people from across the border came to be viewed as outsiders rather than relatives (*lun ruyung*)' (Amster 2006: 215).

Regardless of the separation between community members as a result of political divisions, markers of The Confrontation, such as defensive bunkers against the Indonesians and buildings that housed Commonwealth forces in Pa Lugan, still remain embedded in the landscape as a reminder of the incursion. Furthermore, families display with pride medals awarded by the British for military contribution and weapons used to succeed against the enemy, reinforcing the centrality of this event in the collective Kelabit identity. The lasting impacts of the events of The Confrontation and in particular the relocation of families fostered another level of connection to the landscape resulting from a process clearly marked by their involvement in military campaigns and their experiences of war.[2]

The awakening of heritage preservation in Bario

During the post-war British administration of Sarawak (1946–60), a missionary school was established in Bario and Christianity flourished. The impact of education was felt most profoundly during the 1950s, when the current Kelabit leadership were children. During this period, Harrisson stayed on in Borneo as the Government Ethnologist and Curator of the Sarawak Museum in Kuching from where – as a counterpoint to the work of the missionaries – he was an important agent in promoting the foundations of a modern concept of heritage conservation. Through his ongoing personal relationships and fieldwork in the Kelabit Highlands he raised heritage consciousness in the community; he was able to interpret movable and intangible heritage with authority; and he also developed local approaches to archaeological and anthropological research. Furthermore, he promoted the value of indigenous visual arts and music (later seen as 'intangible cultural heritage') as a foundation component of economic development, and proactively built capacity within the indigenous community to enable its representatives to participate in museum operations.

In Bario during the 1960s and 1970s the question of heritage started to emerge in the thoughts of a new western-educated generation who had adopted Christianity. Kelabit students became aware that there was a lack of continuity with the practices of their grandparents, and that some relatively benign cultural expressions appeared to be at risk of disappearing. As Bala (2009) has argued, Christianity enabled the Kelabit to free themselves from evil spirits and also to embrace a form of modernity but in the process much of the pre-contact culture was submerged. The desire to foreground some practices and assert these as cultural heritage underpins the thinking of the current leadership, and also reflects the wishes of the wider community. For example, in the words of a RKS Council Member, the former Bario school principal Lucy Bulan:

At the time this was happening I don't think people thought about the kind of loss that they would experience. It is much later, I remember in the sixties when we started going to school, when almost everything was gone, that we discovered that even our dances were no longer being practised, and then we started saying 'surely not every thing Kelabit is wrong, it cannot be that everything western is right, it cannot be that everything western is Christian and everything Kelabit is non-Christian, *it can not be, there must be something in our culture that surely can be considered still good*, not un-Christian, in particular'. So, very consciously, we bought back the dancers, which we had thrown away, and there were discussions, I remember, about what are the things that we could still keep doing and what are the sorts of things we must not do anymore.

(S. Wilmot, personal communication, June 2012)

In the years since, this awakening has led to the realisation that the preservation of Kelabit culture necessitates the ability to more clearly articulate heritage values. Thus, the contemporary Kelabit leadership has pursued a heritage strategy in which they have encouraged the assemblage of traditional Kelabit culture, informed by Christianity and modernity, and within a framework that addresses contemporary social, political and economic issues. Bala sees Christianity as a direct outcome of the community's involvement with outside forces during World War II and her work is a significant example of where high-level research is being conducted by community members that goes beyond the recording of historical facts to inform a much deeper understanding of the social conditions that have shaped heritage values. As a Kelabit woman, Bala's research shows that heritage construction is a process in which the community itself is participating and has some agency.

An awareness of the significance of wartime experiences in the affirmation of heritage and identity has also been facilitated in the broader community through more recent external agents. The Malaysian Heritage Group commenced a well-publicised project to locate and preserve World War II aircraft, but perhaps more profoundly, direct exchanges with the Kelabit villagers include interactions with former Allied servicemen. In 1996 and 1997, Major Jim Truscott, an Australian serviceman working for the Special Operations Headquarters, researched *Voices from Borneo; The Japanese War* (nd), which focused on the experiences of Australian servicemen who had participated in Operation SEMUT and the Kelabit people who assisted them. Truscott conducted oral history interviews with wartime survivors and their descendants, a process that facilitated the sharing of memories and revealed the level of emotion that had been buried within the community.

In 2009 this was followed by a television documentary broadcast by PBS, which was titled *The Airmen and the Headhunters* (2009). It tells a powerful story of the crash-landing of an American plane in the Borneo jungle during 1944. Some of the crew were rescued and cared for by indigenous groups in the Kelabit Highlands and, with Harrisson's assistance, they were eventually flown out of Borneo some months later. The film includes dramatic re-enactments of historical events and rare archival footage of Kelabit customs. Above all, however, the heritage significance of these events is reinforced through interviews with surviving American and Australian soldiers involved in the rescue, and local representatives who describe and interpret their memories or understandings of events. These first-hand testimonials showed that there is willingness within the community to express and share their experiences, which they have vested with heritage significance. The research also demonstrated that members of the community were willing to participate in the development of a cross-cultural discourse concerning the shared heritage significance of World War II, based on the values of camaraderie or fellowship that are embodied in these historical events. This is evidenced by the scene in the film that shows community members participating in the re-creation of the innovative bamboo airstrip, which was used to shore up the surface of the rain-soaked valley floor for the evacuation of the airmen by light aircraft.

Furthermore, the way that the community now chooses to remember those experiences is largely in a positive light, placing the Kelabit as victors remarkably free from the typical sufferings of war and beneficiaries of many highly positive aspects of interactions with their military allies. Wartime stories feature prominently in Kelabit recollections of past encounters with foreigners (Commonwealth allies) and are a source of pride and empowerment in recalling victories over their enemies (Japanese and Indonesian).

Heritage, identity and development

The social and economic benefits of tourism have invigorated efforts to address the preservation of Kelabit cultural heritage and to think strategically about sustainable cultural tourism in Bario. For example, the steady increase of young tourists interested in World War II has stimulated a discussion about the use of historical site markers in a context where the historical record is often not watertight, and accordingly there has been some debate about the location of the Harrisson memorial. Furthermore, young tourists are often quick to use social media to disseminate their thoughts and impressions of Bario, and there is now a plethora of amateur internet-blogs providing interpretations of wartime historical events and their significance to local people. Accordingly, the RKS and the Council of Headmen have identified a need to address issues concerning the accuracy of the historical record, including access to archival material, and the representation of their culture. In part to address this they have initiated and supported a study into the benefits of a community-managed museum that would provide a place to engage with Kelabit culture. The museum would help orient and shape the experiences of visitors, and most importantly act as an endorsed agent for strengthening social cohesion and cultural identity within the community.

As a strategy for managing a range of issues associated with the preservation and representation of Kelabit culture, in 2011 Deakin University partnered with the RKS to assist with the Kelabit Highlands Community Museum Development Project. The first stage was designed as a participatory scoping exercise to engage with the community and aimed to understand the level of interest in the concept and the nature and availability of cultural assets that might be utilised. Fieldwork was

Figure 13.2 Local resident displaying a parachute preserved in the Kelabit Highlands.
Source: Jennifer Rowe.

Figure 13.3 Kelabit men discussing The Confrontation and their interactions with Commonwealth forces stationed in Pa Lugan during the 1960s.
Source: Sophie Turnbull.

conducted in Bario in June 2012 by a supervised group of cultural-heritage post-graduate students during which formal consultation was undertaken with a range of community representatives. These included the Council of Headmen, other community leaders from the Baram District Council and the RKS, and a range of longhouse residents. The community as a whole was interested and responsive and the researchers were provided with an opportunity to document tangible material culture and intangible cultural heritage, and to begin to understand the prioritisation of heritage values and the ways in which the community felt these might be most appropriately preserved and interpreted.

It became evident to the researchers as well that this enquiry had reignited an interest within the community to explore the question of Kelabit identity, and what it might mean to be Kelabit. The participation of community members in the consultation process, be it through discussion, display of keepsakes and items of spiritual significance or the sharing of stories, generated excitement and an evident pride in Kelabit culture. An integral component of their cultural heritage is the legacy of World War II and The Confrontation. During the fieldwork the researchers became aware that many objects from the conflict were being kept safely hidden away by community members: the preservation and discussion concerning of material culture such as military medals, Japanese swords and parachutes, is very clear evidence of the impact of island warfare and its social significance in the Kelabit Highlands. For the museum scoping exercise this reinforced the perception that the inclusion of World War II stories, issues and legacies was a critically important subject for the museum to address and that though the museum the community could manage their heritage interpretation and retain agency in the presentation of their experiences of historic events.

Conclusion

The incorporation of the experiences of Kelabit people during World War II and The Confrontation in the discourse addressing heritage and war emphasises the point that heritage construction of this type occurs through cross-cultural dialogue and exchange. In the first place, World War II figures prominently because it is considered to mark the real starting point of radical change for the Kelabit from a pagan to a Christian society, through which western education became available. Significantly for heritage preservation, the war led to a closer association with Harrisson and his concern to awaken cultural heritage acumen in the community during the post-war decades. Furthermore, alongside stories and artefacts that have been passed from one generation to another in a traditional longhouse context, the experiences of the Kelabit people during the Japanese occupation of Borneo have also been made accessible through modern technology, initiated by Allied service-men and researchers. It is clear that experiences of war and the impact of these on the landscape are intimately woven into Kelabit memory and identity. The Kelabit Highlands Community Museum Development Project furthers the aspirations of the community to manage their heritage through a framework that integrates heritage conservation, community development and cultural tourism.

References

Ahmad, A. T. (2015). *Museums, History and Culture in Malaysia* (Singapore: NUS Press).
Amster, M. H. (2006). 'Narrating the border', in A. Horstmann and L. Wadley (eds), *Centering the Margin: Agency and Narrative in Southeast Asian Borderlands* (New York: Berghahn Books), pp. 207–28.
Amster, M. H. (2009). 'Portable potency: Christianity, mobility and spiritual landscapes among the Kelabit'. *Anthropological Forum, 19*(3), 307–22.
Bala, P. (2009). 'An engagement with "modernity"? Becoming a Christian in the Kelabit Highlands of Central Borneo'. *Borneo Research Bulletin, 40*, 173–85.
Bala, P. (2002). *Changing Borders and Identities in the Kelabit Highlands: Anthropological Reflections on Growing Up near an International Border*, Dayak Studies Contemporary Society Series, No. 1 (Sarawak: Institute of East Asian Studies, University Malaysia).
Bulan, R. (2003). 'Boundaries, territorial domains and Kelabit customary practices: discovering the hidden landscape'. *Borneo Research Bulletin, 34*, 18–61.
Coates, K. L. (2007). 'Forest of broken urns. Borneo's unexplored past is dying by the chainsaw'. *Archaeology*, March/April, 33–5.
Gegner, M. and Zino, B. (eds) (2012). *The Heritage of War* (Abingdon: Routledge).
Harrisson, T. H. (1933). 'The Oxford University expedition to Sarawak, 1932'. *The Geographical Journal, 85*(5), 385–406.
Harrisson, T. H. (1959). *World Within. A Borneo Story* (London: The Cresset Press).
Pringle, R. (1970). *Rajahs and Rebels. The Ibans of Sarawak under Brooke Rule, 1841–1941* (New York: Cornell University Press).

Talib, N. (2000). 'Memory and its historical context. The Japanese occupation in Sarawak and its impact on a Kuching Malay community', in P. Lim Pui Huen and D. Wong (eds), *War and Memory in Malaysia and Singapore* (Singapore: Institute of Southeast Asian Studies), pp. 123–38.

Truscott, J. (nd), *Voices from Borneo: The Japanese War.* Available from: http://clarsys. com.au/jt/VfromBor1.pdf [14 March 2014].

Secrets of the Dead: The Airmen and the Headhunters (2009). (DVD) ICON Films for Thirteen in association with Channel 4, National Geographic Channels and International and WNET.ORG, United Kingdom. Available from: www.pbs.org/wnet/secrets/the-airmen-and-the-headhunters-watch-a-preview/451/ [23 June 2015].

Notes

1   See for example, Bala, (2002).
2   For more detail on the Kelabit connections with the land see Bulan (2003).

14 Negotiating the memories and myths of World War II civilian suffering in the railways beneath London and Berlin

Samuel Merrill

Introduction

In the spring of 1945 Londoners and Berliners alike emerged from beneath the ground to face the consequences of World War II (WWII). They surfaced from a host of subterranean spaces including air-raid shelters, bunkers and underground railways. But while the first two of these spaces are widely acknowledged to be physical reminders of the conflict, the latter are less regularly considered as former landscapes of war and are rarely analysed with respect to the wartime memories and myths that they reference (or fail to reference) through commemorative and heritage practices. This chapter remedies this situation by approaching the London Underground (Underground) and the Berlin Untergrundbahn (U-Bahn) and Stadtschnellbahn (S-Bahn) as former landscapes of war. It demonstrates how these landscapes witnessed and continue to play host to an array of WWII civilian experiences, memories and myths, which have repeatedly demanded public negotiation, been produced across and between material, representational and experiential strata, and are influenced by the interplay of a range of mnemonic actors, processes and structures. It charts these subterranean railways' WWII histories and characteristics before highlighting the dominant cultural tropes and mnemonic discourses that shape the remembrance and 'heritagisation' of subterranean experiences of civilians in wartime. Two cases illustrate the extent to which these experiences are commemorated and memorialised within the networks' landscapes today. In Berlin, the commemorative absences and myths relating to the deliberate flooding of the U-Bahn and the S-Bahn at the end of the Battle of Berlin is considered, before attention is shifted to London and the earlier Bethnal Green Tube shelter disaster of March 1943. From here it is suggested that each case's public negotiation can usefully inform the other in ways that highlight the potential for these landscapes to provide unique contexts in which to address the sensitive and often controversial subject of commemorating WWII civilian suffering.

The London Underground's war

The precedent for using the Underground as a public air-raid shelter was established during the Zeppelin raids of World War I. Despite this, however, the British government and London Transport (LT) were initially reluctant to allow the network to fulfil a similar role during WWII, as they feared the development of a 'deep shelter' mentality and the disruption of normal transport services (Calder 1969; Gregg 2001). The military defeat of France, the politicisation of the issue by the British Communist Party and the start of intensive German air-raids led to the authorities' concession, and so, from September 1940 until the end of the war, Londoners seeking shelter vied with paying passengers for space on the platforms of the city's Underground stations (Gregg 2001). The network's deep-level Tube stations and tunnels immediately proved their worth during the sustained bombing of the city by the Luftwaffe [the German Air Force] between 7 September 1940 and 11 May 1941 that became known as the London Blitz.[1] The London Blitz killed close to 30,000 people, seriously injured 51,000 and left 1,400,000 homeless (Field 2002).[2] At its peak in late September 1940 the Underground provided shelter for 177,000 people in one night (ibid.). The Tube's capacity to shelter was soon expanded beyond the operational transport network. In October 1940 parts of the network's unfinished extensions, construction of which had been interrupted by war, including Bethnal Green station, were reassigned to local authorities and converted into public shelters. In addition, by early 1942 eight of ten planned deep-level shelters connected to Tube stations had been constructed, sections of unfinished line extension had been converted for use as factories and a disused station had been reactivated as the headquarters of the wartime Railway Executive Committee and a one-time War Cabinet meeting place (Emmerson and Beard 2004).

The Underground's shelter, however, was not impervious and the Commonwealth War Graves Commission records at least 15 incidents that involved the loss of human life at Underground stations owing to bombing raids (Cooper 2010). Together these incidents claimed around 230 lives although those that actually occurred in Tube station shelters probably numbered around 200 (Ashford 2013). The most serious of these incidents involved direct bombing hits on the stations at Bounds Green (on 13 October 1940, killing approximately 17), Balham (on 14 October 1940, killing approximately 66), Sloane Square (on 12 October 1940, killing approximately 37) and Bank (on 11 January 1941, killing approximately 56). Besides the threat of direct hits Tube shelterers were also exposed to poor sanitary conditions and the risk of acute health issues including emotional stress, anxiety attacks, extreme fatigue and eating disorders (Ashford 2013, Field 2002). Despite these conditions the Underground continued to provide shelter for numerous people even after the end of the Blitz and especially during the V1 flying bomb and V2 rocket raids that occurred between June 1944 and March 1945. On the last evening of their operation, 6 May 1945, the Underground's shelters provided refuge for 260 people in spite of the considerably reduced chance of rocket raids (Gregg 2001). At WWII's end the Underground had proved itself to be remarkably durable and, despite requiring much post-war rehabilitation work, LT had only experienced long-term disruptions to its operations on 23 occasions (Gregg 2001). In comparison the immediate post-war situation that faced the Berliner Verkehrsbetriebe [the Berlin Transport Authority] (BVG), which was responsible for the Berlin U-Bahn, and the Deutsches Reichsbahn [the German State Railway] (DR) that was responsible for the S-Bahn, was far worse.

The war and the Berlin U- and S-Bahn

The first Royal Air Force (RAF) bombing raids to claim civilian lives in Berlin came in late August 1940 and led to the introduction of the Luftschutz-sofort-programm [Air Protection Emergency Programme] in October 1940. This programme sought to rationalise the provision of public air-raid shelters throughout the country (Moorhouse 2010). But of the thousands of smaller public shelters first envisaged for Berlin only around 500 were actually built. These supplemented the construction of three enormous, surface-level, anti-aircraft towers and a number of subterranean bunkers connected to the U-Bahn network, including those at Moritzplatz, Gesundbrunnen and the unfinished Hermannstrasse stations. How-ever, access to these shelters was strictly controlled and forced-labourers, prisoners of war, Jews and service-age men were all denied entrance. Such people and the women, children and elderly with nowhere else to shelter would often seek refuge in subterranean U-Bahn and S-Bahn stations and tunnels (ibid).

These shallow-dug, 'cut-and-cover' constructions offered far less protection than London's deep-level network. As in London they were characterised by overcrowding and a lack of anything beyond basic sanitary and healthcare provisions but at least they provided their occupants with some peace of mind. They also suffered direct bombing hits. For example, in November 1940 a bomb penetrated a S-Bahn tunnel near Stettiner station killing ten Polish shelterers (ibid). The aerial battle of Berlin conducted by the RAF between November 1943 and March 1944, which is reported to have killed somewhere between 4,000 and 7,500, injured between 10,000 and 17,000 and made between 450,000 and 818,000 Berliners homeless, also damaged and destroyed numerous U- and S-Bahn stations (Demps 1982; Rürup 1995). Then in February 1945 the American Eighth Air Force conducted a number of heavy raids on the city that intentionally targeted the railway network in order to disrupt suspected troop and tank movements (Taylor 2005). The first of these, Operation Thunderclap on 3 February 1945, was at first reported to have claimed 20,000 lives but is likely to have actually killed around 3,000, injured 2000 and left 120,000 homeless (Davis 2006). It is not known exactly how many were killed while sheltering in the rail network but some sources report a total of 299 people killed when the Bayerischer Platz, Moritzplatz and Memler Straße (today Weberwiese) U-Bahn stations suffered direct hits during this and a subsequent heavy air-raid on 26 February 1945 (Schomaker 2009).

In late April the ground battle of Berlin began when the Red Army entered the city. This saw what remained of the city's railway system utilised as a strategic network in an urban battleground. The S-Bahn's *Ringbahn* (the network's orbital line) became an improvised inner defence ring, which benefited from the topographical military advantages offered by its elevated sections and cuttings, and, as the battle wore on, subterranean railway stations became makeshift German command posts (Le Tissier 1999). On 26 April the first skirmishes took place in the railway tunnels beneath the city as Soviet troops used any means possible to infiltrate German defensive positions (Read and Fisher 1992; Willemar 1953). Although Berlin's subterranean stations and tunnels were used for covered movements by both sides throughout the battle, in the city centre they remained mostly in German control until the very last phases of the battle (Willemar 1953). Given that the U-Bahn network became entirely inoperable, its tunnels were also used as a means of escape and groups of several hundred German soldiers, civilians and wounded escaped Soviet capture and broke out to the west by walking for extended distances in tunnels beneath enemy lines (Le Tissier 1999). The remnants of the Nazi high command even used the U-Bahn tunnels in the first phases of their escape from Hitler's bunker (O'Donnell 1978).

The exact number of civilian deaths caused by the battle remains unknown. Early estimates placed the number between 100,000 and 150,000 (Ryan 1966) but more recent assessments suggest a figure closer to 22,000 (Antill 2005). For some the battle's end was worse than the battle itself. In its immediate aftermath the female population of the city endured widespread rape by Red Army soldiers whose treatment of German women had shifted with their westward advance from a form of sexual revenge to something more akin to the sexual spoils of war (Beevor 2002a). Estimates of rape victims range between 95,000 and 130,000, of which nearly 10,000 died as a result, often through suicide (ibid). Many women were targeted in sites of shelter such as civilian bunkers and ruined railway stations and tunnels (ibid.). Thus, at the end of WWII the subterranean sections of the U- and S-Bahn presented new risks to Berlin's civilian population. Meanwhile numerous elevated, surface and subterranean sections of track and stations had been destroyed by fighting and around a quarter of the entire U-Bahn network and the whole of the subterranean sections of the S-Bahn now lay flooded (Berger 1948). The network was incrementally returned to service starting a week or so after WWII's end but it only became fully operable to its pre-war extent late in 1950.

Whereas in May 1945 Berlin's transport authorities had presided over a decimated system in a destroyed and vanquished city, LT reflected on the success of its 'business as usual approach' to the war years, amid victory celebrations that softened the edges of its post-war rehabilitation. These very different scenarios, which reflected Britain and Germany's wider contrasting fortunes in WWII, contributed to the foundations of the different cultural tropes and mnemonic discourses that have influenced the ways in which civilian experiences of WWII in the landscapes of the Underground, U- and S-Bahn have subsequently been remembered and heritagised. In turn each of these landscapes' WWII memory and heritage broadly conforms to patterns established by the wider theorisation of subterranean space as a paradoxical site and metaphor that encompasses contrasting notions of safety and danger in both real and imaginary terms (Lesser 1987; Pike 2005; Williams 2008). In other words, the production of heritage and memory, relating to wartime civilian experiences of the railways under London and Berlin, have been influenced by the extent to which each landscape has come to be popularly perceived as having occupied different positions on a spectrum characterised by safety and security at one end and danger and fear at the other.

The Underground: an eponymous setting of security and the Blitz spirit

That the wartime Underground has been so successfully immortalised within London's popular consciousness, through cultural representations including Henry Moore's shelter sketches, Bill Brandt's photography and the artworks of Edward Ardizzone, Feliks Topolski and others, highlights the extent to which it has primarily been appreciated as a site of shelter and safety. Even if some of these representations are ambiguous as to the qualities of the Underground's WWII landscape, and others are clearly propagandistic, they still ultimately communicate 'the popular conception of the wartime Tube as a place of security and peace' (Ashford 2013: 116). The Underground, as such, is one of the eponymous settings for the formation of the 'Blitz spirit' – the new form of British national identity founded on notions of unity, solidarity and resilience, experienced by the civilian population during WWII and a major contributor to what Calder has identified as the myth of the Blitz (1990). Despite his and others' efforts to debunk purely positive historical readings of the Blitz in favour of more nuanced interpretations that highlight how the government nurtured resilient public sentiment in order to protect and reward the people, the myth continues to endure today and primarily casts the Underground as the 'showcase for the morale of civilians under fire' and the 'crucible for a new collective spirit' (Ashford 2013: 116). It endures because, as Noakes has noted, 'problematic and painful memories have little space in the public field of representation of the war' and when 'they are present they are both marginalised and sanitised' (1998, pp32 and 43). The myth of the Blitz has also proved remarkably resilient because of its ability to assimilate counterfactual exercises and negative accounts within its fundamental narrative structure (Ashford 2013).

These factors may explain why in London the commemoration of civilian deaths during the Blitz 'remains partial, fragmented and dispersed' with a post-war commemorative focus on bombed-out churches having been displaced by an unassuming memorial to the victims of the Blitz unveiled in 1999 and a variety of smaller mnemonic references to bombing raids located throughout the city – on occasion subsumed under different commemorative agendas (Moshenska 2010: 6). In the Underground the commemoration of the Blitz's victims is equally fragmented and just two of the most serious direct bombing hits have gained explicit memorialisation. The commemorative strategies pursued for one of these bombings by LT's successor, Transport for London (TfL), show how modes of official memory production and corporate heritage management have contributed to the processes of assimilation, marginalisation and sanitisation associated with the myth of the Blitz.

A memorial plaque to the Balham station bombing that was first installed in 1996 amidst the commemorative excess of the 50th anniversary of WWII was replaced on the bombing's 70th anniversary in 2010 following TfL's acknowledgement that the number of deaths that it had stated was incorrect. The original plaque read: 'In memory of the 64 people killed at this station by a wartime bomb – 14th October 1940'. A lack of historical consensus on the exact number of people killed led TfL to instal a carefully worded replacement that avoided direct reference to the scale of human life lost in the incident (see Figure 14.1). In addition, the new plaque served to rhetorically assimilate the event within the narrative of the Blitz and thus drew on a privileged aspect of Britain's collective memory and national identity. Furthermore, through the new plaque's introduction of two categories of victim (civilians and LT staff) and the official TfL typeface and logo it also functioned to reinforce the transport authority's corporate identity. While the plaque upgraded the bombing's mnemonic and heritage status by assimilating it within the Blitz narrative, in line with TfL's developing design strategy and approach to its negative past (see Merrill 2014), it also simultaneously sanitised and marginalised memory of it. By adopting a standardised mnemonic medium, chosen because of its minimal impact on the everyday operations of the railway network, TfL aimed to operationalise the memory of the wartime bombing. Furthermore, as the plaque's increasing activation during memory flashpoints like Britain's annual Remembrance Day testifies, it has also served to confine remembrance of the bombing to a specific site and a handful of commemorative events in ways similar to other painful WWII memories (see Noakes 1998 and figure 14.1). Another such event, which took place just a few weeks before the unveiling of the new Balham plaque, saw the Blitz return to the Underground in more spectacular fashion. For three days in late September 2010 the London Transport Museum, with the permission of TfL, organised a living history experience called 'Under London' at the disused Aldwych station. The experience involved costumed actors, who recreated scenes from WWII London that conformed to the mostly positive master narrative of the Blitz. The assimilative capacity of this narrative was further demonstrated by a recorded audio message, played at the end of each tour, that announced the number of people killed, injured and left homeless by the air-raids.

The U- and S-Bahn: a contaminated site of threat and victimhood

In Berlin the buried sections of the U- and S-Bahn network occupy a more ambivalent and ominous position in the city's collective cultural consciousness. Whilst unity, solidarity and resilience were surely felt by Berliners sheltering beneath their city, just as Londoners undoubtedly experienced alarm and anxiety under theirs, the way in which the war ended in the German capital has seen historical accounts of sheltering in its subterranean landscapes pervaded by a heighted sense of public fear and chaos (see Evans 2010; Moorhouse 2010). As Evans states, 'these protective havens turned into the deadliest of sanctuaries' (2010: 15). Such fears were further compounded by the later occurrence of armed warfare and rape in the network, not to mention the legacy of its use by remnants of the Nazi high command as a hiding place and means of escape. Thus, Berlin's under-city including its subterranean U- and S-Bahn stations and tunnels has become a culturally and historically contaminated site associated with lingering Nazi threats and memories of civilian suffering. The former is evidenced in numerous cultural representations. For example, the break-out from Hitler's bunker was famously recounted by the popular East German writer and columnist, Heinz Knobloch, in

Figure 14.1 The Balham plaque on Remembrance Day 2013.
Source: Ian Jones, 2013 (http://150greatthingsabouttheunderground.com [31 January 2015]).

a 1982 essay entitled 'Stadtmitte umsteigen' [Change at Stadtmitte] and recently featured in the 2004 film, *Der Untergang* [Downfall]. Since the late 1980s the city's U-Bahn network has also been recurrently used as a signature site for fictional neo-Nazi threats. Some examples include scenes from the Grips Theatre musical, *Linie 1,* first performed in 1986, and Gerhard Seyfried's cult 1990 comic book, *Flucht aus Berlin,* both of which involve their main characters stumbling across ageing Nazis in the bunkers and railways beneath the city. Novels by Yadé Kara (2003) and Chloe Aridjis (2009), which employ visions of Hitler travelling on the U-Bahn to personify the post-unification threat of neo-Nazism, might also be added to this genealogy of cultural representations as can, albeit more tentatively, recent B-movies like *The Depraved* (2011) and *Nazis at the Center of the Earth* (2012).

Meanwhile, the question of German civilian suffering in WWII remains a contentious topic that has often been perceived to be incompatible with the primary aims of the country's changing memory politics. In the immediate post-war years the collective guilt of German civil society was generally downplayed in favour of approaches that emphasised the German civilian population's suffering at the hands of the Nazi regime and their ignorance of its crimes, in order to establish a functioning democratic society (see Herf 1997). But from the late 1960s a new memory discourse emerged in which a 'focus on German crimes eclipsed discussions of German victimization' (Moeller 2005: 168) and by the late 1980s public discussion of German civilian suffering was not possible outside right-wing circles (Nolan 2005). With the turn of the millennium, however, 'German suffering, rather than German guilt' controversially became 'the principal theme in discourses about the past' with a number of publications claiming that the repressed traumatic experiences of German civilians in WWII had to be 'recalled and worked through' (Nolan 2005, pp7 and 9). In fact the supposed silence around German suffering had never really existed (Moeller 2005; Nolan 2005) but the recent return of the perceived need to break this fictional silence rendered the Allied air wars a central topic in a debate that has involved an 'enormous escalation of personal and scholarly interest, political engagement, and emotional investment' in the subject of German victimhood (Nolan 2005: 21). The results of these shifts have been disparate with the most controversial offerings placing German civilian suffering at centre-stage to the exclusion of other narratives and victims, while simultaneously repeating myths that historical scholarship has long disproved (Nolan 2005).

These cultural tropes and mnemonic discourses coalesce around the fear that the commemoration of German civilian suffering might invite forms of neo-Nazi pilgrimage and cloud an emphasis on Nazi crimes. Perhaps unsurprisingly then, there are few explicit references to Berlin's WWII civilian victims in the city's memorial landscape. The Kaiser Wilhelm Memorial Church, Christian Boltanski's 'The Missing House' and the rededicated Neue Wache each pertain to some of the physical and human losses of the city's aerial bombardment but none of them foreground these. Until recently Berlin's transport authorities rarely engaged with the city's difficult WWII past and with occurrences of German civilian suffering even less frequently. In 1998 Deutsche Bahn unveiled the Gleis 17 [Platform 17] memorial at Grunewald S-Bahn station to mark DR's involvement in the deportation of the city's Jews. BVG has also been involved in the installation of memorials that mark the Nazi destruction of Berlin's local Jewish communities, most notably at its Hausvoigteiplatz (in 2000) and Hansaplatz (in 2013) stations. In 2013, BVG also hosted a mini-exhibition at the Alexanderplatz U-Bahn station that focused on the Nazification of the transport authority (see Figure 14.2). None of these efforts, however, explicitly addressed the WWII civilian experiences of the city's subterranean railway networks, which remain mostly 'buried' in psychological as well as physical terms (Merrill forthcoming). The first explicit memorialisation of WWII civilian suffering within the U-Bahn occurred in February 2014 when a small commemorative plaque was unveiled on the 39th anniversary of the bombing raid that killed more than 108 people at what was then Memlerstraße station (Frey 2014) (see Figure 14.3). For the most part, however, the mantel for the heritage management of the Berlin civilian population's negative experiences of WWII has fallen to the Berliner Unterwelten e.V. [Berlin Underworlds Association] (BUe.V.) that formed in 1997 in order to explore and document the city's subterranean architecture. In 1999 BUe.V successfully campaigned to have the Gesundbrunnen U-Bahn station bunker included on the city's heritage list and today the bunker acts as the association's headquarters and museum, from where it runs tours to other U-Bahn station shelters across the city. The museum and these tours now provide one of the few places where Berliners and tourists can gain insight into the civilian population's experience of WWII and the narratives that are otherwise largely absent in the city's heritage and tourism sectors. However, BUe.V. has, at times, fallen prey to some of the controversies associated with the topic of German civilian victimhood. This can be illustrated by reference to the association's involvement in the production of a German-Swiss documentary called *Bunker: Die Letzten Tage* [Bunker: the last days] that is discussed further below. This documentary covered the flooding of the U- and S-Bahn at the end of the battle of Berlin.

The flooding of the U- and S-Bahn

Despite having been noted by numerous eyewitnesses and featuring in a number of historical reconstructions, no single definitive account of the wartime flooding of Berlin's subterranean rail network exists. Instead multiple accounts diverge in their description and explanation of the flood and often differ on issues such as its extent, timing, and most controversially its causes. Meyer (1992), does however, establish that the major flooding was triggered by the professional detonation of explosives in the North–South S-Bahn tunnel beneath the Landwehr Canal on the morning of 2 May 1945.

Figure 14.2 The 'From Red to Brown: the BVG after 1933' exhibition at Alexanderplatz U-Bahn station in 2013.
Source: Author, 2013.

Figure 14.3 The small plaque commemorating the WWII bombing of Memlerstraße U-Bahn station at the station that is now named Weberwiese station.
Source: Author, 2014.

Meyer's research was the result of an attempt by Berlin's Kreuzberg district assembly to memorialise the flood's victims in 1989 but these plans were abandoned when it became evident that it was impossible to say beyond doubt who had ordered and carried out the detonation and exactly how many people had lost their lives as a consequence. Most accounts attribute responsibility for the flood to an official order given either by Hitler or another member of the Nazi high command in order to stem a subterranean Soviet advance (Beevor 2002b; Boldt 1947; O'Donnell 1978). However, no evidence of a written order exists. Thus Meyer speculated that explosives were laid in preparation for such an order and then later spontaneously detonated by either SS officers or Soviet troops (1992). In the immediate post-war aftermath city authorities prepared themselves to recover 10,000 corpses from the network but in fact only around 90 bodies were officially retrieved, leading Meyer to later estimate that between 100 and 200 people had been killed as a direct result of the flooding. While press reports highlighted the shortfall in expected victims (Slupski 1945) the myth that thousands of people had died as a result of the flood still circulated widely. This myth has recurrently withstood contradictory evidence (Black 2010). Like the myth of the Blitz in Britain it connected to a national memory politics, which in Germany sought to make the recent past more comprehensible through the application of the western metacategories of good and evil in order to allow the German civilian population to identify as the innocent victims and survivors of Nazism (Black 2010; Moeller 2005; Till 2005). In the late 1940s and early 1950s, for example, sensationalised fictional and journalistic accounts shaped the flood's narrative in the city's collective memory and provided gruesome theories to explain the shortfall in recovered victims (Black 2010).

The myth of the thousands drowned has resurfaced since the 1950s, in some instances reflected through the nationalist lenses of Germany's WWII adversaries. For example the flood features in Yuri Ozerov's 1970–71 Russian film series, *Osvobozhdenie* [Liberation]. Here a cleansing deluge coalesces with a heroic Soviet liberation. Soviet troops rescue innocent German women and children not only from an overcrowded U-Bahn station that is rapidly filling with water but also from a Nazi regime that has ordered the flooding, thus reinforcing the antifascist foundational narrative, which in the 1970s still crucially underpinned both Soviet and East German national identities. The myth is further reinforced by Ennio De Concini's 1973 British-made *Hitler: The Last Ten Days*, in which General Krebs protests the so-called 'flood order' when it is issued by a suitably hysterical and demented Hitler, played by Alec Guinness – 'but, my Führer, the tunnels of the subways are now our field hospitals. There are thousands of wounded soldiers down there, thousands of women, children and old people, they would all be drowned'. Writing in the early 1990s Meyer noted how the story of the flood 'was known to nearly all Berliners in some form or another' (1992: 7) and although the flood has probably weakened in the collective memory of the city, current conditions allow its myth to prevail. The *Bunker: Die Letzten Tage* documentary dedicated significant attention to the flood but did so in a sensationalist manner by interlacing scenes taken from *Liberation* and without discrediting the myth that thousands had drowned. Elsewhere reference to the flood has been omitted altogether, most curiously from the otherwise historically accurate, award-winning *Downfall*.

A lack of mnemonic and historical closure surrounding the flood and its victims, as reflected by its memorial absence, allows the myth of the drowned thousands to be re-emphasised by uncontextualised versions of the WWII past that controversially foreground German civilian suffering at the expense of related narratives and other victims. Paradoxically, at the same time the controversy surrounding the so-called 'Germans as victims' discourse and the uncertainties surrounding exactly who was responsible for the flood continue to inhibit any act of physical memorialisation. In this way the case of the Bethnal Green Tube shelter disaster can be instructive insofar as efforts to gain greater memorialisation for the disaster have had to overcome wider, inhospitable, cultural and mnemonic discourses.

The Bethnal Green Tube shelter disaster

On the evening of 3 March 1943, 173 people were crushed to death on a stairwell leading to the Bethnal Green Tube shelter when the fear of an anticipated bombing raid and the unrecognised sound of a salvo of anti-aircraft rockets led to a panicked surge towards the shelter's entrance. In fact, no bombs fell in the area that evening.

A highly censored account of the incident appeared in the national press two days later and a secretive and rapid official inquiry was completed within three weeks and then withheld from the public until January 1945, owing to the fear that it might be used by enemy propagandists (Dettman 2010). The inquiry emphasised the psychological and environmental causes of the disaster but ultimately attributed it to 'a number of people losing their self-control at a particularly unfortunate place and time' (Coates 1999: 60).

These psychological causes stand in stark contrast to the notions of public behaviour recognised to be the hallmark of the Blitz spirit and their refutation has become a fulcrum around which a recent campaign to have the disaster properly memorialised has formed. In 2007 the Stairway to Heaven Memorial Trust (SHMT) was established to raise the £550,000 required to build a memorial that had been designed a year earlier by a local architect. The SHMT, including local community members that were directly affected by the disaster such as survivors and victims' relatives, has emphasised the initial, official, cover-up of the disaster in order to claim that the disaster is absent from the city's collective memory of WWII and that the physical causes of the disaster, which included the insufficient shelter entranceway, poor lighting and the lack of a central banister (Coates 1999) were its primary cause as opposed to the panic of the crowd.

While the disaster's perceived forgotten status predates the SHMT's campaign and remains prevalent in the British press (see Lack 2003; Hardman 2008; Taylor 2009; Warren 2011), the disaster has, in fact, commanded modest waves of cultural remembrance since the early 1970s. In 1975 it was the subject of a television adaptation. In 1991 it became the subject of a Frank Tovey song on his *Grand Union* album, in 1992 the first historical account of the disaster appeared (Kendall 1992) and in 1993 the local council installed a memorial plaque at the station to mark the disaster's 50th anniversary. Thus the forgotten disaster was in fact the first WWII incident to be explicitly remembered in the Underground and amongst the earliest explicit occurrences of civilian suffering to be commemorated in London. The SHMT's memorial campaign that deemed this plaque unfitting for such a disaster marks the crescendo of a mnemonic process that has seen the disaster move 'from being marginal to, and almost invisible within, the dominant cultural memory of the Blitz to a central position within representations of London at war' (Noakes and Pattinson 2014: 17). The disaster's strengthening mnemonic status is confirmed by the rhetorical support given to the campaign by Britain's last three Prime Ministers, by recurrent academic attention (see Bourke 2005; Dettman 2010; Freedman 1999; Moshenska 2010; Noakes 1997, 1998; Noakes and Pattinson 2014) and by its recent use by Jessica Kane as the basis for her historical novel, *The Report* (2010). Additionally, the 70th anniversary of the disaster in 2013 saw the launch of a digital oral history and archive project involving researchers from the University of East London working in collaboration with the SHMT and local survivors, witnesses and victims' relatives. By mid-2015 this initiative had resulted in the publication of an oral history book and a schools' teaching pack (both available in electronic as well as physical forms), and the creation of two 30-minute online audio tours, one designed for adults and the other for children, which are spatially connected to the memorial via a QR code featured on a new enamel plaque attached to the railings surrounding the Tube station entrance. The assimilative power of the myth of the Blitz might be at work again but ultimately it now appears to be partially reliant on the local community's opposition to the original diagnosis that public panic was the main cause of the disaster. It might be acknowledged, then, that the myth has become self-perpetuating and retroactive in ways that see it evoked in society from the bottom up as much as the top down.

The memorial itself, which when complete will see an inverted hollow teak stairwell suspended above the entrance where the disaster occurred, was opposed in the first instance by TfL on the grounds that it would hinder the operation of the station, present health and safety risks, and infringe on the organisation's 'airspace' (LBTH 2007). TfL's objections buoyed local misconceptions that their wartime predecessor had been complicit in the causes and official cover-up of the disaster and eventually resulted in the memorial being relocated 3.5 metres away from the intended position. Construction began in 2012 so that the unfinished memorial could form the focal point of commemorations planned for the 70th anniversary (see Figure 14.4). On the 72nd anniversary, in March 2015, the Trust's secretary announced that the charity had reached its fundraising target and that the

Figure 14.4 The unfinished 'Stairway to Heaven' memorial on the 70th anniversary of the Bethnal Green Tube shelter disaster in 2013.

Source: Author, 2013.

memorial's final element would be installed by the end of the year. In part this was thanks to a donation of £10,000 pledged in April 2014 by the Mayor of London, Boris Johnson, on behalf of TfL's London Underground subsidiary, which was presumably an attempt to broker reconciliation between the transport authority and the local community. Conversations with some of the SHMT's representatives suggest that once the memorial is complete the trust might seek an official government apology for the disaster's initial handling, especially in light of the official government apology that was recently granted for the Hillsborough stadium disaster. Thus, as Noakes and Pattinson have noted elsewhere (2014), the completion of the memorial will not mark the end of contestation over the disaster's remembrance and representation not least because both of these remain partial and contingent. There remains, for example, little space within the event's interpretation 'for the entrenched anti-Semitism of that period that saw Jewish residents of Bethnal Green widely blamed for the disaster' (Noakes and Pattinson 2014: 18; Freedman 1999; Bourke 2005) and the ambiguity of attributing innocence and calm or guilt and panic to a crowd in which the actions of some are likely to have contributed to their own and others' fate is also rarely acknowledged. Given the sensitivity of these narratives it is perhaps not surprising that they have so far most thoroughly been explored in a work of fiction. Kane's character Bertram (2010), for example, provides the personification of the blurred boundaries between victim and perpetrator – an individual wracked by guilt, and to a far lesser extent relief, after surviving a crush to which he actively contributed.

Reflections

The WWII pasts of the railways under London and Berlin and their constitutive narratives of civilian suffering have gained varying degrees of expression within and beyond their landscapes as determined by the convergence of a range of mnemonic actors, processes and structures. In the city of WWII's victors, the Underground has remained a home front, primarily perceived as a secure and safe site around which it has been possible to forge a new national identity reinforced by the wider myth of the Blitz spirit. This myth has endured as a dominant cultural trope and mnemonic discourse in ways that have seen it first marginalise and sanitise and more recently assimilate the negative collective memories of civilian experiences beneath London. In the city of WWII's vanquished the U- and S-Bahn became battlefronts that witnessed widespread and varied forms of civilian suffering in forms that rendered them a contaminated site of danger with limited positive, formative, cultural currency. Culturally associated with the fear of a lingering Nazi threat and drawn into the complicated and controversial mnemonic discourses surrounding German victimhood the civilian experiences of WWII under Berlin remain, for the most part, absent and uncommemorated.

Such differences have primarily been highlighted in reference to the wartime flooding of the U- and S-Bahn and the Bethnal Green Tube disaster. Both case studies index the potential risks of the mythological sufferings of urban civilian populations during WWII. However, they also provide insights as to how to negotiate the social memories that, in some cases, contribute to or are the result of such myths in ways that might inform each other's continuing remembrance and public representation. The efforts of the SHMT highlight that it is possible to carve out commemorative space for events that contradict a nation's dominant mnemonic discourse. This is a process that should arguably be emulated for the flooding of the U- and S-Bahn in order to approach a level of commemorative closure that will inhibit the persistence of historically inaccurate and potentially politically dangerous myths. Meanwhile, the mnemonic debates related to German victimhood in which the U- and S- Bahn flooding is embroiled might also provide the perspectives that can ensure that the future interpretation of the Bethnal Green disaster does not succumb to the positive assimilative powers of the wider myth of the Blitz. The future commemoration, memorialisation and heritagisation of these wartime incidents, as informed by one another, may, therefore, have the potential to contribute to the responsible approach for handling WWII examples of civilian suffering recommended by Nolan. She advocates an approach that amongst other objectives seeks to 'capture the multiplicity of diverse, often contradictory experiences and reactions' that are contextualised chronologically, causally and comparatively (2005: 31). This chapter has followed such an approach in order to demonstrate that the landscapes of the Underground, the U-Bahn and the S-Bahn, once populated by thousands during WWII and today used by millions in their everyday lives, can provide a unique and innovative site in which to consider the question of remembering civilian suffering.

References

Antill, P. (2005). *Berlin 1945: End of the Thousand Year Reich* (Oxford: Osprey).

Aridjis, C. (2009). *Book of Clouds* (New York: Black Cat).

Ashford, D. (2013). *London Underground: A Cultural Geography* (Liverpool: Liverpool University Press).

Beevor, A. (2002a). 'They raped every German female from eight to 80'. *The Guardian*, 1 May. Available from: www.theguardian.com/books/2002/may/01/news.features11 [31 January 2015].

Beevor, A. (2002b). *Berlin: The Downfall 1945* (London: Penguin Books).

Berger, R. (1948). 'Die Wiederingangsetzung der U-Bahn im Jahre 1945'. *Straßen- und Tiefbau*, 2(11), 308–14.

Black, M. (2010). *Death in Berlin from Weimar to divided Germany* (New York: Cambridge University Press).

Boldt, G. (1947). *Die letzten Tage der Reichskanzlei* (Hamburg and Stuttgart: Rowahlt Verlag).

Bourke, J. (2005). *Fear: A Cultural History* (London: Virago Press).

Bunker: Die Letzten Tage (2003). Documentary directed by M. Reuter, and G. Hodge (Germany and Switzerland: Salzgeber and Co Medien GmbH).

Calder, A. (1990). *The Myth of the Blitz* (London: Jonathan Cape).

Calder, A. (1969). *The People's War: Britain 1939–1945* (London: Jonathan Cape).

Coates, T. (1999). 'Tragedy at Bethnal Green: report on an inquiry into the accident at Bethnal Green Tube station shelter' (London: The Stationery Office).

Cooper, N. (2010). 'Analysis of casualty and fatality figures'. Available from: www.nick cooper.org.uk/subterra/lu/tuawcafa.htm [31 January 2015].

Davis, R. B. (2006). *Bombing the European Axis Powers. A Historical Digest of the Combined Bomber Offensive 1939–1945* (Maxwell AFB, AL: Air University Press).

Demps, L., (1982). 'Die Luftangriffe auf Berlin. Ein dokumentarischer Bericht'. *Jahrbuch des Märkischen Museums*, *8*, 7–44.

Der Untergang (2004). Film directed by O. Hirschbiegel (Germany: Constantin Film Produktion).

Dettman, S. (2010). *The Bethnal Green Tube Shelter Disaster of 1943: A Stairway to Heaven* (London: The East London History Society).

Emmerson, A. and Beard, T. (2004). *London's Secret Tubes* (Harrow Weald: Capital Transport).

Evans, J. V. (2010). 'Life among the ruins: sex, space, and subculture in zero hour Berlin', in P. Broadbent and S. Hake (eds), *Berlin: Divided City, 1945–1989,* (New York and Oxford: Berghahn Books), pp. 11–22.

Field, G. (2002). 'Nights underground in darkest London: the Blitz, 1940–1941'. *International Labor and Working-Class History*, *62*, 11–49.

Freedman, J. R. (1999). *Whistling in the Dark: Memory and Culture in Wartime London* (Lexington, KY: University Press of Kentucky).

Frey, T. (2014). 'Erinnerung im U-Bahnhof: Gedenktafel für Bombentote von 1945 enthüllt'. *Berliner Woche*, 27 February. Available from: www.berliner-woche.de/nachrichten/bezirk-friedrichshain-kreuzberg/friedrichshain/artikel/36732-gedenktafel-fuer-bomben tote-von-1945-enthuellt/ [31 January 2015].

Gregg, J. (2001). *The Shelter of the Tubes* (Harrow Weald: Capital Transport).

Hardman, R. (2008). 'The Bethnal Green Tube tragedy saw 173 people crushed to death making it the war's worst civilian disaster. But why was it censored from history?' *Daily Mail*, 27 February. Available from: www.dailymail.co.uk/news/article-521490/The-Bethnal-Green-Tube-tragedy-saw-173-people-crushed-death--making-wars-worst-civilia n-disaster-But-censored-history.html [31 January 2015].

Herf, J. (1997). *Divided Memory: The Nazi Past in the Two Germanys* (Cambridge MA and London: Harvard University Press).

Hitler: The Last Ten Days (1973). Film directed by E. De Concini (UK: Tomorrow Entertainment).

Kane, J. F. (2010). *The Report* (London: Portobello Books).

Kara, Y. (2003). *Selam Berlin* (Zurich: Diogenes).

Kendall. D. (1992). 'The Bethnal Green Tube disaster'. *East London Record*, *92*(15), 27–35.

Knobloch, H. (1982). *Stadtmitte Umsteigen: Berliner Phantsien* (Berlin, Hauptstadt der DDR: Buchverlag Der Morgen).

Lack, J. (2003). 'The hush-hush catastrophe'. *The Guardian*, 15 February. Available from: www.theguardian.com/lifeandstyle/2003/feb/15/weekend.jessicalack [31 January 2015].

Le Tissier, T. (1999). *Race for the Reichstag: the 1945 Battle for Berlin* (London and Portland, OR: Frank Cass).

Lesser, W. (1987). *The Life below the Ground: A Study of the Subterranean in Literature and History* (London and Boston, MA: Faber and Faber).

London Borough of Tower Hamlets (LBTH) (2007). 'Delegated Report: Town Planning Application. Ref No: PA/06/02326'. 15 January 2007.

Merrill, S. (2014). 'Excavating buried memories: mnemonic production in the railways under London and Berlin', unpublished PhD thesis (London: UCL).

Meyer, K. (1992). *Die Flutung des Berliner S-Bahn-Tunnels in den letzten Kriegstagen: Rekonstruktion und Legenden* (Berlin: Kunstamt Kreuzberg).

Moeller, R. G. (2005). 'Germans as victims? Thoughts on a post-Cold War history of World War II's legacies'. *History and Memory*, *17*(1–2), 145–94.

Moorhouse, R. (2010). *Berlin at War* (New York: Basic Books).

Moshenska, G. (2010). 'Charred churches or iron harvests? Counter-monumentality and the commemoration of the London Blitz'. *Journal of Social Archaeology*, *10*(1), 5–27.

Nazis at the Center of the Earth (2012). Film directed by J. L. Lawson (USA: Asylum).

Noakes, L. (1998). *War and the British: Gender, Memory and National Identity* (London: IB Tauris).

Noakes, L. (1997). 'Making histories: experiencing the Blitz in London's museums in the 1990s', in M. Evans and K. Lunn (eds), *War and Memory in the Twentieth Century* (Oxford and New York: Berg), pp. 89–104.

Noakes, L. and Pattinson, J. (2014). 'Introduction: Keep calm and carry on – the cultural memory of the Second World War in Britain', in L. Noakes and J. Pattinson (eds), *British Cultural Memory and the Second World War* (London: Bloomsbury), pp. 4–24.

Nolan, M. (2005). 'Air wars, memory wars'. *Central European History*, *38*(1), 7–40.

O'Donnell, J. P. (1978). *The Bunker* (Boston, MA: Houghton Mifflin).

Osvobozhdenie (1970) and (1971). Film directed by Y. Ozerov (Russia: Mosfilm).

Pike, D. L. (2005). *Subterranean Cities: the World beneath Paris and London, 1800–1945* (Ithaca, NY and London: Cornell University Press).

Read, A. and Fisher, D. (1992). *The Fall of Berlin* (London: Pimlico).

Rürup, R. (1995). *Berlin 1945: Eine Dokumentation* (Berlin: Verlag Willmuth Arenhövel).

Ryan, C. (1966). *The Last Battle: The Classic History of the Battle for Berlin* (New York: Touchstone).

Schomaker, M. (2009). 'Die U-Bahn im 2. Weltkrieg'. Available from: www.berliner-untergrundbahn.de/ [10 March 2014].

Seyfried, G. (1990). *Flucht aus Berlin* (Berlin: Rotbuch Verlag).

Slupski, G. (1945). Pontonfahrt im S-Bahn-Tunnel. *Berliner Zeitung*, 7 October, p. 2.

Taylor, F. (2005). *Dresden: Tuesday 13 February 1945* (London: Bloomsbury).

Taylor, J. (2009). 'The Blitz tragedy that Churchill erased from history'. *The Independent*, 19 February. Available from: www.independent.co.uk/news/uk/this-britain/the-blitz-tragedy-that-churchill-erased-from-history-1625964.html [31 January 2015].

The Depraved (2011). Film directed by A. Fetscher (Germany: Papermoon Films).

Till, K.E. (2005). *The New Berlin: Memory, Politics, Place* (Minneapolis, MN and London: University of Minnesota Press).

Warren, J. (2011). 'Bethnal Green Tube disaster: Winston Churchill covered up Britain's worst civilian disaster'. *Daily Express*, 26 March. Available from: www.express.co.uk/posts/view/236947/Bethnal-Green-Tube-disaster-Winston-Churchill-covered-up-Britain-s-worst-civilian-disaste [31 January 2015].

Willemar, W. (1953). *The German Defense of Berlin* (United States Army, European Command).

Williams, R. (2008). *Notes on the Underground: An Essay on Technology, Society, and the Imagination* (new edn) (Cambridge, MA and London: MIT Press).

Notes

1   While originally it was only the network's deep-level lines that were known as the 'Tube' this term is now commonly used synonymously with the 'Underground' to refer to the whole network including its cut-and-cover and surface sections.

2   Air raids across Britain between 1939–41 are believed to have killed 43,000 people initially and subsequently a further 17,000.

15 Remembering wars in Vietnam

Commemoration, memorialisation and heritage management

William Logan

Unlike most of the chapters in this volume that deal with the World Wars, this chapter is concerned with more recent conflicts, commemoration strategies and war heritage management, and an Asian setting – Vietnam. In concentrating here on Vietnam's major twentieth-century wars and some of the battlefields and memorials related to them, the aim is to show how their study might reinforce, extend or raise questions about approaches taken to the World Wars and to the study of landscapes of war generally. As is well known, Vietnam has been the scene of constant struggle for most of its 3,000-year existence as a recognisable political entity. This has involved internecine conflicts between rival war lords and their clans, battles to subdue surrounding political entities such as Champa and to take their lands, and wars of resistance and independence against the Chinese, the French and the United States, followed most recently by the 1979 border war with China that was an after-shock from the Cambodian catastrophe under Pol Pot. This chapter concentrates on Vietnam's two mid-twentieth-century Indochinese Wars of Independence, neither of which was part of the World Wars. While the components of French Indochina – Tonkin, Annam and Cochin-China in today's Vietnam, and Cambodia and Laos – contributed men to the French armies in World Wars I and II, no World War battles were fought on Vietnamese territory. During World War II – or at least from the Fall of France in 1940 until the Japanese *coup de force* in March 1945 – the French remained in charge of the administration of French Indochina.

The First Indochinese War was fought against French colonial control. It commenced in 1946 (although nationalist insurgencies started almost as soon as the French arrived to set up their colonial outposts in the mid-nineteenth century) and ended with the French defeat at Dien Bien Phu in 1954. The Second Indochinese War was against the Americans and their allies (1955–72). In the West this is usually referred to as the Vietnam War; the Vietnamese call it the American War. Both of these wars were long and complicated and have been much written about, especially by the French and Americans. For the purposes of this chapter, I will focus on four landscapes of war and make a point of showing how they are viewed by the Vietnamese themselves. I have discussed the views of foreigners elsewhere (see Logan 2006; Logan and Witcomb 2013; Logan and Nguyen 2012; Logan 2013). The first landscape of war is the 1954 Dien Bien Phu battlefield in north-western Vietnam on the Lao border, from the First Indochinese War. From the Second Indochinese War, three landscapes are studied more briefly: the Long Tan battlefield in Vung Tau-Ba Ria province (formerly Phuoc Thuy province), where Australian and a mix of Viet Cong and regulars from the northern People's Army of Vietnam (PAVN) clashed in August 1967; the nearby village of Binh Ba which was the scene of violent confrontation between Vietnamese and Australian troops in June 1969; and the Long Hai complex, built on a rugged peninsula near Vung Tau to memorialise the contribution of the Viet Cong to victory over the United States and its allies.

The chapter has four aims, the first of which is to appraise the three aspects that heritage scholars and practitioners standardly consider:

1   the commemoration of wars by nations and societies;
2   the memorialisation or building of memorials and development of memorial practices around them, usually related to specific wars or campaigns and events within them; and
3   war heritage management – that is, the identification, registration, conservation and interpretation of the physical relics of war on battlefield sites.

Although not the principal interest of this chapter, it should be acknowledged that war museums separated from the battlefields, such as the War Crimes Museum in Ho Chi Minh City, the Dong Nai Museum in Hoa Binh and the Hoa Lo Museum in Hanoi (Logan, 2009), are important in conserving movable artefacts and play an educational role that is essential to effective commemoration.

The notion of 'landscapes of war' taken in the wider, non-physical sense is also important; that is, the way that wars and battles have meaning for individuals, families, local communities and nation-states. In looking at how battlefields are identified and registered, therefore, the heritage concept of significance is central. Clarifying the ways in which battlefield relics are significant is the second key aim of the paper. This leads to a questioning of the physical conservation of these relics, notably asking to what end and with what effect such work is carried out. In relation to commemoration, I am especially interested in what happens when individual and family interests clash with those of the state.

The third aim is to tease out the complications that commemoration faces when the conflict was not simply against a foreign occupying power or invading force but involved groups within a state fighting each other in a civil war. The assistance given by some Irish to the Central Powers in World War I comes to mind. In France the civil conflict aspects of World War II are not much talked about even now, nearly 70 years after the end of the war. Few French or foreign tourists know about the Musée Jean Moulin at Montparnasse and even fewer visit. In Italy, civil war came closer to breaking out during World War II – indeed, to the point that allied leaders made strategic decisions to prevent the leftists from gaining control. Vietnam is in many ways little different. Here the struggle to create a single, independent, national state became caught up in the formation of geopolitical blocs from early in the twentieth century and in the Cold War from mid-century.

Centuries-old tensions between north and south were complicated by ideological divisions throughout the country. The separation of North Vietnam from South Vietnam at the end of the First Indochinese War reinforced both the dominance of the communist nationalists under Ho Chi Minh in the northern Democratic Republic of Vietnam and the civil war in the Republic of Vietnam in the south between the communist Viet Cong and the anti-communist, pro-Western government of the Republic of Vietnam and its supporters. The two Vietnams were reunified in April 1975 after the capture/fall of Saigon and renamed the Socialist Republic of Vietnam. The chapter asks how the two wars are commemorated in the reunified state when one side in the civil war gained and remains in power. The question is complicated by Vietnam's ethnic diversity and the legacy of the involvement of some ethnic minority groups during the wars, as well as the continuing interference in Vietnam's internal politics by overseas Vietnamese, both from the Kinh Viet majority and from several ethnic minorities.

The fourth aim is to look for changes in attitudes towards wars and battlefield heritage in Vietnam and to seek signs of a softening of enmity. Nguyen Thanh Binh and I have made the point elsewhere (Logan and Nguyen 2012: 43) that the binaries of Vietnamese vs French and North vs South that have provided the usual framework for discussions of Vietnamese history and politics were always too simplistic. There were and are still today important differences *within* Vietnam, as well as within France, the United States and Australia, towards what should be commemorated and memorialised and why and how. These contrasts are based on different personal and family connections with the two Indochinese wars, different memories and different understandings of the political context of the wars and of the role of politics in shaping Vietnam's war heritage. Attitudes are never fixed and even the official Vietnamese heritage discourse has shifted perceptibly since 1954 in the case of Dien Bien Phu and 1975 in the case of the Vietnam/American War. This complexity must be recognised if the significance of landscapes of war is to be evaluated and protected and if light is to be shed on universal questions related to war and its remembrance – questions such as how does memorialisation alter as the generations that experienced a particular war first-hand pass away? At what point do pain and grief die and old hostilities disappear? And when, and under what conditions, can states begin to reuse hallowed battlefield land?

Commemoration

The Battle of Dien Bien Phu

The French had developed the 'Navarre Plan', named after its architect General Henri-Eugène Navarre, in which the French army would establish a fortified base in a valley called Dien Bien and airlift soldiers into a ring of surrounding armed positions. As it turned out, Navarre had made a disastrous strategic blunder and left his men totally unprepared for the guerrilla tactics adopted by the nationalist Viet Minh forces, the use of massive numbers of troops to drag artillery onto the ridges overlooking the valley and the mobilisation of farmers to provide continuous food supplies to the Vietnamese troops. The battle, which raged for eight weeks from 13 March to 7 May 1954, saw all the French fortresses destroyed, 62 French planes downed and 30 cannon and 6 tanks taken. The French forces under Brigadier-General Christian de la Croix de Castries capitulated only hours before the opening of negotiations on Indochina at the Geneva Peace Conference.

What is the significance of the battle? Is it so significant that the battlefield should be protected? If so, in what way? As mentioned, 'significance' is the key concept in identifying, evaluating and conserving heritage. The Burra Charter (1970) requires that a clear and convincing Statement of Significance is established at the identification stage, one that channels future management. The World Heritage system developed under UNESCO's 1972 World Heritage Convention is based on the concept of Outstanding Universal Value (OUV), although the requirement for a Statement of OUV did not come until 30 years later. In the heritage field it is now common to refer to 'values-based conservation' as international best practice. There are, of course, many kinds of value when considering battles and battlefields. It may be possible to identify and evaluate a battle site on the basis of its impact on the conduct of the war itself or on geopolitical alignments and subsequent world, regional or national history. Emotional value is also extremely important for this type of heritage and this relates to human loss and suffering both for the military personnel involved and their families and friends, but also for the people and communities who were, to use the shameful contemporary term, 'collateral damage'. Aesthetic values often contribute to the ability of the place to inspire, emotionally move or evoke a strong human response.

The Battle of Dien Bien Phu ranks highly at the global level. It is one of the great battles of the twentieth century with anti-colonial political ramifications that spread across Asia. In terms of battle strategies it also marked the shift from formal troop manoeuvres to guerrilla tactics. The significance of the battle for the two sets of military personnel was plain. For the French a humiliating defeat foreshadowed the loss of Algeria, the Suez debacle and the rapid decline of French imperial power in the second half of the twentieth century. Available casualty statistics are unreliable and contradictory. But it is estimated that around 11,000 military personnel were garrisoned at Dien Bien of whom 19 per cent were French regulars, 26 per cent Foreign Legion of whom half were German nationals, 19 per cent from French colonial Africa and 36 per cent Indochinese, including men from the Hmong ethnic minority. It seems that 2,000–3,000 French military were killed in the fighting and 5,000–6,500 wounded. The number captured – 11,000 – given by Association Nationale des Combattants de Dien Bien Phu (online, nd) cannot be right, since that is the generally accepted total number of French troops at Dien Bien Phu. Nevertheless large numbers were taken on a 'long march' to jungle prisons near the Chinese border or in Thanh Hoa in central Vietnam. Of these, more than 8,000 perished in captivity. Windrow (2004, pp646–7) reckons this amounts to a 60 per cent casualty rate, one of the worst battle statistics of the twentieth century. As late as 2009 2,350 French nationals and 2,867 French Legionnaires were still unaccounted for (Advocacy and Intelligence Index, 2009).

By contrast, for the Vietnamese it was a stunning victory on most counts. The colonial masters had been defeated. Although about 8,000 Viet Minh forces perished and 15,000 were wounded, the loss was quickly overlain by official messages of heroism and dedication to the national cause. It has long been established in heritage studies that all countries select certain places to reinforce the national story, particularly the official narrative. In relation to communal conflict and war, however, some of Southeast Asia, such as Indonesia and Cambodia, seems to prefer to 'forgive and forget'. Communist Vietnam is perhaps an exception: the value of Dien Bien Phu in supporting the state ideology and in nation building is too great for such communal amnesia. The ancient struggle for independence against the Chinese is recalled at the Hai Ba Trung temple in Hanoi commemorating the two sisters who fought off the Chinese in 39–43 CE and at Bach Dang River where invading Chinese forces were turned on their heels in 938 CE. But these are relatively unimportant as places of celebration today, the historic facts lost in the mists of time. From the Second War of Independence (Vietnam War) Khe Sanh and other sites in the Demilitarized Zone (DMZ) are exploited for foreign tourists, but there are few sites where the celebration and commemoration of the North's victory are *officially* focused. The April 1975 storming of the presidential palace in Ho Chi Minh City – now Reunification Palace – comes close but seems to be more visited by foreign tourists than Vietnamese. Perhaps the old US Embassy building in Ho Chi Minh City – site of America's ignominious departure – might have acquired national heritage significance but the USA quickly pulled it down once diplomatic relations were re-established in 1995.

Dien Bien Phu stands out, then, as the site of major national commemoration and associated memorialisation and battlefield heritage management. Since 1954 commemoration ceremonies at Dien Bien Phu have been considered among the most important public events in Vietnam (Logan and Nguyen 2012: 53). Every five years large victory ceremonies have been organised, bringing together senior political leaders and heroes from the battle to pay tribute to martyrs of the battle, praise significant contributions to the national independence struggle and express determination to overcome remaining difficulties. Activities to commemorate the Dien Bien Phu victory are organised in schools, state-led institutions and mass organisations, and have been in many forms, including street parades, public performances, exhibitions, storytelling competitions and school outings and camps.

The Battle of Long Tan

If, however, Dien Bien Phu is significant globally and seen by the Vietnamese government as a glorious milestone on the path to national independence and prosperity, where does the Battle of Long Tan rank? For Australia it has acquired iconic status, coming to represent the whole of Australian involvement in the Vietnam/American War. What do the Vietnamese make of it? For the Vietnamese matters are more complicated: not only does it mean different things to the north and the south but it also fits less well into the official national narrative. In military terms it was not highly significant, a sideshow between communist troops and the Australian allies of the United States.

During the Vietnam War Australian troops were based at Nui Dat in Phuoc Tuy province, where the Viet Cong generally held sway. The first Australian Task Force arrived in mid-1966, many of the troops being National Servicemen, enlisted following a highly controversial birthday ballot. Shortly after their arrival, in mid-afternoon on 18 August, D Company of the 6th Battalion, Royal Australian Regiment (6 RAR), was patrolling in the Long Tan rubber plantation five kilometres east of Nui Dat when the lead platoon (11 Platoon) encountered the main body of the Viet Cong 275 Regiment. This has been estimated at 2,500 men, mostly local villagers who doubled as Viet Cong guerrillas, as well as regulars from the North. Helicopters and tanks gave support and the Viet Cong fled. During the night both sides evacuated their dead and wounded. In the morning there were still 245 Viet Cong bodies in the battle area. Eighteen Australians had been killed, including 11 National Servicemen, and 24 were wounded.

The contrast in military significance and casualty numbers between Dien Bien Phu and Long Tan is enormous. The Vietnamese government tolerates foreign memorials at both battlefields – the only two permitted in Vietnam. It is fairly clear that the memorials and commemoration services at Dien Bien Phu and Long Tan have been allowed because this helped set favourable conditions for attracting French and Australian aid and business investment. In the case of Dien Bien Phu, moreover, the Vietnamese were the victors and can afford to be magnanimous. The Long Tan case is more difficult for the Vietnamese authorities. They try to portray it as their victory – 'a death blow to the mercenary expeditionary army' (Ho 1995: 280) and the casualty figures they published are different from those given by the Australians (McNeill 1993: 367–8). But telling a different narrative has made it possible to let the Australians use the Long Tan memorial site. To allow foreigners to celebrate a victory over the Vietnamese on Vietnamese soil simply would not have fitted with the story of the war that the government and military want remembered. Long Tan thus becomes a victory like Dien Bien Phu, albeit on a minor scale.

On the other hand the treatment of servicemen from the Army of the Republic of Vietnam (ARVN) and other supporters of the southern Republic has been quite different. The Hanoi government said it had no way of estimating the number of ARVN dead (Shenon 1995). ARVN cemeteries were bulldozed after 1975. ARVN veterans and their families have been unable to remember their dead publicly or as a group, and grieving could only occur within the family. Supporters of the Southern regime went to re-education camps and others disappeared quietly into the general Vietnamese population. Many fled the country as *Viet kieu* (Overseas Vietnamese), to live in diaspora communities mostly in the USA, France, Australia and Canada, where many keep alive old animosities as a way of maintaining ethnic solidarity in the host countries and some engage in anti-communist activities designed to subvert the Hanoi regime (Le 2009).

Memorialisation

In the Socialist Republic of Vietnam, the one-party state governance arrangements set the context for political and bureaucratic decision-making. Memorials are seen as part of the effort to build a unified socialist (communist) nation and the state determines what memorials are permitted. Such decision making remains locked in the civil war mindset and there is no opportunity yet to acknowledge officially or even publicly the lives lost on the southern side or the places, campaigns and events of significance to those who opposed the northern army and the Viet Cong. War cemeteries are scattered across the country and especially in the central provinces – but not for the ARVN dead, many of whose cemeteries were bulldozed and abandoned after 1975.

Dien Bien Phu

Until the 1990s internal travel within Vietnam was restricted under a travel permit system and poor transport conditions. A trip to Dien Bien Phu from Hanoi, for instance, was by road and took five days. This meant that very few Vietnamese could go to the battlefield to grieve for their dead. Memorial ceremonies at the site were for senior officials and military personnel. Around the fringes of the ceremonies were the former soldiers who had followed General Vo Nguyen Giap's order to stay behind after the battle and create a permanent township. The ceremonies were well covered by the national media, initially the press but increasingly

Figure 15.1 Urban development cutting into Dien Bien Phu's war landscape.
Source: W. Logan.

Figure 15.2 The Victory Statue at Dien Bien Phu.
Source: W. Logan.

also television. The memorials constructed at Dien Bien Phu reflected the political use of war heritage by the state. The largest monument ever constructed in Vietnam is the Victory Monument atop D1 hill, inaugurated on 30 April 2004 to mark the 50th anniversary. In a typical socialist realist style, it stands 12.6m high above a

3.6m base and consumed 220 tonnes of copper. Unfortunately it was built in a rush and the base quickly began to collapse. At least 20 officials were punished and another large sum of money has been spent on making good the statue.

Long Tan

By comparison the memorialisation at Long Tan is minimalist in the extreme – a simple cross in the midst of a rubber plantation. A set of protocols has been imposed by the Vietnamese authorities to prevent the Australian government from conducting large-scale ceremonies on Vietnamese soil. No military medals or uniforms are to be worn, no flags raised or displayed and no music played. Speeches made at the site have to be low-key and short. Groups visiting the site cannot be larger than 20 to 30 people and they must always have a permit from the local police to do so. Permanent interpretation signage cannot be put up and the local police hold the memorial plaque. A non-government organisation – the Australian Vietnam Volunteers Resource Group – looks after the site (although some small government funding is provided through the Australian consulate in Ho Chi Minh City).

Enforcement of the restrictions means there can be no equivalent to the Anzac Day services at Gallipoli, Villers-Bretonneux in France or Hell Fire Pass in Thailand. Moreover, at least from the Vietnamese side, it has been seen as a joint memorial. Thus, while the original plaque honouring the Vietnamese dead is no

Figure 15.3 The Long Tan Cross in its rubber plantation setting.
Source: W. Logan.

Figure 15.4 The Long Tan Cross with its dedication plaque.
Source: W. Logan.

longer there, there is an urn for the burning of incense, a traditional way of honouring the dead in Vietnam. Over the years, however, more and more Australians (and smaller numbers of New Zealanders) have wanted to visit the site, especially on Anzac Day (25 April) and Long Tan Day (18 August). Although the restrictions remain in place, the number of visitors at these two ceremonies has grown in recent years to more than 600, suggesting a need to renegotiate the protocols in coming years.

Binh Ba

Another contrast is seen at Binh Ba, five kilometres north of the Anzac base at Nui Dat. It was a neat little village of around 3,000 farmers and rubber plantation workers in 1969 when it became engulfed in a battle that was part of Operation Hammer (O'Neill 1968: 30). The area had been under the control of the South Vietnamese army but, in response to a Viet Cong attempt to take the village, the 5th Battalion of the Royal Australian Regiment (5RAR) attacked the village on 6–8 June and met and defeated a combined force of PAVN regulars (Regiment 33) and Viet Cong. It could be argued that this was a more strategically important battle than that at Long Tan in August 1967. It was the biggest tank battle since World War II. In addition there was also close-quarter house-to-house fighting. According

Figure 15.5 The Binh Ba mass grave.
Source: W. Logan.

Figure 15.6 Pavilion with stele listing the North Vietnamese soldiers killed at Binh Ba.
Source: W. Logan.

to one military historian (Coulthard-Clark 2001: 291), the heavy losses suffered by the Viet Cong forced them to leave the province temporarily and, although the Australians did encounter communist units in the following years, the Binh Ba battle was the last large-scale clash.

This battle is largely unknown to Australians. Binh Ba does not fit the Anzac legend forged at Gallipoli in World War I whereas Long Tan, with its David and Goliath imagery, clearly does (Logan 2013). One Australian soldier was killed in the battle of Binh Ba and ten wounded. Here the memorialisation is by the Vietnamese, remembering the large number of northern soldiers killed. The interpretation given in the meeting room, however, does not portray the site as one of defeat. The only Australian 'presence' is a few letters by Australians and photos of visiting Australian vets pinned up in the meeting room. It was a vicious battle with unpleasant cleaning-up operations, including the mass burial of Vietnamese dead, and the battle had a devastating moral and physical impact on the village. Most of the bodies in the Binh Ba mass grave have since been returned to the North. Even today the bodies of northern soldiers are being disinterred from official war graves in the South and returned to family plots in village cemeteries in the North. Shame rather than heroism colours the Binh Ba landscape of war and the Australian letters and photos on display in the meeting room suggest that at least some Australian veterans see the need for atonement.

Long Hai

Figure 15.7 The main pavilion at the Long Hai memorial park.
Source: W. Logan.

Figure 15.8 President Ho Chi Minh watches over the lists of Viet Cong dead.
Source: W. Logan.

The dead memorialised at Binh Ba are regular soldiers of the PAVN. The contribution of the region's Viet Cong is memorialised at Minh Dam, site of the Viet Cong's secret base in the Long Hai hills on the peninsula east of Vung Tau. Here again we find lists of the dead with military registration, birthplace and date of death, overseen by President Ho Chi Minh. The main pavilion is quiet but grand, and surrounded by minor pavilions, exhibitions and pathways through the rocky terrain that successfully hid the Viet Cong from the enemy. No memorials exist to the southern dead and wounded.

Heritage management

Identification, registration and conservation

War heritage in Vietnam is managed by the state and its bureaucratic structures to demonstrate the authorised war narrative. The Long Hai hills and the mass grave at Binh Ba were identified as highly significant sites by the Vietnamese authorities and are closely managed, as are parts of the much more important and extensive Dien Bien Phu battlefield. Long Tan, on the other hand, is not an official Vietnamese heritage site and attempts by Australia to add it to the Australian Heritage List would require sensitive bilateral negotiations. Australia's failure to achieve such an agreement with the Turkish government over Gallipoli suggests it will be necessary to depend on Vietnam's continuing goodwill in order to maintain memorial ceremonies at Long Tan.

In terms of heritage registration, at Dien Bien Phu General Giap's initial thought was not to keep the physical evidence of the battle. Rather, he saw the soldiers' 'new task' as being to return the plain to the local people for cultivation purposes (Vo 2001: 386). Nevertheless other leaders took a different view and parts of the Dien Bien Phu battlefield were inscribed on the national historical and heritage site list in 1962. The registration was extended in 1981. Dien Bien Phu is not on Vietnam's World Heritage Tentative List. It probably should be because of its international significance, but such a nomination would probably face enormous difficulties, both in subduing the national story in favour of the international, and in countering the resistance that might be expected from France.

At Dien Bien Phu the Vietnamese Ministry of Culture and Information and its provincial counterparts have drawn up and implemented at least six conservation plans and associated projects since 1959. In 1984 the Dien Bien Phu Gallery House opened (Logan and Nguyen 2012, pp53–5). This was later converted to Dien Bien Phu Museum with popular battlefield dioramas and battlefield artefact displays. The remains of Giap's headquarters at Muong Phang 40km away, the French military headquarters in de Castries vault, and military infrastructure and artillery at A1 hill have received most attention. The climate and termites always create enormous problems for conserving Vietnam's timber and metal structures and in 1989 the sites underwent renewal using concrete replicas. For the 50th anniversary in 2004 and the 55th anniversary in 2009 US$23.5 million was spent on new victory monuments, new museum exhibits and further restoration of vestiges, again using durable materials.

Interpretation

It is now commonplace to remark that the victors write the history of wars. The wars in Vietnam are an exception in that far more has been written by the French and the Americans and it is their narrative that has influenced world readership. Even recent historians, cultural students and museologists such as Christina Schwenkel (2009) and Carol Wilder (2013) still focus mostly on dispelling the trauma felt by the American veterans, their families and the American state itself, although both make serious efforts to introduce Vietnamese people and their stories into the discussion.

The relatively little Vietnamese scholarship that exists tells a different story and visitors to Vietnam are often surprised by the interpretation provided. Like political and bureaucratic decision-making, the official line is still generally locked in mindsets of the past. There are, however, some signs of a softening of interpretations, as in the Hoa Lo prison museum in Hanoi where the virulent anti-American line has been toned down by the curators in recent times (Logan 2009). Bao Ninh's critically acclaimed novel *The Sorrow of War* (1993) helped open up more complex issues of memory and commemoration. Its enormous popularity gave the book and its author protection from the state's censorship machinery. It allowed recognition of the personal pain and family suffering that is suppressed in the official story of heroism. It is ironic that General Giap noted the reality of battle fatigue and demoralisation in mid-April 1954; he called them 'the new phenomena', but such an admission did not fit with construction of strong national identity at the time and was not absorbed into the official story of the battle until his 2001 memoir (Vo 2001: 326).

There has also been considerable public criticism of the Dien Bien Phu memorials, especially the Victory Monument (Logan and Nguyen 2012: 58). Given that the media are still subject to state monitoring and occasional direct censorship, the fact that such criticism has been published suggests that it reflects the views of at least some of Vietnam's ruling elite. The essential point of this criticism is in fact the unexceptionable and universal one that the archaeological remains and physical memorials are too simple to express the traumatic impact of the battle and the quasi-sacred value that the battlefield has for veterans and the nation (Lai Chau People's Committee 2002). One visiting veteran is quoted in a recent, officially endorsed publication as saying he was 'sad, because the historic battle had left nothing, vestiges were roughly and carelessly restored… [so] how could our descendants when seeing [them] understand the historic battle' (Dao Thanh Huyen *et al.* 2009: 201). Critics see ceremonies and educational activities as more important.

The Dien Bien Phu memorials are out of kilter with traditional Vietnamese ways of remembering the dead. The Taoist and Confucian legacies of the centuries of Chinese dominance provide that sacred places are normally marked by a temple or shrine housing an altar where people burn incense and pray to gods, heroes and ancestors. It is only at the cemetery adjacent to A1 hill that notions of courage, sacrifice and respect are shown in the dignified lines of soldiers' graves. Here people can quietly burn incense and pray. The design, incidentally, is not unlike that found in cemeteries created by the Commonwealth War Graves Commission after World War I although no evidence has yet been located to show a direct linkage in the source of inspiration. The cemetery gate, statues and incense burners provide the local Vietnamese touch.

The future

How can the horror of battle be read in the landscape as it is today? Dien Bien Phu is a place of wonderful beauty; not the place of horror it was in 1954. It is also now a regional urban growth pole and a major provincial centre. The hills where battles raged are now interspersed with and being eaten into by tongues of urban development, and a network of major roads has been overlaid with little apparent concern for heritage. As at the Hoa Lo Museum, however, Vietnamese pragmatism may prevail at Dien Bien Phu and a planning compromise may be reached in which both development and conservation are possible (Logan 2006). The bigger, universal questions facing battlefield management are whether memorialisation and conservation are sustainable economically and physically and whether they achieve the primary goal of supporting commemoration. It is clear that the conservation of physical vestiges can never capture the trauma of those who experienced a battle. We are usually forced to select particular pieces of the battlefield to memorialise, rather than the whole, since alternative economic uses of the land are considered more important. Memorialisation is also limited by the representational style used and the message given. In the case of Dien Bien Phu, socialist realism, an art influence resulting from the 35 years when Vietnam was part of the Soviet bloc, is now only fashionable in Vietnamese Communist Party circles and the ideological messages will date as creeping pluralism continues to overtake the Party and the state.

Perhaps commemoration through ceremonies and education is the most that can be achieved in the medium to long run. The role of interpretation centres on battlefields therefore takes on a more important role and expenditure might be better directed towards the provision of high-quality infrastructure, multi-media exhibitions and collections than towards attempts to give permanence to battlefield vestiges by using cement or building more and bigger memorial statues. Public commemoration activities may survive while the one-party state dominated by the Vietnamese Communist Party prevails. However, demographic change has already radically altered attitudes in Vietnam. The generation of people who personally remember the two Indochinese Wars is passing. Two-thirds of Vietnamese were born after 1975 and their primary interest is in achieving higher living standards, by which is meant material wealth for most and the right to worship freely for some. In the end commemoration is likely to survive, if it survives at all, by retreating into the private home, around the family, back within the traditional mode of remembering and honouring the dead.

If 'battlefield heritage' is to survive for Vietnamese people it may primarily be through tourism and interpretation centres rather than through the conservation of physical relics *in situ*. Even this is far from guaranteed. Domestic tourism to Dien

Bien Phu peaked in 2004, the 50th anniversary of the battle, but even with the opening up of highway and air connections Vietnamese visitors remain few in number. Not many international tourists visit the site yet but battlefield tourism is booming elsewhere and with promotion might be lucrative here in future. Tourism exploitation of battlefield sites does, however, raise ontological, ethical and practical issues in relation to respecting the need for them to continue functioning as places of personal and community healing and of education for peace.

There are many types of war landscape and battlefield site in terms of spatial context and each offers different tourism possibilities. In Vietnam Long Tan battlefield and memorial site sit in a relatively remote agricultural setting, the Binh Ba memorial site is in the middle of an equally remote village, the Long Hai memorial pavilions are surrounded by hills and forest although not far from the rapidly growing tourism city, Vung Tau, while Dien Bien Phu's landscape of war is being eaten into by a major provincial city. Each requires a different heritage planning strategy, if the significance of the landscape is to be maintained for the different involved and affected actors. Developing an effective planning strategy for war landscapes can be difficult if not impossible owing to their scale. Multiple ownership of the allotments that make up the landscape can sometimes make an integrated strategy impossible, although is less of an obstacle where governments own all of the allotments, for instance as national parks, or are able to easily override the wishes, needs and rights of private landholders.

Sitting over all of this discussion is a final question: 'battlefield conservation – to what end?' Heritage is about what we want to do with the past today. It is political; it is not merely a technical matter, nor is it just about improving physical techniques and management systems. Heritage, if it uses public funds and limits individual property rights, needs to perform a useful and significant function in today's world. We in the heritage industry need to go beyond the mere physical protection of war heritage and to use it as a vehicle for questioning war itself and challenging governments that drag people into conflicts. Heritage is too often exploited to bolster nationalism, even jingoism. This is not an acceptable professional aim. Instead, our professional aim must be to understand other people's heritage, to minimise fears of difference and to build tolerance. With regard to war heritage, this means building dialogue between former enemies, finding commonalities rather than differences and celebrating the achievement of peace rather than the prosecution of war.

References

Advocacy and Intelligence Index (2009). 'Advocacy and Intelligence Index for Prisoners of War Missing in Action'. Available from: www.aiipowmia.com/reports/exam5.html, [12 October 2009].

Association Nationale des Combattants de Dien Bien Phu (nd). 'Dien Bien Phu: le site officiel et historique de la bataille'. Available from: www.dienbienphu.org (home page) [14 October 2009].

Australia ICOMOS (2013). *The Burra Charter: The Australia ICOMOS Charter for Places of Cultural Significance*, 4th edn (Melbourne, Australia: ICOMOS).

Bao Ninh (1993). *The Sorrow of War: A Novel of North Vietnam* (London: Martin Secker & Warburg).

Coulthard-Clark, C. (2001). *The Encyclopaedia of Australia's Battles,* 2nd edn (Crows Nest, NSW: Allen and Unwin).

Dao Thanh Huyen *et al.* (2009). *Chuyen nhung nguoi lam nen lich su – Hoi uc Dien Bien Phu 1954–2009* [The Stories of People who made History – Memories of Dien Bien Phu 1954–2009] (Hanoi: Nha Xuat ban Chinh tri Quoc gia [National Political Publishing House]).

Ho Son Dai (ed.) (1995). *Lich su Ba Ri – Vung Tau khang chien (1945–1975)* [Resistance history of Ba Ria – Vug Tau (1945–1975)] (Hanoi: Nha xuat ban Quan doi Nhan dan [People's Army Publishing House]).

Lai Chau People's Committee (2002). 'Du an dau tu bao ton ton ta ova phat huy gia tri khu di tich chien thang Dien Bien Phu – Lai Chau' [Investment, Conservation, Repair and Value-enhancement Project of the Dien Bien Phu Battlefield Complex – Lai Chau] Appendix: Opinions of the Army's Leaders (Lai Chau: Lai Chau People's Committee).

Le, C. N. (2009). '"Better dead than red": anti-communist politics among Vietnamese Americans', in I. Zake (ed.), *Anti-Communist Minorities in the US: Political Activism of Ethnic Refugees* (New York: Palgrave Macmillan), pp. 189–209.

Logan, W. (2013). 'The Battles of Binh Ba and Long Tan, Vietnam: difficult war heritage and the disconnect between significance and memorialisation', University of Melbourne Faculty of Architecture and Building symposium 'Traditionalism, Colonialism, and Modernism: Asian Heritage Transformed', 3–4 October.

Logan, W. (2009). 'Hoa Lo Museum, Hanoi: changing attitudes to a Vietnamese place of pain and shame', in W. Logan and K. Reeves (eds), *Places of Pain and Shame: Dealing with 'Difficult' Heritage* (London: Routledge).

Logan, W. (2006). 'Dien Bien Phu, Vietnam: managing a battle site, metaphoric and actual'. *Outre-Mers: Revue d'histoire,* 350–1 (special issue: 'Sites et monument de mémoire'), 175–92.

Logan, W. and Nguyen, T. B. (2012). 'Victory and defeat at Dien Bien Phu: memory and memorialisation in Vietnam and France', in M. Gegner and B. Ziino (eds), *The Heritage of War* (London: Routledge), pp. 41–63.

Logan, W. and Witcomb, A. (2013). 'Messages from Long Tan, Vietnam: memorialisation, reconciliation and historical justice'. *Critical Asian Studies, 45*(2), 255–78.

McNeill, I. (1993). *To Long Tan: The Australian Army and the Vietnam War 1950–1966* (St Leonards, NSW: Allen and Unwin).

O'Neill, R. (1968). *Vietnam Task: The 5th Battalion The Royal Australian Regiment, 1966/7* (Melbourne: Cassell Australia).

Schwenkel, C. (2009). *The American War in Contemporary Vietnam: Transnational Remembrance and Representation* (Bloomington: Indiana University Press).

Shenon, P. (1995). '20 years after victory, Vietnam's Communists ponder how to celebrate'. *New York Times,* 23 April. Available from: www.nytimes.com/1995/04/23/world/20-years-after-victory-vietnamese-communists-ponder-how-to-celebrate.html?pagewanted=all&src=pm [12 February 2012].

Vo Nguyen Giap (2001). *Dien Bien Phu, diem hen lich su – hoi uc do Huu Mai the hien* [Dien Bien Phu, the Rendezvous of History – A Memoir edited by Huu Mai] (Hanoi: Nha xuat ban Quan doi Nhan dan [People's Army Publishing House]).

Wilder, C. (2013). *Crossing the Street in Hanoi: Teaching and Learning about Vietnam* (London: Intellect Press).

Windrow, M. (2004). *The Last Valley: Dien Bien Phu and the French Defeat in Vietnam* (London: Weidenfeld and Nicolson).

16 Nation-building and the development case for cultural heritage

Solomon Islands

Julien Barbara

Introduction

This chapter considers cultural heritage from a development perspective. What is the case for donors to support cultural heritage activities more explicitly and systematically as part of their aid programmes? How might advocates for cultural heritage support as a development programme overcome donor reluctance to fund such programmes as a more important part of development programmes? To date, advocates for cultural heritage support have tended to base their case on a narrow range of arguments centred on the worthiness of cultural heritage activities (UNESCO 2011)[1] and/or their economic potential as a source of tourism revenue and jobs.[2] While these are important reasons to support cultural heritage, arguments based on the normative and economic potential of cultural heritage can be easily marginalised as worthy yet unaffordable in the context of scarce donor funding. This chapter argues that a different case needs to be made for why scarce donor resources should be diverted away from core donor priorities such as basic service delivery (i.e. health and education) towards cultural heritage programmes. Such a case can be made but requires a more sophisticated understanding of the political economy of development and why donor support for cultural heritage activities might be an effective aid investment. This requires an understanding of the challenge of development as a collective action problem – how societies might overcome social differences to better collaborate to support national development through growth-enhancing investments.

Using the case of Solomon Islands, this chapter considers the ways in which support for cultural heritage might be understood as a relevant complement to more orthodox forms of donor support. Solomon Islands is a highly diverse society facing a range of development challenges including the legacies of recent violent conflict and unfinished processes of post-colonial nation- and state-building. As a result of these legacies Solomon Islands is a highly fragmented political community and this greatly complicates prospects for national collaboration to overcome development challenges. To date, donor support for Solomon Islands has focused on the state-building side of the development problem. While donors have recognised the need for nation-building, they have struggled to find sensitive ways to support and engage with what must be an indigenous process. Support for cultural heritage offers donors a tangible way of engaging positively with processes of nation-building and the formation of more cohesive political communities.

This chapter begins by considering how the development challenge facing many developing countries can be understood as a collective action problem. In this light it assesses how the development situation in Solomon Islands is an example of an acute collective action problem. The chapter then considers how cultural heritage support from donors might respond to issues of social and political fragmentation in ways useful to the resolution of collective action problems, such as those experienced in Solomon Islands. The chapter concludes with a brief consideration of how cultural heritage practitioners might strengthen the case for cultural heritage support by responding directly to the development challenges that donors, and their partner countries, are grappling with.

Development as a collective action problem

The challenge of economic under-development centres on the inability of societies to mobilise scarce resources in support of inclusive and sustainable economic growth. Poverty-reducing, and transformational, economic development requires societies to collaborate to redirect national resources from low- to high-productivity economic activities – a process that inevitably involves winners and losers, generating political conflict. In materially developed societies, formal and informal institutions have evolved over time to help societies manage the peaceful redirection of resources into highly productive areas to support improvements in material living standards. The development experiences of successful 'late developers' who have experienced rapid economic growth, such as China and the miracle economies of East Asia, are notable for their successful national mobilisation and the strategic redirection of scarce resources to support growth and capitalise on opportunities arising from high-growth markets (North *et al.* 2007; Slater 2010).

Successful development requires a capacity for societies to mobilise collectively to overcome collective action problems. Collective action refers to the willingness of people or groups with different interests to agree to work together to resolve an economic and/or political problem to their long-term mutual benefit, but which will require some immediate restraint or sacrifice (Laws 2013: 9). Effective collective action requires societies to develop hard and soft infrastructures to support collaboration (Jenkins 2013). Hard infrastructure includes public goods, security, law and order, effective legal systems, investments in health and education and physical infrastructure (roads, telecommunications). It also includes a functional state apparatus capable of centralising and re-allocating resources to development ends (Nixon 2006; OECD 2014). Soft infrastructure refers to public cultures and norms that encourage peaceful political competition in support of common or national interests. This includes a national leadership and political groups willing to think about development problems in a collective sense and support national mobilisation efforts to overcome them. David Booth from the influential UK-based Overseas Development Institute notes that a fundamental prerequisite for successful development is a national leadership for which national development is a priority. Booth (2012: 540) argues that 'the most important development issue is whether countries are governed by people for whom national development is a central objective'.

A key development challenge facing many developing countries is to develop a political culture that facilitates trust and collective action. A characteristic feature of many under-developed societies is high levels of conflict (frequently violent), political, economic and social fragmentation, and state fragility leading to poor governance (World Bank 2011). Fragility and conflict greatly complicate prospects for collective action and the emergence of a developmental politics capable of overcoming political and social fragmentation, resulting instead in social groups in divided societies viewing development challenges in competitive and conflictual terms (Collier 2009; Fukuyama 2012). Concerted national action in support of development presupposes a sense of the national interest and collective or public good. It also requires trust between elite and wider social groups (Putnam 2002) and confidence that self-sacrifice and the pooling of resources will be mutually beneficial, leading to higher growth and more societal resources to distribute to constituents/citizens.

If it is accepted that an important development challenge is one of collective mobilisation, then a key development problem in the face of high diversity, conflict and social fragmentation is how to support the emergence of a political culture that can mobilise diverse social groups in support of mutually beneficial national development strategies. This inevitably requires a consideration of broad historical processes of nation- and state-building and the ways in which highly diverse societies have developed progressively, and come to recognise, their collective self-interests.

Following from this, a key challenge for donors is how to support fragile and conflict-affected societies to bridge social divisions to enable a more developmental or collective political frame. This is a particularly difficult development problem for donors to address because it implies working in highly charged and political spaces involving sensitive issues of national identity, nation-building, sovereignty and politics. To date, donors have shied away from substantively seeking to support the construction of soft infrastructures upon which to build inclusive political communities. Instead, they have preferred to focus on strengthening hard infrastructure, through state-building focused on institutional strengthening, 'good governance' and capacity-building.

The limitations of such an approach have been all too painfully exposed in the challenges of post-conflict reconstruction in Iraq and Afghanistan, where ambitious state-building programmes have arguably faltered because they focused on abstract state-building programmes without a complementary focus on nation-building and the construction of inclusive political communities (Borgerhoff 2006). The failure of reconstruction processes focused predominantly on technical and physical reconstruction rather than the fostering of inclusive communities has forced donors to recognise the need for more rounded forms of post-conflict engagement that deal with problems of nation-building and the construction of peaceful political communities willing to work together in support of effective political and economic development. While this is a welcome development, donors have struggled to identify tangible ways in which to support nation-building. How might donors support processes of nation-building in positive ways? The following sections will consider the case of Solomon Islands and how cultural heritage programmes might be well placed to bridge this policy divide.

The development challenge in Solomon Islands as a collective action problem

Solomon Islands faces significant economic and social development challenges. In 2012 Solomon Islands ranked 143rd out of 186 countries in UNDP's human development index (UNDP 2013), ranking it one of the lowest Pacific Island countries, coming in only above Papua New Guinea. Relative poverty remains endemic across Solomon Islands, with around 80 per cent of the population dependent on subsistence farming for their livelihoods. Solomon Islands has a constrained economic future (Haque 2013). The country earns income through logging, fisheries and cash crops. It's major export, timber, is under significant pressure and may soon be exhausted. It is not clear what new economic sectors might emerge. Given its broad economic and social challenges, Solomon Islands has required heavy donor subsidy to provide basic services and maintain security. The country is one of the most aid-dependent, with aid equating to one-third of its annual national income (World Bank 2013) and is expected to remain heavily dependent on donor support for generations. Challenges of poverty and economic under-development are exacerbated by high population growth rates at around 2.3 per cent. Around 40 per cent of the population is under 15 years of age.

There are many reasons for Solomon Islands' development predicament. At the most basic level this reflects the extreme social and geographic diversity of the country. Comprising some 1,000 widely dispersed islands in the south-west Pacific, Solomon Islands' 90 inhabited islands are highly culturally and linguistic diverse, with over 70 languages spoken. Of the approximately 550,000 Solomon Islanders, some 80 per cent live in rural areas. The capital, Honiara, has a population of some 80,000, and is both a major focus for internal migration and an important melting pot, but also a source of political tension in a country where provincial identities predominate. Haque (2013) observes that, as a result of the diversity, fragmentation and geographic isolation from major markets, Solomon Islands faces acute structural economic challenges resulting in high cost structures that make it uncompetitive.

The legacy of recent violent civil conflict also weighs heavily on the country. Known as the 'tensions', this erupted in 1998 and only ended with the arrival of an international peacekeeping force, the Regional Assistance Mission to Solomon Islands (RAMSI), in 2003. There were many factors leading to the tensions (Braithwaite *et al.* 2010; Allen and Dinnen 2010). The conflict had a strong ethnic dimension, arising from grievances between two dominant ethnic groups – Malaitans and Guadalcanese – over issues of economic opportunity and recognition. Local grievances were stoked by perceptions of inequitable local development and the marginalisation of key groups from perceived development opportunities. Economic grievance made ethnic groups susceptible to political manipulation by opportunistic leaders, precipitating the conflict and a governance crisis. The tensions had a high cost in human lives – an estimated 200 deaths and the mass displacement of communities from the capital, Honiara – and the broader degradation of the Solomon Islands state and economy. The conflict quickened processes of state demise and social fragmentation as ascendant Malaitan groups and associated elites used the opportunity of the tensions to plunder state resources. As a result of the tensions, latent ethnic divisions hardened.

Another factor undermining development prospects in Solomon Islands is state weakness and the limited capacity of the state to support effective development policies (Barbara 2014). This partly reflects the colonial legacy of under-investment. As a British protectorate, Solomon Islands suffered historically from a colonial power that was generally uninterested in its territory and invested little in its institutional development. At independence in 1978 the Solomon Islands state was institutionally weak and lacked infrastructural power (Mann 1984) to extend its authority across its territorial inheritance and deliver basic services (law and order, education, health). The history of post-colonial Solomon Islands is in one sense the history of the gradual degradation of the state's already tenuous hold on its territory as it was overwhelmed by the demands and expectations of independence and government (Dinnen 2008). The issue of state failure, reflected in the inability of the state to deliver basic services to its geographically dispersed citizens, has been identified as an important factor underwriting citizen frustrations leading to the tensions and has framed post-conflict donor responses (Barbara 2008; Braithwaite *et al.* 2010). Central to RAMSI's intervention has been a concerted state-building programme to support development and improve the legitimacy of the state in its citizens' eyes (Braithwaite *et al.* 2010: 77).

Political instability and state fragility have been exacerbated by a weak sense of national identity. The path to independence in Solomon Islands was not characterised by the broad assertion of a national identity to resist the colonial power. In Solomon Islands, the eagerness of the colonial power to divest itself of responsibility for governing was central to the decolonisation process. The weak sense of national identity binding post-colonial Solomon Islands was acknowledged by one of the country's founding fathers, Solomon Mamaloni (Mamaloni 1992), who characterised his country as a 'nation conceived but never born'. Writing in 1995, Jourdan (1995: 127) observed that the urban-based middle classes in Solomon Islands were beginning to construct a sense of national identity, but that the post-colonial state had yet to develop 'needed ideological and institutional infrastructure' to support the process. The ethnicised tone of the tensions quickly reversed these processes, underscoring their fragility. Subsequent national leaders and governments have struggled to re-engage with nation-building. The result is that to this day national identity exerts only a weak influence on communities throughout the country. For example, it is notable that the presence of a large international stabilisation force with RAMSI has generated only muted 'nationalist' opposition (Barbara 2014). Localised identities – the village, island, province –

remain the predominant conceptual frame for Solomon Islanders. According to Dinnen (2008: 347):

> [l]iving mostly in rural villages, bonds of kinship, shared language and ties to ancestral land, along with moral frameworks drawing on kastom and Christianity, provided the basis for individual identities and allegiance rather than abstract notions of 'citizenship' or 'nationality'.

High social diversity, coupled with a weak state unable to assert its authority over its citizenry, and the absence of a cohering sense of national identity, manifests in a fragmented political community. Absent strong centralising and unifying infrastructures and forces, politics, including the politics of development, is understood in highly localised terms. In Solomon Islands, political competition is intense and highly personalised, with politicians competing for office on the basis of parochial promises and issues. Solomon Islands' first-past-the-post electoral system means individuals can get elected with very low mandates, and voted out with relative ease at subsequent elections. High political turnover – around 50 per cent of elected representatives at each election – means that power is transient and ephemeral (Dressel and Dinnen 2014) and undermines prospects for government continuity. Governments are formed as a result of intense post-election bargaining, with governing coalitions formed amongst self-interested MPs focused on securing material resources to reward local supporters and strengthen prospects for local re-election (Steeves 2011). There are no genuine political parties that concentrate local interests into a coherent national program (Alasia 1997). The political challenge, then, centres on securing office for short periods of time and using that time to distribute the material benefits of office to supporters.

These factors combine to undermine prospects for collective action to resolve development problems. Strong centrifugal forces limit incentives for political collaboration focused on national issues in favour of very local priorities. This is reflected in the persistence of highly personalised understandings of the development challenge in Solomon Islands. MPs tend to think of themselves and be understood by their constituents as 'personalised agents of "development"' (Dinnen 2008: 350) whose primary role is to extract resources from the central state and distribute them locally. This has the effect of fracturing already scarce resources and limited prospects for economic concentration necessary for economic growth.

The impact of this fragmented politics is compounded by Solomon Islands' limited economic development options. The country's economic future remains highly uncertain, having only just passed the national income level that preceded the tensions in 1998 (Haque 2013). Solomon Islands' growth model is dependent on intensive resource extraction – primarily logging – and to a lesser extent cash crop production. Logging has provided economic rents that have supported high levels of post-conflict economic growth (Hameiri 2012). However, logging revenues have primarily benefited private interests and the state has struggled to capture an adequate share with which to fund services and public goods. With the looming exhaustion of timber resources, and no clear alternative in sight, the country faces a profound existential challenge about alternative development trajectories and its economic future. The World Bank considers Solomon Islands will remain highly aid-dependent for generations to come (Haque 2013).

These factors add up to a constrained development future for Solomon Islands and underline the need for strong political leadership to chart a path to future prosperity. But there is limited national infrastructure – state, social, political – to encourage and enable a collective approach to the development challenges facing the country. A key development question centres on how might a stronger collective outlook be supported as a basis for exploring alternative development futures. An important part of a more positive development future will be the capacity of the country's leaders and citizens to collaborate to resolve collective action problems that limit the state's capacity to provide growth-enhancing public goods. This in turn will require Solomon Islands leaders and citizens to agree to invest in state capacity to act as a positive development factor, and to shift the frame of development from a personalised to a national level.

The development case for cultural heritage support

If unfinished processes of nation-building and the construction of inclusive political communities are a key development deficit in post-conflict environments such as Solomon Islands, then activities that contribute tangibly to positive forms of nation-building and the formation of inclusive political communities become crucially important. But donors have struggled to incorporate nation-building activities into their development programmes in substantive or direct forms.

There are two major reasons for this. The first is the political sensitivity inherent in nation-building processes and the importance of local ownership in driving them. Historically, successful nation-building has been an elite-led programme involving the deliberate mobilisation of state power and the deployment of nationalist ideologies to build citizen loyalty to the state and create a politically mobilising sense of national identity (Smith 1991; Anderson 2001). Such processes have been politically contentious, requiring the invention of tradition and the construction of common histories. The existence of external threats has also been important in galvanising nationalisms to construct new nations. In many cases, key development partners have been former colonial powers and the very external threat against which anti-colonialism was mobilised, making it particularly fraught for donors to engage in this space. Donors are acutely aware of the risks of being accused of being neo-colonial and interfering in local politics, and reluctant to step into such highly charged spaces.

The second is limited donor understanding of *how* to effectively support positive nation-building processes, in terms of specific programmatic actions that they can fund and support with technical assistance. Whereas it is easy for donors to support the construction of infrastructure or the delivery of services, it is much more difficult to support the construction of a national identity, which is intangible, amorphous and contested. Moreover, orthodox development activities can be measured, and thus subject to rigorous cost–benefit analyses. For example, it is possible to assess how many children have been vaccinated, and whether donor funds were spent in worthwhile and effective ways. It is difficult to measure the effectiveness of donor support for the construction of inclusive national identities, and thus difficult to justify aid investments for cultural heritage on the basis of economic opportunity cost.

The result is that in post-conflict contexts, such as Iraq, Afghanistan and Timor-Leste, donors have tended to focus support on strengthening what Jenkins (2013: 119) has described as 'hard' infrastructure – rebuilding physical infrastructure and state institutions. In Solomon Islands, for example, RAMSI spent some A\$2.6 billion between 2003 and 2013 (Heyward-Jones 2014), providing security and development support, focused on the reconstruction of core state institutions such as the parliament, the justice system, public service and the finance ministry (Barbara 2014). This was complemented by bilateral and multilateral development programmes, most of which focused on rebuilding infrastructure (roads, ports, hospitals) and improving service delivery. In the case of RAMSI, donors actively eschewed engaging with questions of nation-building and unfinished processes of peace and reconciliation, which, being highly sensitive and political, were explicitly framed as a responsibility for national leaders (Barbara 2014). This was despite donors recognising the absence of nation-building as a long-term impediment to post-conflict reconstruction and development. (Hard infrastructure supports nation-building indirectly, by providing connecting infrastructure – e.g. roads, telecommunications equipment – and supporting state effectiveness to provide common services to citizens.)

Donors have struggled to support what Jenkins calls the 'soft' side of state-building – the reconstruction of societies and peoples (Jenkins 2013: 119) – because in many cases they do not know what they might assist with. Where donors have engaged with nation-building, it has often been incidental to core development objectives such as improving literacy. For example, arguably the most substantive way in which donors have become involved in the ideational aspects of nation-building is through support for education – what Jourdan (1995: 127) has described in a Pacific context as one of the 'three stepping stones to national consciousness'. Nevertheless, while education can be a key foundation for nation-building (Fukuyama 2012; Anderson 2000; Smith 1991), donor support for it has tended to focus on technical assistance and resourcing. The potential for nation-building and political formation that education represents has been either unconsidered or treated as a fortuitous side-effect. While donors routinely consider the gender or environmental consequences of 'core' aid investments, they have largely avoided considering the nation-building potential of major development investments.

Support for cultural heritage provides a concrete way for donors to engage with issues of nation-building. Importantly, such support has a clear nation-building dimension. Dealing directly with issues of history, memory and identity, cultural heritage institutions (museums, universities, heritage sites, arts organisations) have significant potential to help communities overcome fragmentation and high social diversity in post-conflict environments. Bandarin *et al.* (2011: 20) note that cultural heritage 'has been seen to play crucial roles in processes of recovery and recon-struction not only in the wake of natural disasters, but also in the framework of post-conflict reconciliation efforts'. Likewise, Jenkins (2013: 119) directly links cultural heritage to the soft side of state-building:

> [w]here heritage is utilized to play a role in the construction of the nation and the people, in memory and identity. For it can play a role in legitimizing myths and identifying symbolic, historic events, and implicitly informs the construct-ion of infrastructure, institutions and other aspects of life.

Crucially, support for cultural heritage institutions provides politically feasible and programmatically viable ways for donors to engage with nation-building issues. Recognising the strengthening of institutions and the building of institutional capacity as state-building activities, donors can provide support for cultural instit-utions in concrete ways. This includes by providing support for cultural heritage administration and management, skills development and general capacity-building, and resource supplementation for cash-strapped organisations.

The rationale for such support from a development perspective lies in the construction of institutional fora that can potentially provide space for sensitive national conversations and empower local actors to support, in long-term and dynamic ways, the construction of inclusive national identities. Part of the development attraction of a long-term cultural heritage programme lies in the potential of cultural heritage institutions to support dynamic and evolving nation-building processes. If supported appropriately, cultural heritage institutions have convening power to help broker shared identities. As enduring institutions, cultural heritage institutions can support ongoing social conversations about history and national identity in ways that complement other reconciliation and education programmes. Indeed, given the contestable nature of national identities and nationhood, and the potential for cultural heritage institutions to become captured by competing political factions (see, for example, the contested nature of history in Timor-Leste – Leach 2003), donors in post-conflict states can potentially provide institutional support in ways that encourage cultural heritage institutions to develop in inclusive directions. Funding can be linked to clear expectations of inclusive institutional development so that cultural heritage institutions contribute positively to broader processes of peace-building and positive nation-building.

Donor engagement in potentially sensitive spaces such as cultural heritage ultimately requires domestic consent and obtaining this may be one of the largest impediments to donor engagement in the area. Host governments can be as wary as donors about allocating scarce resources to cultural heritage projects, and equally indifferent to the nation-building potential of cultural heritage and its development significance. Finally, host governments may be complicit in propagating exclusive national identities and disinterested in or outright hostile to efforts to challenge this.

A challenge for donors, therefore, is to engage with partner governments to advocate the merits of cultural heritage as having development importance. In the Pacific, governments on the whole have been permissive of donor support for cultural heritage activities. The four-yearly Festival of Pacific Arts is a prestigious, donor-funded event that host Pacific Islands states value highly. In Solomon Islands, the experience with RAMSI – which in many respects constituted an intrusive form of state-building – shows that successive governments have been permissive of creative donor engagement in sensitive areas (Barbara 2014). There is every reason to expect that future Solomon Islands governments would welcome targeted donor support for cultural heritage, as a modest part.

Foana'ota and White (2011) have lamented that the Solomon Islands government has historically been ambivalent in its support for its formal cultural heritage institutions: '[t]he weak level of interest is related to the lack of understanding of the potential contributions of these kinds of institution to a broad spectrum of national interests, beyond the oft-repeated areas of education and tourism'. This ambivalence is reflected in the launch of Solomon Islands' first cultural policy in 2012, which only vaguely acknowledged the role of cultural heritage institutions. Importantly, however, the policy acknowledges the government's need to engage with donors more systematically. This suggests the time may be right for donors to engage with authorities and play a more active role in encouraging Solomon Islanders to think about the importance of cultural heritage and its connection to broader processes of nation-building in a more formal and institutional sense.

Conclusion: making a stronger case for cultural heritage

To the degree that a developmental argument has been used to justify greater funding for cultural heritage programmes and institutions, such arguments have tended to be made in very normative and instrumental terms, emphasising the inherent importance of cultural heritage and/or its tourism potential. While the intrinsic worth of cultural heritage is of course an important argument in its own right, and the economic benefits of cultural heritage activities are not inconsequential for some developing countries, there is a broader development argument that can be mounted in support of more systemic donor support for cultural heritage. This argument recognises the development challenges facing many countries as collective action problems, whereby fragmented political communities struggle to cooperate to support growth-enhancing policies in their long-term interests. Where weak collective action is a root cause of under-development, policies that support the strengthening of inclusive political communities through positive nation-building may be important in helping them overcome impediments to growth. While donors have struggled to find concrete ways to support nation-building, support for cultural heritage potentially provides a tangible means of doing so.

By emphasising the contribution cultural heritage institutions can make to crucial but intangible processes of nation-building, the development case for cultural heritage is strengthened, moving beyond a niche activity to a more compelling way for donors to engage with politically sensitive processes of political stabilisation. While such arguments should not be overstated and support for cultural heritage will never displace donor prioritising of core development activities such as support for health, education and basic infrastructure, such arguments may help legitimise modest support for cultural heritage as a useful complement to these activities. Modest programmes of support for cultural heritage deserve greater consideration as part of a diversified portfolio of donor tools that they can use to support positive, locally led, nation-building processes.

References

Alasia, S. (1997). 'Political parties and government in Solomon Islands'. State, Society and Governance in Melanesia Discussion Paper, No 97/7, State, Society and Governance in Melanesia Program (Canberra: Australian National University).

Allen, M. and Dinnen, S. (2010). 'The north down under: antimonies of conflict and intervention in Solomon Islands'. *Conflict, Security and Development*, 10(3), 299–327.

Anderson B. (1983). *Imagined Communities, Reflections on the Origin and Spread of Nationalism*, 2000 and 2001 editions used (London: Verso).

Bandarin, F., Hosagrahar, J. and Albernaz, F. S. (2011). 'Why development needs culture'. *Journal of Cultural Heritage, Management and Sustainable Development*, 1(1), 15–25.

Barbara, J. (2014). 'From intervention to partnership: prospects for development partnership in Solomon Islands after RAMSI'. *Asia and the Pacific Policy Studies*, 1(2), 395–408.

Barbara, J. (2013). 'Post-statebuilding: the Australian experience in Timor-Leste and Solomon Islands', in D. Chandler and R. Sisk (eds), *International Statebuilding: Concepts, Themes and Practices, A Routledge Handbook* (London: Routledge), pp. 327–38.

Barbara, J. (2008). 'Antipodean statebuilding: the Regional Assistance Mission to Solomon Islands and Australian intervention in the South Pacific'. *Journal of Intervention and Statebuilding*, 2(2), 123–49.

Booth, D. (2012). 'Aid effectiveness: bringing country ownership (and politics) back in'. *Conflict, Security and Development*, 12(5), 537–58.

Borgerhoff, A. (2006). 'The double task: nation- and state-building in Timor-Leste'. *European Journal of East Asian Studies*, 5(1), 101–30.

Braithwaite, J., Dinnen, S., Allen, M. and Charlesworth, H. (2010). *Pillars and Shadows: State Building as Peace Building in Solomon Islands* (Canberra: ANU Press).

Collier, P. (2009). *Wars, Guns and Votes: Democracy in Dangerous Places* (London: Vintage).

Dinnen, S. (2008). 'The Solomon Islands intervention and the instabilities of the postcolonial state'. *Global Change, Peace and Security*, 20(3), 339–55.

Dressel, B. and Dinnen, S. (2014). 'Political settlements: old wine in new bottles?' Development Policy Centre Policy Brief 9, February (Canberra, ACT: Development Policy Centre).

Foana'ota, L. and White, G. (2011). 'Solomon Islands cultural policy? A brief history of practice', in E. Hviding and K.M. Rio (eds), *Oceania: Social Movements, Cultural Heritage and the State in the Pacific* (Wantage, Oxon: Sean Kingston Publishing), pp. 273–299.

Fukuyama, F. (2012). *The Origins of Political Order from Prehuman Times to the French Revolution* (New York: Farrar, Straus and Giroux).

Hameiri, S. (2012). 'Mitigating the risk to primitive accumulation: state-building and the logging boom in Solomon Islands'. *Journal of Contemporary Asia*, 42(3), 405–26.

Haque, T. (2013). 'Economic transition in Solomon Islands'. SSGM Discussion Paper 2013/10, State, Society and Governance in Melanesia Program, Australian National

University. Available from: http://ips.cap.anu.edu.au/sites/default/files/2013_10 final.pdf [1 February 2015].

Heyward-Jones, J. (2014). 'Australia's costly investment in Solomon Islands: the lessons of RAMSI'. Analysis: The Lowy Institute, Sydney. Availalable from: www.lowyinstitute.org/files/hayward-jones_australias_costly_investment_in_solomon_islands.pdf [1 February 2015].

Jenkins, T. (2013). 'Introduction to the special issue on cultural interventions'. *Journal of Intervention and Statebuilding, 7*(2), 119–24.

Jourdan, C. (1995). 'Stepping-stones to national consciousness: the case for Solomon Islands', in R. J. Foster (ed.), *Nation-Making: Emergent Identities in Post-Colonial Melanesia* (Ann Arbor: University of Michigan Press), pp. 127–49.

Laws, E. (2013). 'Governance, politics and development in the Pacific'. Developmental Leadership Program Background Paper 14 (Birmingham: The Developmental Leadership Program).

Leach, M. (2003). 'Privileged ties: young people debating language, heritage and national identity in East Timor'. *Portuguese Studies Review, 11*(1), 137–50.

Mamaloni, S. (1992). 'The road to independence', in R. Crocombe and E. Tuza (eds), *Independence, Dependence, Interdependence – The First 10 Years of Solomon Islands Independence* (Honiara, Solomon Islands: Institute of Pacific Studies, USP Honiara Centre and Solomon Islands College of Higher Education), pp. 7–18.

Mann, M. (1984). 'The autonomous power of the state: its origins, mechanisms and results'. *European Journal of Sociology, 25*(2), 185–213.

Nixon, R. (2006). 'The crisis of governance in new subsistence states'. *Journal of Contemporary Asia, 36*(1), 75–101.

North, D., Wallis, J., Webb, S., and Weingast, B. (2007). 'Limited access orders in the developing world: a new approach to the problems of development'. World Bank Policy Research Working Paper No. 4359 (Washington, DC: The World Bank).

OECD (2014), *Fragile States 2014: Domestic Revenue Mobilisation in Fragile States.*

Putnam, R. D. (ed.) (2002). *Democracies in Flux: The Evolution of Social Capital in Contemporary Society* (New York: Oxford University Press).

Slater, D. (2010). *Ordering Power: Contentious Politics and Authoritarian Leviathans in South Asia* (Cambridge: Cambridge University Press).

Smith, A. (1991). *National Identity* (London: Penguin).

Steeves, J. (2011). '"Unbounded politics" and the democratic model in Solomon Islands: the 2010 national elections'. *Commonwealth and Comparative Politics, 49*(3), 342–58.

UNDP (2013). 'Human Development Report 2013. The rise of the South: human progress in a diverse world'. (New York: United Nations Development Programme).

UNESCO (2001). *UNESCO Universal Declaration of Cultural Diversity,* 2 November. Available from: http://portal.unesco.org/en/ev.php-URL_ID=13179&URL_DO=DO_TOPIC&URL_SECTION=201.html [1 February 2015].

World Bank (2013). *Solomon Islands – Country partnership strategy for the period FY2013–2017* (Washington, DC: World Bank). Available from: http://documents.worldbank.org/curated/en/2013/05/17747045/solomon-islands-country-partnership-strategy-period-fy2013-2017 [1 February 2015].

World Bank (2011). 'World development report: conflict, security and development' (Washington, DC: World Bank). Available from: http://siteresources.worldbank.org/INTWDRS/Resources/WDR2011_Full_Text.pdf [1 February 2015].

Notes

1   Normative arguments centre on the intrinsic importance of culture and recognition of cultural identities as central to processes of inclusive development. UNESCO's 2001 *Universal Declaration of Cultural Diversity* identifies cultural diversity as 'one of the roots of development understood not simply in terms of economic growth, but also as a means to achieve more satisfactory intellectual, emotional, moral and spiritual existence'.

2   Bandarin *et al.* (2011: 18) note that cultural tourism accounts for some 40 per cent of total tourism revenue, with developing countries accounting for some 47 per cent of tourism arrivals and 36 per cent of tourist revenues in 2009.

17 Commemoration and interpretation of World War II in the Solomon Islands

A practitioner's perspective

Rowena MacDonald

This chapter looks at the development of the Solomon Scouts and Coastwatchers monument and accompanying interpretative display in Honiara in 2011, and the interpretation of World War II history at the redeveloped Solomon Islands National Museum, opened in 2012. It places these recent developments in a historical context, tracing the shift in World War II commemoration in Solomon Islands from an emphasis on foreign combatants, to a more recent recognition of the contribution of Solomon Islanders. The Solomon Scouts and Coastwatchers monument and its accompanying educational activities mark a discernible shift in the nature of World War II commemoration and interpretation in Solomons, from a foreign focus prior to the Tensions (1998–2003), to local genesis and ownership following that period.

The chapter is written from a museum practitioner's perspective. It is drawn from my experience as a volunteer at the Solomon Islands National Museum in 2011 and 2012, when I worked with the Museum team developing a display about the Solomon Scouts and Coastwatchers in World War II, then redeveloping the Museum's permanent exhibition about the history and culture of Solomon Islands.[1] It offers a case study in the commemoration and interpretation of war history in a fragile post-conflict state, and the role these activities play in efforts to develop shared historical narratives that might contribute to the unfinished process of national reconciliation.

The chapter starts with a brief consideration of the contemporary context of Solomon Islands and a summary of its World War II history. It surveys the commemoration of World War II and sporadic efforts at preservation and interpretation of World War II heritage in the pre-Tensions period, before discussing the shift in commemorative and interpretative focus in the post-Tensions period. It explores the nation-building efforts evident in the development of the Solomon Scouts and Coastwatchers monument and the redevelopment of the Solomon Islands National Museum gallery, and concludes with consideration of the significance of the increased local engagement in World War II commemoration and broader cultural heritage ventures.

The Solomon Islands context

Solomon Islands is a small Pacific nation of about 550,000 people, geographically dispersed over more than 900 islands covering 1600km of ocean, and culturally diverse, with more than 70 languages spoken. Solomon Islands was a British Protectorate from 1893 until Independence in 1978. During World War II the Solomon Islands, and particularly the largest island, Guadalcanal, was the site of fierce battles as Allied troops fought to turn back advancing Japanese forces.

It is a developing country, with limited income from fishing, forestry and mining and receives almost 50 per cent of its national income from international aid donations (World Bank 2013). While the shift of people from rural to urban areas has been accelerating since the 1960s, the majority of people still live a largely subsistence lifestyle in rural communities. It is also defined as a post-conflict fragile state, in which the government is struggling to provide basic services such as security, health and education to its people.

The country is still recovering from a period of civil unrest known as the 'Tensions' from 1998 to 2003, when ethnic tensions mostly on Guadalcanal escalated into violent clashes between rival militant groups, and the government virtually collapsed (Braithwaite *et al.* 2010). In 2003 the Solomon Islands government invited the Australian-led Regional Assistance Mission to Solomon Islands, known as RAMSI, to come and help restore peace, stability and economic development (Barbara 2008).

Solomon Islands in World War II

Solomon Islands became an unlikely theatre of war in 1942, after Japanese forces had swept through Southeast Asia, Papua New Guinea and into Western Solomons. By May 1942 the Japanese occupied Tulagi, the capital of the British Solomon Islands Protectorate, and had begun building an airfield on the island of Guadalcanal. On 7 August 1942, US troops landed at Tulagi and Guadalcanal, where they seized the airfield. It was only after six months of bitter fighting on land, at sea and in the air that the Allies repelled the Japanese, securing their hold on Guadalcanal. There, Allied forces, including American, New Zealand, Australian, British and Pacific Islanders, won a critical victory which marked a turning point in the Pacific War. Finally the Japanese advance had been stopped.

Fierce fighting continued in the Western Solomon Islands through 1943 as the Allies pushed the Japanese back, eventually forcing their withdrawal from Solomon Islands and Papua New Guinea. Allied troops continued to slowly force the Japanese back until Japan's surrender in 1945. About 90,000 Allied and Japanese soldiers lost their lives during the Solomons conflict, as well as an unknown number of Solomon Islanders.

Pre-Tensions commemoration and interpretation of World War II

Because Solomon Islands, and Guadalcanal in particular, were such significant sites of conflict for both the USA and Japan, World War II has been heavily memorialised there. Prior to the Tensions, this memorialisation focused predominantly on foreign combatants, for a foreign audience of tourists, veterans and their families. Memorialisation took several forms, including formal monuments, both large and small, funded by foreign governments and veterans' organisations, which have provided the focus for commemorative ceremonies; and private collections of relics and artefacts. Most monuments and commemorative activities were funded and maintained by international donors, and few had strong connections to the Solomon Islands state or broader community.

Interpretation of the history and significance of the war was limited, and efforts at preservation of material culture sporadic. The Solomon Islands National Museum has been the key state agency in the field, but has been poorly equipped to meet its mandate to preserve and collect the nation's World War II heritage.

Commemoration of World War II

One of the earliest formal commemorations happened on the 25th anniversary of the US landing on Guadalcanal, 7 August 1967, when US veterans attended memorial services in Honiara with Solomon Islander veterans. On the 50th anniversary in 1992 more than 1,500 US veterans attended the dedication of the US War Memorial, built on a prominent hilltop site in Honiara by the American Battle Monuments Commission and US Guadalcanal veterans. Since then, this has been the site of annual commemorative services, including the 70th anniversary in 2012.

The Japanese Peace Memorial was built in Honiara in 1984. Here, low-key ceremonies are held when veterans, their families and friends visit Guadalcanal. It is also used as the place where Japanese bones collected from the battlefield are cremated so the ashes can be taken back to Japan.

The first of the combined services attended by American and Japanese veterans occurred in 1997, when the Japanese invited American veterans to their service at this Memorial on 6 August and Japanese veterans attended the American service the next day. Japanese veterans' associations have also built smaller monuments at various locations, mainly around Guadalcanal (Innes 2011).

In 1989 the Guadalcanal-Solomon Islands War Memorial Foundation dedicated a monument to decorated Solomon Scout Sir Jacob Vouza. In 1942 Vouza volunteered to serve with the Coastwatching unit on his home island of Guadalcanal. While scouting near Henderson Airfield after the US landing in August 1942, Vouza was interrogated by Japanese soldiers. Badly wounded, he managed to escape and warn US troops of a planned Japanese attack. Vouza became the local head of the Solomon Scouts, and accompanied the US Marines on many combat missions against the Japanese. He was so respected by US troops that he was made an honorary Sergeant Major in the US Marines, and awarded the Silver Star and Legion of Merit by the USA. In 1979 Vouza received a knighthood from Britain (Innes 2011).

The Jacob Vouza monument lists the Allied units that fought in the Solomons campaign, including Solomon Islanders serving as Scouts and Coastwatchers. While its plaque honours 'all Solomon Islanders who fought alongside the Allies', the monument's main focus is on one individual's heroism. Until 2012 this was the only official monument that highlighted the involvement of Solomon Islanders in the War.

Figure 17.1 US War Memorial, Honiara.
Source: R. MacDonald.

Figure 17.2 Japanese Peace Memorial, Honiara.
Source: R. MacDonald.

Figure 17.3 Monument to Sir Jacob Vouza, Honiara.
Source: R. MacDonald.

Preservation and interpretation of World War II material heritage

The physical remnants of the fierce fighting are still visible everywhere, particularly on Guadalcanal. After the war, when the former capital of Tulagi had been destroyed, the new capital was established at Honiara, the site of many early battles, and of the US headquarters after the defeat of the Japanese. Iron Bottom Sound off Honiara is named for the dozens of ships, submarines, planes and other war wreckage that litter its floor. Efforts at preservation and interpretation of this physical heritage have been sporadic.

The Solomon Islands National Museum is mandated to collect, preserve, safeguard, record, develop and promote the tangible and intangible cultural heritage of the Solomon Islands, including its World War II heritage (Solomon Islands Government 2011: 23). The Museum administers the Protection of Wrecks and War Relics Act 1980. It houses a collection of relics, and displays a small number of these in its permanent exhibition. It undertakes surveys to record World War II sites and aims to assist local communities to establish mini-World War II museums in communities. With limited resources and an enormous number of war sites and relics spread across such a large area, the Museum is struggling to make an impact in the collection and preservation of World War II heritage. The museum is also developing long-term plans to establish a dedicated World War II gallery in Honiara.

Individuals have set up several private museums of World War II relics, including the Vilu War Museum, about 15km outside Honiara, where a series of small Japanese and US monuments have been built. This privately run outdoor

Figure 17.4 John Wesley timber yard relics, Honiara.
Source: R. MacDonald.

museum holds a collection of World War II wrecks and artefacts gathered from various locations on Guadalcanal, including planes, guns and ammunition. Other customary landholders have gained income from providing access for visitors to battlefields and relic sites across Solomon Islands. (Kwai 2014: 87)

A Honiara timber yard houses a diverse array of relics assembled by local European collectors, ranging from the small personal effects of Japanese and Allied soldiers, through weapons, to a tank in the process of being restored.

While the relics of war are highly visible in Solomons, there is little interpretation of the material on display. Some of the war memorials, such as the American, include a narrative of the battles that took place, but none explains in any detail the involvement of Solomon Islanders in the conflict, or its impact on their lives.

Post-Tensions commemoration and interpretation of World War II

The post-Tensions period has seen World War II commemoration and interpretation playing a role in efforts to build a sense of national pride and identity, by highlighting the contributions of Solomon Islanders to events of global significance and interpreting history from a Solomon Islands perspective.

The Solomon Scouts and Coastwatchers monument and its accompanying interpretative display at the Solomon Islands National Museum mark a discernible shift in the focus of World War II commemoration and interpretation in Solomons, from foreign to local genesis and ownership. These commemorative activities are central in nascent efforts to develop shared historical narratives that might contribute to the unfinished business of reconciliation.

Solomon Scouts and Coastwatchers

The Coastwatchers formed a network of observers organised by the Royal Australian Navy and stationed on Pacific islands from New Guinea to the New Hebrides. As the Japanese swept south in 1941–42, expatriate volunteers in Solomon Islands were called on to stay behind and hide in enemy-held territory to gather intelligence on the Japanese. Using telegraph-radios they transmitted reports to other listening posts, which passed the reports to the Coastwatchers headquarters in Townsville, Queensland. Most Coastwatchers were civilians, and included government officials, plantation managers and gold miners. Geoffrey Kuper on Isabel Island was the only Solomon Islander in charge of a Coastwatching station. The Coastwatchers relied on the help of Solomon Islanders to operate and to survive.

The information Coastwatchers provided was critical to the success of the Allies' Solomons campaign. They gave early warning of Japanese air attacks on Henderson Airfield, and Japanese shipping and land movements. As Allied forces drove the Japanese north in 1943, the Coastwatchers used their intimate knowledge of the islands and their people to help guide the Allied advance.

Members of the British Solomon Islands Protectorate Defence Force, known as Solomon Scouts, formed a crucial part of the network of Coastwatchers. They gathered intelligence, moved heavy radio equipment if a station had to be hastily relocated, captured Japanese prisoners-of-war and rescued Allied airmen or sailors stranded in Japanese-held territory. The Scouts also served as guides and carriers for Allied troops, and some fought in regular combat.

Many more ordinary Solomon Islanders gave vital support to the Coastwatchers and Allied troops. They helped the Coastwatchers hide, spied on the Japanese and provided food and other support. Sometimes whole villages, including women and children, played their part. All helped turn back the advancing Japanese forces, leading to the retreat and eventual surrender of Japan in 1945 (Innes 2011).

Solomon Scouts and Coastwatchers monument

The Solomon Scouts and Coastwatchers Memorial Trust was established in 2009, coordinated by Australian expatriate businessman and long-term Honiara resident Sir Bruce Saunders. The Trust is headed by former Solomon Islands Prime Minister Sir Peter Kenilorea and made up of Solomon Islanders, including Michael Ben and Michael Liliau, both sons of Solomon Scouts, and long-term expatriates such as Saunders. They raised money largely from private and corporate donations, both locally and overseas, to fund creation of the Monument located on Commonwealth Street at Point Cruz, near the port in central Honiara. About 60 per cent of the funding came from within Solomon Islands and the remainder from the USA, Australia and New Zealand (Solomon Scouts and Coastwatchers Memorial Trust 2013). The Monument was designed and constructed by prominent local artist Frank Haikiu.

Titled 'Pride of Our Nation', the Monument was a conscious effort at nation-building, designed to build Solomon Islanders' pride in their collective history, and an attempt to overcome the regional and ethnic divisions that led to the 'Tensions' between 1998 and 2003 (Saunders 2012).

The Monument shows a life-size Coastwatcher standing looking through binoculars, surrounded by three Solomon Scouts, one operating a radio, another looking and pointing to the horizon and the third squatting ready with a rifle. Haikiu's concept was 'to create a sculpture that any Solomon Islander could look at and say "that could be me"'. (Solomon Scouts and Coastwatchers Memorial Trust 2013). More abstract or symbolic iconography was considered for the monument during its design, but it was decided that a figurative style was more likely to be meaningful to Solomon Islanders (Saunders 2012).

For a monument intended to celebrate the contribution of Solomon Islanders, its iconography is intriguing. The European Coastwatcher stands in a commanding pose at the centre of the sculpture, his scale apparently larger than that of the Solomon Scouts who squat around him in what could be interpreted as more subservient poses.

The Monument was dedicated on 7 August 2011, when several Solomon Scout veterans attended. On the same date in 2012, a roll of honour was added to it, listing the names of all known Scouts and Coastwatchers. Significantly, the names are listed in alphabetical order, not grouped according to province or ethnic group, in a conscious effort to emphasise the unifying power of their wartime contribution.

Figure 17.5 Pride of Our Nation statue by Frank Haikiu, Solomon Scouts and Coastwatchers Monument, Honiara.

Source: R. MacDonald.

Figure 17.6 Solomon Islands National Museum permanent exhibition, Honiara.
Source: R. MacDonald.

Figure 17.7 Solomon Islands National Museum permanent exhibition, Honiara.
Source: R. MacDonald.

The honour roll also thanks 'all Solomon Islanders who played a role in assisting the Allies during World War II'.

The final plinth for the Monument, featuring a ship's anchor of the period donated by the Australian National Maritime Museum, was dedicated in August 2013 to honour the Royal Australian Navy, which created the Coastwatchers network. Inclusion of this element marked the completion of the Monument (Solomon Scouts and Coastwatchers Memorial Trust 2013).

The 2012 ceremony, on the 70th anniversary of the US landing, was a major event, attended by visiting military and political dignitaries and launched by the Solomon Islands Prime Minister Gordon Darcy Lilo. The Solomon Islands government had not contributed money to the original monument appeal launched in 2011, but did provide funding for inclusion of the roll of honour in 2012 and landscaping the street in which the Monument sits.

The Monument now joins the US War Memorial as a key site for annual commemorative activities staged to mark the anniversary of the US landing, transforming the event from a private ceremony to a national celebration (Kwai 2014: 102). In recent years Solomon Islands Veterans Day has been established to coincide with the anniversary of the landing of US Marines on Guadalcanal, with a view to gradually shifting the focus of commemoration from the USA to Solomon Islands. The Monument has also become a key site at which visiting dignitaries pay their respects. Annie Kwai has summarised the positive response of both the local and international community to the Monument since its launch in 2011 (Kwai 2014: 102).

The Memorial Trust saw the dedication of the Monument as the central part of a broader campaign to educate Solomon Islanders about their World War II history. They supported local student Anna Annie Kwai in her successful application for an AusAID scholarship to undertake her masters in history at Australian National University, focusing on the history of the Solomon Scouts and Coastwatchers. Kwai was awarded her masters in 2014 and is now working on maintenance of the Monument and continuing efforts to communicate the history she has documented. Her research has also contributed to the inclusion of the Solomon Scouts and Coastwatchers in the newly developed curriculum material covering World War II history for Solomon Islands secondary schools (Solomon Islands Curriculum Development Unit 2013).

In 2011 a series of radio programmes was broadcast on the Solomon Islands Broadcasting Corporation featuring readings in Solomons *pijin* of oral histories by Scouts recorded by Hawaii's East West Centre in the 1980s (White 1988). A video of a Solomon Islands battlefield tour conducted by military historian John Innes has been released by the Trust, accompanied by a series of ten booklets providing detailed background on the battles, including the role of the Solomon Scouts and Coastwatchers (Innes 2011).[2]

Scouts and Coastwatchers display

Another part of this educational initiative was a historical display about the Solomon Scouts and Coastwatchers, which I developed as a volunteer in collaboration with the Solomon Islands National Museum. The display consisted of four graphic panels that were set up under a tent in Commonwealth Street near the Monument on the day of its dedication in 2011, and attracted much interest. The day after the Monument ceremony the display was relocated to the Museum's exhibition gallery, where it remains.

The display provides background on how the war came to Solomon Islands, the role of the Solomon Scouts and Coastwatchers and individual stories, including those of Sir Jacob Vouza, and Eroni Kumana and Biuku Gasa who saved future US President John F. Kennedy and his crew after their torpedo boat was sunk in Western Province in 1943. It is more narrative than commemorative in its approach. The original display included the draft honour roll listing the names of all who served as Solomon Scouts and Coastwatchers, to give people a chance to review and correct the list before it was finalised for inclusion in the Monument. The draft honour roll has now been removed from the museum display, leaving the panels telling the story of Solomon Islanders' involvement in World War II.

The Monument and the accompanying display do not fully reflect the complexities of Islander participation in the war alongside Allied troops. For example, the display team decided after much consideration not to include reference to examples of Solomon Islanders supporting the Japanese rather than the Allies. It was decided that, given the space constraints, 'collaboration' with the Japanese had not been widespread enough to warrant inclusion, particularly given the commemorative context. White and Laracy have said 'the issue of Islander loyalty is much more complex than usually acknowledged in written accounts of the war' and that 'many Islanders approached both sides with wariness, pragmatism and humanity' (White and Laracy 1988: 3). Essentially, it was decided that the issue of Islander loyalty was ultimately too complex to be adequately explored within the constraints of this display.[3]

Interpretation of World War II in the Solomon Islands National Museum

In the year following the completion of the Solomon Scouts and Coastwatchers Monument and display, the Solomon Islands National Museum (SINM) redeveloped its permanent exhibition, including additional displays on World War II heritage. The redevelopment was part of the intense cultural activity in Honiara accompanying the 11th Pacific Arts Festival, hosted by Solomon Islands in July 2012 and funded by the Secretariat of the Pacific Community.

The new exhibition, opened in July 2012, surveys the prehistory, history and culture of Solomon Islands using cultural and historical artefacts, archival documents and photographs, interpretative panels and an audio-visual display. It was developed by the SINM team with assistance from local and international contributors,[4] and funded by the Solomon Islands government, using funds provided by the Secretariat of the Pacific Community for the Pacific Arts Festival.

The Museum was established in 1969 by a group of expatriate volunteers, bringing together collections of ethnographic material acquired as gifts by colonial officers, and since developed over the life of the museum (Foana'ota and White 2011). In addition to its World War II material, the collection includes ethnographic and historical material, photographs, audio-visual recordings, archaeological material and a small number of natural history specimens.

The SINM has an active archaeological programme, working with local and overseas academics from a range of disciplines to research and document important cultural heritage sites. It has also played a role in supporting the development of custom houses and cultural centres in regional areas to record, preserve and pass on cultural practices. The success of these initiatives has been mixed, in part owing to insecure funding.

Since its establishment, the SINM has not been a high priority for often short-lived national governments. Responsibility for the institution has been moved more than 30 times between government departments since the Museum became a government-funded body in 1972 (Foana'ota and White 2011). Funding has been discontinuous and maintaining staff has been an ongoing problem for the SINM. It is a small institution, currently with a staff of nine, having few resources but vast responsibilities as the main cultural heritage institution in the country.

The Museum was closed during the period of the 'Tensions', during which it was broken into four times, and valuable collection items such as shell money were stolen (Foana'ota and White 2011). Since then staff have been working to reinvigorate the SINM, improve its facilities and rebuild its programmes and community relationships. Redevelopment of its permanent gallery exhibition in 2012 was a significant step in the continuing rejuvenation of the institution.

Of course World War II, while critical in its impact, is only one chapter in the long history of Solomon Islands, so its representation in the exhibition is necessarily limited. The exhibition includes the Solomon Scouts and Coastwatchers display, enhanced by a small selection of war relics from the SINM's collection.

Other content about World War II focuses on its impact on Solomon Islanders, and particularly its role in exposing them to the wider world. In addition to those who served as Scouts and Coastwatchers, thousands of men worked for the Solomon Islands Labour Corps, which helped Allied forces by carrying supplies, gardening and cooking for the troops. Working closely with US and Allied troops, they were exposed to new ideas from outside the Solomons. They observed the apparent equality of African-American and white troops, and were introduced to the idea that Solomon Islands could become independent. As a result, the relationship between Solomon Islanders and their European colonisers changed forever (Dinnen 2008).

After the war, Solomon Islanders demanded more control of their country's government. They organised several protest movements, including the Maasina Rule movement in the late 1940s and the smaller Moro movement in Guadalcanal in the 1950s. Along with a world-wide shift towards decolonisation, these movements led Solomon Islands toward independence. So the interpretation of World War II in the exhibition focuses largely on Solomon Islanders' role, and its massive impact on Solomons society, rather than on the more common narrative of the key battles, told from the perspective of the foreign combatants.

The exhibition also features a small display on the Tensions and their aftermath, including a brief summary of the period, images of Solomon Islanders' involvement in peacemaking efforts and objects representing the impact of RAMSI. A video commissioned by RAMSI featuring women discussing their experiences, including the impact of the Tensions, is also included in the gallery's audio-visual display (RAMSI 2012).

This sits alongside displays highlighting the diverse range of cultural practice across Solomon Islands, and the long story of Solomons societies before European contact. The aim was not to promote one homogeneous national identity through the exhibition, but to celebrate the richness, diversity and longevity of Solomons cultures, while exploring the history that Solomon Islanders share.

Through its new permanent exhibition the SINM is also attempting to play a nation-building role, by celebrating the diversity of Solomons cultures while presenting the unifying narrative of the country's journey from colonial protectorate to independent nation, including its World War II history. Interestingly, the nation-building objective was not explicitly articulated by the SINM team in the planning of the exhibition, but emerged during the development of the content and was recognised as a potential outcome of the exhibition only in retrospect.

Conclusion

The Solomon Scouts and Coastwatchers Monument and the redeveloped exhibition at the SINM are examples of cultural heritage playing an active role in the ongoing process of reconciliation. Through the Monument and its accompanying activities, the commemoration and interpretation of one conflict is being used in an attempt to heal the wounds of another, more recent conflict. These ventures focus on telling stories from the perspective of Solomon Islanders, encouraging pride in their struggles and achievements and highlighting their common history.

The positive community response to the Monument, the SINM redevelopment and the Pacific Arts Festival demonstrates an interest among Solomon Islanders in engaging with their own history and culture. An opportunity now exists to tap into this interest and provide more avenues for community engagement with inclusive commemorative activities and Solomons-focused cultural heritage ventures.

While post-Tensions efforts at nation-building through cultural heritage have clearly been significant, it remains to be seen whether the momentum generated in recent years will be maintained. Continued state fragility poses a major obstacle to efforts to further develop local engagement with cultural heritage in general, and inclusive commemorations in particular. State institutions such as the SINM have insufficient resources and limited capacity to pursue their broad mandate. Dependence on donor support or philanthropy for such ventures makes long-term planning difficult, and increases pressure to focus on activities catering to tourist and expatriate audiences in order to attract resources.

Both the Solomon Scouts and Coastwatchers Monument and the Museum redevelopment relied heavily on funding from international donors and participation by expatriate or overseas contributors. While this reflects the reality of the challenges involved in pursuing cultural heritage ventures in a post-conflict fragile state, it does raise questions about the extent of local ownership of and commitment to the nation-building rationale of these activities.

Recent developments do reflect increased government recognition of the importance of cultural heritage. The release of *The Solomon Islands National Cultural Policy Framework* in 2013 (Solomon Islands Government 2013), the first such policy, sets out directions for Solomon Islands to refocus and invest in its culture sector. In 2014 the Solomon Islands government allocated approximately Solomon Island $3.8m in its Development Budget to assist the SINM to work towards building a new National Museum.

The Memorial Trust is now exploring the possibility of developing a World War II museum, focusing less on the relics of war than on the stories of Solomon Islanders' experience and participation. This may dovetail with plans for the SINM to develop a dedicated World War II gallery.

The increase in locally generated and Solomons-focused cultural heritage ventures bodes well for post-conflict reconciliation and the long-term challenges of nation-building that still face the country. Support will still be required from the international donor community to facilitate these efforts and help develop local capacity. This is an opportunity that the donor community should be encouraged to support.

References

Barbara, J. (2008). 'Antipodean state-building: the Regional Assistance Mission to Solomon Islands and Australian intervention in the South Pacific'. *Journal of Intervention and Statebuilding*, 2(2), 123–49.

Braithwaite, J., Dinnen, S., Allen, M. and Charlesworth, H. (2010). *Pillars and Shadows: State Building as Peace Building in Solomon Islands* (Canberra: ANU E Press).

Dinnen, S. (2008). 'The Solomon Islands intervention and the instabilities of the post-colonial state'. *Global Change, Peace and Security*, 20(3), 339–55.

Foana'ota, L. (2007). 'The future of indigenous museums: the Solomon Islands case', in N. Stanley (ed.), *The Future of Indigenous Museums: Perspectives from the Southwest Pacific* (New York: Berghahn Books).

Foana'ota, L. and White, G. (2011). 'Solomon Islands Cultural Policy?: A Brief History of Practice', in E. Hviding and K. M. Rio (eds), *Made in Oceania: Social Movements, Cultural Heritage and the State in the Pacific* (Wantage, Oxon: Sean Kingston Publishing), pp. 273–299.

Guide to Guadalcanal Battlefields (2011). DVD, SIBC and Trad Records, available from BJS Group of Companies, Honiara, Solomon Islands.

Innes, J. (2011). 'Guide to the Guadalcanal battle field'. Unpublished document, available from BJS Group of Companies, Honiara.

Kwai, A. (2014). 'Islanders in the Second World War: a Solomon Islander perspective', MA History thesis (Canberra: ANU).

RAMSI (2012). *Mere Blong Iumi: Stori Blong Oloketa*. DVD (Honiara: RAMSI).

Saunders, Sir Bruce (2012). Personal communication, 9 August.

Solomon Islands Curriculum Development Unit (2013). *Social Studies for Solomon Islands: Year 8 Learner's Book* (Melbourne: Pearson).

Solomon Islands Government, Ministry of Culture and Tourism (2013). *Solomon Islands Nasinol Policy Framework blong Kalsa* (Honiara: Secretariat of the Pacific Communities).

Solomon Islands Government (2011). 'Ministry of Culture and Tourism Strategic Plan 2011 to 2014'.

Solomon Scouts and Coastwatchers Memorial Trust (2014). *The Monument* Newsletter, Issue no. 7, February.

Solomon Scouts and Coastwatchers Memorial Trust (2013). *The Monument: Pride of Our Nation* brochure (Honiara).

White, G. (1988). *Bikfala Faet: Olketa Solomon Aelanda Rimembarem Wol Wo Tu; The Big Death: Solomon Islanders Remember World War II* (Fiji: Solomon Islands College of Higher Education and University of the South Pacific – Solomon Islands Centre and Institute of Pacific Studies).

White, G. and Laracy, H. (1988). *Taem Blong Faet*: WWII in Melanesia. *O'O A Journal of Solomon Islands Studies*, Special Issue, No 4 (Honiara: University of the South Pacific).

World Bank (2013). *Solomon Islands – Country partnership strategy for the period FY2013–2017* (Washington, DC: World Bank).

Notes

1   For part of my time at the Museum I worked under the Australian Volunteers for International Development programme, which is an Australian government initiative.

2   Brisbane-based military historian John Innes conducts battlefield tours around Honiara and Tulagi. His work acknowledges the contribution of Solomon Islanders, and was a key source in development of the display on the Solomon Scouts and Coastwatchers in the National Museum and this chapter.

3   Since the display was developed, Anna Annie Kwai has further explored the concept of Islander 'loyalty', concluding that 'the reasons that lured or motivated Islander participation in war alongside Allied troops were varied in nature, reflecting the complexities of the politics of colonialism and war, their interactions with and transformations of Islander worldviews' (Kwai 2014).

4   Tony Heorake, Museum Director, managed the redevelopment project. Ben Burt, Anthropologist and Curator at the British Museum co-curated the main exhibition with Rita Sahu, Ethnologist at the Solomon Islands National Museum and the author. Content for the Archaeology gallery was developed by Peter Sheppard at University of Auckland, with input from Martin Gibbs and Melissa Carter from the University of Sydney, and the Museum's Field Archaeologist John Keopo. Others who contributed include University of Queensland historian Clive Moore, former director of the Solomon Islands National Museum Lawrence Foana'ota, and Bishop Terry Brown from the Anglican Church of Melanesia.

18 Conclusion

Keir Reeves

This book has investigated the intersection between the themes of battlefield commemorative events, warscapes, heritage-related travel and tourism and memory. In doing so the contributors have explored a number of sites and themes that highlight the enduring appeal of key battlefield events and also the continued resonance of these commemorative events to the wider community well into the present day. Indeed, for many attending, a commemorative event such as Anzac Day in Darwin, a peace memorial at Ieper or a World War II-era Solomon Islands war service monument is their first and most intense direct engagement with battlefield events and more broadly the memory of war.

Lieux de mémoire is a pivotal concept in the era of the boom in memory studies and has wide currency amidst the centenary of World War I. Clearly, Nora's influential concept is irresistible in attempts to make sense of key sites and associated cultural memories and commemorative events. However his concept is primarily a historical tool that can tend towards nostalgia when assessing the significance of battlefield events. Nora's notion of the *lieux de mémoire* has been one that has resonated through many chapters of this volume. However we have argued in terms of the design and intellectual premise of this book that a more interdisciplinarily conceived, methodologically driven approach has in turn provided new insights and understandings about the heritage of commemorative battlefield events.

On one hand commemorating battlefield events is about remembering a conflict at a certain place and a certain time. Given that we are in the middle of the centenary celebrations of the Great War it is understandable that the bulk of this volume privileges interpretation of the World War I events. The Great War continues to cast a long shadow. Indicative of this is the ongoing, indeed increasing, level of public interest, scholarly academic research, travel to key destinations (referred to by some as pilgrimages) and official, governmental, commemorative responses.

This theme of interpreting and assessing the longitudinal significance of the Great War has driven much of the discussion that has sustained the first half of this book. In it key events such as Fromelles, Vimy Ridge, Ieper are interrogated and lesser-known events such as the anti-conscription response of the Victorian Trades Hall to World War I in Australia provides a welcome counterpoint in terms of a commemorative event. The formal state response (in this case Flanders, the key theatre of World War I and site of the bloodiest conflicts) is neatly encapsulated in the chapter by Vandael *et al.,* while Stichelbaut *et al.* provide the reader with a clear grounding in landscape analysis (a key aspect of the book, as the title suggests) through their revealing aerial-photographical approach that explored the shifting Western Front throughout the conflict.

The second half of the book concentrates on later conflicts of the twentieth and early twenty-first centuries and discusses strategies commemorating World War II, the Vietnam War and other conflicts. New, more subtle themes emerge in this second part of the book. Barbara's chapter about the role of RAMSI is also one about the significance of recent conflict in successful attempts at reconstituting the state formation of the Solomon Islands. Reeves and Cheer's analysis of John Frum Day in Tanna, Vanuatu closely reads an event in terms of its enduring, intangible heritage of World War II that continues to captivate and fascinate visitors in the present day.

However, a final word of caution is required when considering heritage of battle-field commemorative events. The ongoing appeal, visitor numbers, government response and public interest in World War I, particularly that associated with the centenary celebrations, is unprecedented. Nonetheless, throughout the second half of book examines the interest in commemorative events that are not as prominent World War I commemoration. There, the significance of later conflicts of the twentieth and twenty-first centuries is not always obvious. Some are at risk of becoming what Nancy Wood described as *lieux d'oubli,* sites of oblivion (Wood 1999). That is to say, they are sites that are potentially avoided in public memory. The ongoing legacy of John Frum Day beyond its touristic value is not as obvious as commemoration of the Somme. Logan's chapter explores and interrogates the still contested and in large part unresolved legacy of the Vietnam (American) War and for many the process of remembering, or indeed the desire to remember and commemorate battlefield events, is not clear. This issue of resolving difficult heritage will be brought into a clearer focus with the next-wave centenary commemorating World War II during the next quarter of this century.

But for this book the focus has predominantly been on the twentieth century, though we have also included the earlier event of the Gate *Pā* in the New Zealand Wars and the later conflict in the Solomon Islands during the early twenty-first century. *Battlefield Events: Landscape, Commemoration and Heritage* has explored the reasons why commemorative events are held and explained the ongoing appeal of key twentieth-century battles, as well as analysing the complex interactive combination of heritage, history, tourism, travel and memory that explains the phenomenon of battlefield events.

Reference

Wood, N. (1999). *Vectors of Memory: Legacies of Trauma in Postwar Europe* (Oxford: Berg).

Index